ASTON VILLA
REVIEW 1993

Published by Sports Projects Ltd

ACKNOWLEDGEMENTS

Aston Villa Review 1993
First published in Great Britain in June 1993
by Sports Projects Limited

© 1993 Sports Projects Limited
188 Lightwoods Hill, Smethwick, Warley,
West Midlands B67 5EH.

ISBN 0-946866-09-0

Printed and bound in Great Britain
by Butler & Tanner Limited

Editor: Dennis Shaw

Statistics: Trevor Hartley

Photographs: Bernard Gallagher, Sports Projects
and Terry Weir

Design, layout and graphics: Bernard Gallagher,
Trevor Hartley, Phil Lees, Nadine Goldingay
and Scott Anderson

Special thanks to: Steve Stride, Pam and Dave
Bridgewater

KEY

❏	Player booked
■	Player sent off
32	Figure in goals column indicates time of goal
†56	First substitute and time of substitution
†	First player substituted
‡56	Second substitute and time of substitution
‡	Second player substituted

Note: In friendly games, where several substitutes may have appeared, additional symbols are used in the following order: #, §, ††, ‡‡, ##, §§.

A new concept which takes the reader on an interesting and eventful journey

At first glance Aston Villa Review 1993, might appear to be the usual club year book. In reality, it is no such thing.

This publication is a completely new concept in that it takes the reader on an interesting and eventful journey, from first kick of the season to last.

In so doing it provides all the important details, statistics, facts and figures and breathes life into the characters who make up Aston Villa FC's staff on the playing side.

What is the manager REALLY like? What did he have to say about that fabulous result and performance or that terrible defeat?

When and how were the goals scored, who got booked, what was the attendance, how did the build-up to the game shape up?

The book gives you the linesmen, the team changes, the fluctuating league positions, the substitutions.

But it is not just a record book. This is a reading book, too. There is a comprehensive report on every first team match in all competitions and they are written is such a way that you can start at Ipswich and read through, fiction-style, to Loftus Road.

It is humbly hoped that the story emerges as a good 'read' in addition to being a total work of record, compiled with the valued help of Trevor Hartley of Sports Projects.

Aston Villa Review 1993 is the first of a series, presented in such a way that it will sit snugly on the bookshelf as a lasting work of reference, alongside next year's, the year's after that and so on.

The year of launch was deliberate because it coincides with the introduction of the FA Premier League. Start now and purchasers will have the makings of a collection which could increase in value.

What's more, those who took up the offer to order in advance and have their name included in the book as subscribers even have their own personalised copy to pass on to their family for posterity.

It is too late now to catch up on that particular aspect if you missed out. But the chance will arise again in twelve months time when, remember, there will be a European tale to tell.

The book is an official publication, written and presented as an on-going service to supporters who are an integral part of Aston Villa FC.

Dennis Shaw, May 1993.

CONTENTS

CONTENTS

Saturday 15th August 1992 • Portman Road • 3.00pm

IPSWICH TOWN 1   ASTON VILLA 1

Half-time 1-0 • *Attendance* 16,818
Referee Alf BUKSH (London)
Linesmen M.D. DEARING and J.L. ELWIN

Blue Shirts with White Sleeves, White Shorts		Goals	Claret and Blue Shirts, Blue Shorts		Goals
1	Craig FORREST		1	Nigel SPINK	
2	Phil WHELAN		2	Earl BARRETT	
3	Neil THOMPSON		3	Steve STAUNTON	
4	Mick STOCKWELL ‡		4	Shaun TEALE ❑	
5	John WARK		5	Paul McGRATH	
6	David LINIGHAN		6	Kevin RICHARDSON †	
7	Geraint WILLIAMS		7	Tony DALEY	
8	Paul GODDARD		8	Garry PARKER	
9	Gavin JOHNSON ❑	33	9	Ray HOUGHTON	
10	Jason DOZZELL †		10	Dalian ATKINSON	83
11	Chris KIWOMYA		11	Steve FROGGATT	

Substitutes			*Substitutes*	
	Eddie YOUDS †70			Cyrille REGIS †52
	Simon MILTON ‡89			Ugo EHIOGU
Gk	Jason WINTERS		Gk	Les SEALEY

BEFORE	P	W	D	L	F	A	pts	AFTER	P	W	D	L	F	A	pts
Villa	0	0	0	0	0	0	0	Villa	1	0	1	0	1	1	1
Ipswich	0	0	0	0	0	0	0	Ipswich	1	0	1	0	1	1	1

FACTFILE

History is made as the new FA Premier League kicks off... New rule allows any two from three substitutes named... Ray Houghton makes his Villa League debut... Dalian Atkinson scores against his former club... There's a familiar look to Villa's new jersey - a traditional link to the style worn in the 1890's.

It's a whole new ball game!

The new FA Premier League swings into action. Good to have the ball rolling again after months of politics in breaking away from the Football League.

Maybe it IS merely the former First Division with a change of name and management. But only time will tell if the new format will work.

The first obvious change is the referee in a new green top, having discarded the traditional black. Also, new attention is focussed on goal-keepers, now barred from handling back passes played deliberately with the feet.

Like a year earlier, when the season kicked off at Hillsborough, it is Villa's lot to 'break in' new-comers from the lower division. It won't be easy.

Portman Road Ipswich is a-buzz with antic-ipation. Visiting Villa are full of big names, with Ray Houghton a new recruit from Liverpool and Dalian Atkinson back at his original 'home'.

There are some missing faces, too. Dwight Yorke is on international duty with Trinidad and Tobago while Cyrille Regis is demoted to the subs bench because of nagging Achilles tendon trouble.

The front pair are Atkinson and Tony Daley. Sounds OK. But the chemistry is not right. This much emerges as Steve Froggatt feeds some good balls across but no-one is on the end of them. No-one has to tell manager Ron Atkinson that there is a piece missing from his jig-saw. Be patient. He'll find it.

After an undistinguished start, there is much to applaud. Houghton's Anfield quality is in evidence. He motors across the width of the field, probing and supplying.

Along with Garry Parker and Kevin Richard-son, and with Froggy doing his stuff down the flanks, Houghton provides high promise in midfield.

To confirm it, a goal is needed. By now it's Ipswich who have pounced with a Gavin John-son strike after 32 minutes. Supporters could be in for a long and disappointing journey home unless finish can be added to the build-ups.

Another problem arises early in the second half when a tackle leaves Richardson with a dead-leg and substitute Regis is on.

Strangely the enforced re-grouping brings an improvement. With Houghton more central, Daley wide on the right and Regis alongside Atkinson.

Persistency by Villa creates hesitancy in front of the home goal and seven minutes from time Regis squares the ball to Atkinson who joyful-ly nets against his old club.

The danger of first-day defeat is thus avoid-ed with a well-justified draw. Too early yet to judge Villa's potential but it is impossible to escape the feeling that something extra is need-ed up front. Elsewhere all the signs are favourable. Close season suggestions that Earl Barrett is unsettled can be discounted. He looks England-class at right back and recognises that there is no way the Paul McGrath-Shaun Teale partnership can be disturbed.

First match verdict: Satisfactory for starters but manager Ron Atkinson's team building programme is clearly not completed. His search for a striker will go on.

Atkinson scores Villa's first of the season

Wednesday 19th August 1992 • Villa Park • 8.00pm (delayed)

ASTON VILLA 1 LEEDS UNITED 1

Half-time 0-0 • Attendance 29,151

Referee Keith HACKETT (Sheffield)
Linesmen M.E. ALEXANDER and D.C. MADGWICK

Claret and Blue Shirts, White Shorts	Goals		White Shirts, White Shorts	Goals
1 Nigel SPINK			1 John LUKIC	
2 Earl BARRETT			2 Jon NEWSOME	
3 Steve STAUNTON			3 Tony DORIGO	
4 Shaun TEALE			4 David BATTY †	
5 Paul McGRATH			5 Chris FAIRCLOUGH	
6 Kevin RICHARDSON			6 Chris WHYTE	
7 Tony DALEY			7 Eric CANTONA ‡	
8 Garry PARKER			8 Rod WALLACE	
9 Ray HOUGHTON			9 Lee CHAPMAN	
10 Dalian ATKINSON	77		10 Gary McALLISTER	
11 Dwight YORKE †			11 Gary SPEED	84
Substitutes			*Substitutes*	
Cyrille REGIS †29			Steve HODGE †h45	
Ugo EHIOGU			Gordon STRACHAN ‡78	
Gk Les SEALEY			Gk Mervyn DAY	

BEFORE	P	W	D	L	F	A	pts	AFTER	P	W	D	L	F	A	pts
Leeds	1	1	0	0	2	1	3	Leeds	2	1	1	0	3	2	4
Villa	1	0	1	0	1	1	1	Villa	2	0	2	0	2	2	2

FACTFILE

Villa's opening game of the season at Villa Park... Dorigo, Hodge and Day are three former Villa players in the Leeds squad... Home debut for Ray Houghton... Dalian Atkinson scores his first 'home' goal for Villa... Eric Cantona is the first Frenchman to play in a League match at Villa Park since Didier Six in 1984.

Defensive error lets in Leeds

The Villa Park league programme opens with the visit of the reigning champions and just one team change, Dwight Yorke returning to the exclusion of Steve Froggatt.

Home supporters are keen to see new signing Ray Houghton in action and to judge if Villa have progressed since Leeds fired four goals past them the previous November.

Immediate signs are that while the quality of Villa's game is in good shape with clear signs of improvement the reigning champions will have no difficulty in maintaining the high standards set in the previous campaign.

The return of Yorke, last season's top scorer with 17 goals, proves ill-fated. A heavy collision with Chris Whyte sees him hobble off to be replaced by Cyrille Regis after only 29 minutes.

English football is renowned for its pace, its excitement, the stamina and the sheer physical commitment of its players.

This is an outstanding example. Two evenly-matched sides give all they have to cancel each other out, though Villa are looking likely winners when Dalian Atkinson strikes his second goal in two games in the 77th minute. Kevin Richardson's corner is helped on by the influential Regis for Atkinson to squeeze a shot between John Lukic and the post.

Leeds followers, including manager Howard Wilkinson, must now fear that all is lost. It would be, too, but for the most irritating of goals from Villa's viewpoint.

Only six minutes remain when Welsh cap Gary Speed is fleetingly released in front of goal. Nigel Spink comes out to close him down, there is some misunderstanding between defenders, no doubt due to the new goalkeeper law, and Speed's shot goes through Spink's legs. A dreadful anti-climax for Villa. A not undeserved

escape for Leeds. With expectations of the new Premier League sky-high, opinions vary on the merit of the match.

In the interview room afterwards reporters are taken aback by Wilkinson's assessment. "That was as good a performance by Leeds as any since I came to the club," he said before stressing "bearing in mind the degree of difficulty of the match.

"There were no cheap tackles, no cheap passes, no cheap shots. Everything had to be hard earned."

Wilkinson is clearly impressed with Villa, scant consolation when four points have drifted out of the first six. The 'plus' points for Villa are the welcome signs of a team framework continuing to emerge. Also the sheer pace of Tony Daley and Dalian Atkinson has continually unhinged Leeds' championship defence.

Other lesser rearguards are going to face a similar problem if Villa can steer clear of injuries. In the centre of midfield, Kevin Richardson and Ray Houghton, two deeply experienced performers who have both won top honours elsewhere, are forging an understanding which can only improve with more and more matches under their belt.

On the debit side, the odd chance has been wasted - that missing striker problem again! - while a defensive error has resulted in the opportunity to kick-off the home programme with an impressive victory has been allowed to slip away.

Dalian Atkinson celebrates his goal

Saturday 22nd August 1992 • Villa Park • 3.00pm

ASTON VILLA 1 SOUTHAMPTON 1

Half-time 0-0 • Attendance 17,894

Referee Kelvin MORTON (Bury St. Edmunds)
Linesmen J.B. ROBINSON and P.M. ROBERTS

Claret and Blue Shirts, White Shorts	Goals	Red and White Striped Shirts, Black Shorts	Goals
1 Nigel SPINK		1 Tim FLOWERS	
2 Earl BARRETT		2 Jeff KENNA	
3 Steve STAUNTON		3 Micky ADAMS	78
4 Shaun TEALE		4 Terry HURLOCK	
5 Paul McGRATH		5 Richard HALL	
6 Kevin RICHARDSON		6 Kevin MOORE ❑	
7 Ray HOUGHTON		7 Matthew LE TISSIER ❑ †	
8 Garry PARKER		8 Glenn COCKERILL	
9 Dwight YORKE †		9 Kerry DIXON	
10 Dalian ATKINSON	65	10 David SPEEDIE	
11 Steve FROGGATT ‡		11 Francis BENALI	

Substitutes	*Substitutes*
Frank McAVENNIE †37	Iain DOWIE †37
Ugo EHIOGU ‡76	Tommy WIDDRINGTON
Gk Les SEALEY	Gk Ian ANDREWS

BEFORE		P	W	D	L	F	A	pts	AFTER		P	W	D	L	F	A	pts
14	Villa	2	0	2	0	2	2	2	12	Villa	3	0	3	0	3	3	3
18	Soton	2	0	1	1	1	3	1	17	Soton	3	0	2	1	2	4	2

FACTFILE

Dalian Atkinson continues his goal a game sequence... On-trial Frank McAvennie makes his Villa debut as substitute – and sets up the equaliser for Atkinson... It's Villa's third successive 1-1 draw, two at home, as Villa make a welcome return to the TV screens on 'Match of the Day'.

Late goal steals points from Villa

Attention is now firmly fixed on whether Villa can deliver enough goals to match the standard of their build-ups which, at times, has been outstanding.

As a possible short-term 'fix' Frank McAvennie has been taken on trial and is included as sub.

With Tony Daley out with a knee problem Steve Froggatt returns while Dwight Yorke has got over the injury sustained against Leeds.

The Saints are not the most welcome of visitors. They have a mean, destructive style of play which, folks suspect, will be even more pronounced with the sale of England striker Alan Shearer to Blackburn Rovers.

Villa boss Ron Atkinson would have liked him. But not at £3.6m...!

Dalian Atkinson and Yorke are again the front pair, neither of them the 'target man' type to capitalise on any crosses Froggatt or Ray Houghton may provide.

Villa's football is more a measured build-up from defence through midfield rather than the old-fashioned up-and-unders.

Southampton block the route to goal in sheer numbers.

Before half-time a further disruption arrives when Yorke goes off for the second successive match, this time a bang in the back being the problem.

The 'bonus' here is a chance for McAvennie, admittedly rusty and short of match-play and above his best playing weight.

The visitors are visibly playing for a point and though McAvennie makes spirited efforts to break them down, Southampton increasingly look capable of getting one.

Twenty minutes into the second half and Atkinson conjures his third goal in successive

games. A healthy if belated return on the £1.6m paid to Spanish club Real Sociedad a year earlier is now arriving.

McAvennie heads across goal from Steve Staunton's forward pass and Atkinson volleys in from close range. Unhappily, as in the previous match, Villa cannot hold on, Micky Adams evading substitute Ehiogu to get on the end of Kerry Dixon's pass.

Three games, three 1-1 draws, three goals from Dalian Atkinson. Not a bad start. But not a good one either.

On top of the limited scoring threat a problem has arisen with conceding 'bad' goals through lapses in concentration.

Plenty of time to get it right but a win is needed for a spark to ignite the new season.

The manager's insistence on playing a 'possession' style of game is being met by players who rarely resort to cruder 'get rid of it' methods.

One clear improvement this season is the pristine state of the playing surface compared to the horrors of 1991-92.

Work carried out during the summer by groundsman Tony Eden has brought almost miraculous results while the decision to play reserve games at Walsall's Bescot Stadium has proved a wise one in terms of avoiding overuse.

Dalian Atkinson, on target again!

Tuesday 25th August 1992 • Goodison Park • 7.30pm

EVERTON 1 ASTON VILLA 0

Half-time 0-0 • *Attendance* 22,372
Referee Martin BODENHAM (Looe, Cornwall)
Linesmen T. A. ATKINSON and M. A. RILEY

Blue Shirts, White Shorts		Goals	Claret and Blue Shirts, Blue Shorts		Goals
1	Neville SOUTHALL		1	Nigel SPINK	
2	Alan HARPER		2	Earl BARRETT	
3	Andy HINCHCLIFFE		3	Steve STAUNTON	
4	John EBBRELL		4	Shaun TEALE	
5	Dave WATSON		5	Paul McGRATH	
6	Gary ABLETT		6	Kevin RICHARDSON	
7	Mark WARD		7	Tony DALEY	
8	Peter BEARDSLEY		8	Garry PARKER †	
9	Paul RIDEOUT †		9	Ray HOUGHTON	
10	Barry HORNE		10	Dalian ATKINSON	
11	Maurice JOHNSTON	88	11	Steve FROGGATT	

Substitutes			*Substitutes*	
	Peter BEAGRIE †48			Cyrille REGIS †89
	Matthew JACKSON			Ugo EHIOGU
Gk	Jason KEARTON		Gk	Les SEALEY

BEFORE		P	W	D	L	F	A	pts	AFTER		P	W	D	L	F	A	pts
6	Everton	3	1	2	0	5	2	5	2	Everton	4	2	2	0	6	2	8
12	Villa	3	0	3	0	3	3	3	16	Villa	4	0	3	1	3	4	3

FACTFILE

Villa's first defeat of the season... Everton start the season with wins over both Villa and Manchester United and draws with Norwich and Sheffield Wednesday... Paul Rideout, a recent signing for Everton from Rangers, plays against his former club.

Close game goes Everton's way

Results have not been quite living up to all the pre-season promise of an exciting season as Villa head for Goodison Park to face an Everton side who, in contrast, have started well.

Too much has rested on Dalian Atkinson whose three single goals have earned the three 1-1 draws so far while destructive defensive errors have also crept in.

England winger Tony Daley, who missed the home game with Southampton is back, replacing Dwight Yorke.

The encouraging signs in team-building terms are that the defence and, in the main, the midfield, are becoming settled units. It is the final component which is missing, in the shape of another reliable goalscorer.

General team shape looks good as does the capacity to play sensible possession football. Earl Barrett is justifying the manager's belief that, while his 'natural' position is central defence, he has all of the attributes of an international-class right back.

Those who anticipate a match for the purist are not to be disappointed. Everton build from the back, through midfield, with Peter Beardsley in England form. Yet Villa are even better and by half-time are leading 'on points' if not in actual goals, though the home team conjure the most dangerous moment of all.

Beardsley, having seen ex-Villa striker Paul Rideout and Mo Johnston waste a number of openings , decides to go it alone. Dribbling forward past three opponents he attempts to chip Nigel Spink from near the 18-

yard line. Momentarily the Villa keeper is alarmed until Beardsley's shot swerves narrowly wide of its target. For Villa Barrett has been a constant threat in raising down the right-hand touchline but the quality of his finishing pass has sometimes been suspect.

After the break Everton boss Howard Kendall sends on the tricky, ball-playing winger Peter Beagrie in place of the injured Rideout and he gets in some telling crosses.

Villa survive some close shaves but continue to be the better side overall and are frustratingly close to taking the lead via a Steve Froggatt blast against the post.

A fourth successive draw is right on the cards but Beagrie and Everton always look capable of sneaking the winner, and so it proves with only two minutes to go.

One unfortunate feature of Villa's early games has been their nasty habit of conceding such late goals and this one leaves them with only three points from a possible 12 and a low place in the early league table.

Gary Ablett and Beardsley set up the chance for Johnston, who had been close on two or three occasions, to beat Spink.

"Villa played attractive football, hit the woodwork a couple of times and caused us problems," said Kendall. "Tonight you have seen two highly-committed teams in an exciting contest which could have gone either way."

Atkinson is not displeased with the general form of his team but the fact that his side loses on the first occasion his namesake fails to score does not escape him.

Four games, no wins. He needs that new striker.

Earl Barrett

Saturday 29th August 1992 • Bramall Lane • 3.00pm

SHEFFIELD UNITED 0 ASTON VILLA 2

Half-time 0-1 • *Attendance* 18,773

Referee Roger MILFORD (Bristol)
Linesmen E. LOMAS and T. LYNCH

Red and White Striped Shirts, White Shorts		Goals	Claret and Blue Shirts, White Shorts		Goals
1	Simon TRACEY		1	Nigel SPINK	
2	Kevin GAGE		2	Earl BARRETT	
3	Tom COWAN		3	Steve STAUNTON	
4	John GANNON		4	Shaun TEALE	
5	Brian GAYLE ❑		5	Paul McGRATH	
6	Paul BEESLEY		6	Kevin RICHARDSON	
7	Mitch WARD		7	Ray HOUGHTON	
8	Mike LAKE †		8	Garry PARKER	4, 86
9	Alan CORK ‡		9	Cyrille REGIS †	
10	Brian DEANE		10	Dalian ATKINSON	
11	Glynn HODGES		11	Stephen FROGGATT ❑	

Substitutes			*Substitutes*		
	Adrian LITTLEJOHN †45			Ugo EHIOGU †72	
	Carl BRADSHAW ‡57			Frank McAVENNIE	
Gk	Alan KELLY		Gk	Les SEALEY	

BEFORE		P	W	D	L	F	A	pts	AFTER		P	W	D	L	F	A	pts
13	United	4	1	1	2	7	8	4	11	Villa	5	1	3	1	5	4	6
18	Villa	4	0	3	1	3	4	3	19	United	5	1	1	3	7	10	4

FACTFILE

Villa's first win in the new FA Premier League and their first win at Bramall Lane since September 1961... Garry Parker's goals are his first away from home for Villa in the league, his only previous away goal was in last season's FA Cup win at Derby.

Blades blunted as Villa move up

And so to Bramall Lane, where Sheffield United can be confidently expected to play a totally different type of game to Everton in the previous fixture.

The Dave Bassett Hounds will be out hunting in marauding packs, chasing everything that moves in search of their prey, tossed forward mainly by the aerial route.

Can Villa sustain their contrasting brand of football in such circumstances? Or will they be dragged into the kind of up-and-under forays which United favour?

Ron Atkinson has called for more goals from midfield as a means of taking the pressure off strikers who could be feeling the pressure to produce. He has called in Cyrille Regis up front and named Frank McAvennie on the bench.

A feeling of confidence grows from the kick-off and, after only four minutes, Garry Parker provides the lead.

From Steve Staunton's throw-in he steadies himself, allows the ball to run into a tempting position from 25 yards out and fires his stunning drive past Simon Tracey.

Yes, Villa CAN play cultured ground-level passing moves, despite United's feverish attempts to unsettle their rhythm. That message comes through loud and clear.

The hub of it all is the centre of midfield where Parker, perked by his first goal of the season, is in fine shape. The ex-Forest schemer is striking up a superb understanding with skipper Kevin Richardson, the always-on-the-move link man and with Ray Houghton, busy as always on the right-hand side.

As Villa's intricate play builds up promisingly, United attempt to unsettle them with their bustling style and all-out efforts to knock long balls forward without delay.

The home team's offside trap can be a shade troublesome, too, but Regis is capable of holding the ball up and waiting his moment to pounce, until he limps off mid-way through the second half.

As at Goodison a few days days earlier, chances are wasted and it is not until the 86th minute that Parker collects a second goal and pins a more fitting scoreline to the occasion.

Again, Parker beats Tracey with a long-range drive which confirms his status as a magnificent all-round performer who could well eventually add senior England caps to the under-21s already in his locker.

Ironically, Villa's miss of the match, among many, is down to Dalian Atkinson, who ought to have made it 2-0 long before Parker finally sealed it.

The £1.6m signing from Spanish club Real Sociedad, heads a Houghton centre over the top when it looks easier to score. "I thought it was the goalkeeper's ball, but he missed it and that completely threw me," he explains.

This one certainly wasn't Dalian's Day... he was denied what looked a clear penalty by referee Roger Milford when Brian Gayle yanked the Villa forward back by his shirt to floor him well inside the area.

At the back Paul McGrath is sound as ever in intercepting United's bombardment of high balls while Nigel Spink plays his part when he leaps to turn a Brian Deane header over the bar.

Shaun Teale supports him well, reliable as always, while Earl Barrett continues to grow in stature in his right back role.

As for Parker... 'you wanted goals from midfield gaffer? You got 'em...'

Garry Parker

Wednesday 2nd September 1992 • Villa Park • 7.45pm

ASTON VILLA 1 CHELSEA 3

Half-time 1-2 • *Attendance* 19,125

Referee Peter FOAKES (Clacton-on-Sea)
Linesmen A. STREETS and S.W. DUNN

Claret and Blue Shirts, White Shorts		Goals	Blue Shirts, Blue Shorts		Goals
1	Nigel SPINK		1	Dave BEASANT	
2	Earl BARRETT ❏		2	Steve CLARKE †	
3	Steve STAUNTON ❏		3	Gareth HALL	
4	Shaun TEALE		4	Vinnie JONES	
5	Paul McGRATH		5	Paul ELLIOTT	
6	Kevin RICHARDSON	31	6	Mal DONAGHY	
7	Ray HOUGHTON		7	Eddie NEWTON	42
8	Garry PARKER		8	Robert FLECK	39
9	Cyrille REGIS †		9	Mick HARFORD	
10	Dalian ATKINSON		10	Andy TOWNSEND	
11	Stephen FROGGATT		11	Dennis WISE	57

Substitutes		*Substitutes*	
	Frank McAVENNIE †70		David LEE †45
	Ugo EHIOGU		Joe ALLON
Gk	Les SEALEY	Gk	Nick COLGAN

BEFORE		P	W	D	L	F	A	pts	AFTER		P	W	D	L	F	A	pts
10	Chelsea	5	1	3	1	6	6	6	9	Chelsea	6	2	3	1	9	7	9
14	Villa	5	1	3	1	5	4	6	15	Villa	6	1	3	2	6	7	6

FACTFILE

Robert Fleck scores his first goal for Chelsea... The Londoners record their first win at Villa Park since 1966-67 when they won 6-2... Villa are beaten at home for the first time in eight games.

Fleck wrecks Villa's challenge

Tony Daley, who missed the previous game with a knee injury is out again and fears arise that it could be a long job, perhaps requiring surgery.

The team is thus unchanged from last Saturday and hopes are high that, having recorded the first win of the season, this third home game will provide the opportunity to keep up the good work. In the event, deep disappointment is in store.

By now Ron Atkinson has taken a firm step towards solving that recurring goal-scoring problem with an offer of around £2.5m to Liverpool for Dean Saunders.

The Villa manager had hoped to set up a deal in principle for the Welsh international the previous day but there are complications regarding the fee, which would be a club record signing.

Atkinson and Liverpool manager Graeme Souness have verbally sanctioned a deal. Now the fine details are being discussed between the clubs as Atkinson and supporters cross their fingers and hope that a move is agreed.

The attendance figure of fewer than 20,000 is a disappointing one, especially as the club are, tranfer-wise, operating in the Big League. The economic recession is biting deep. Clearly fans have to select their games carefully.

This one gets underway on a promising note as Villa take the lead with a 31st minute goal from midfield to add to the pair provided by Garry Parker at Bramall Lane. Once more this was a shot from outside the penalty area, by Kevin Richardson, which goes in off the underside of the bar.

Ray Houghton, Richardson, Garry Parker and Steve Froggatt are working well as a midfield unit and it seems more than the likely that the 1-0 lead will be extended.

Chelsea's game looks fragmented and uncertain by comparison with Villa's. The one exception in Chelsea's ranks is Scottish striker Robert Fleck, signed for £2.1m from Norwich City. He radiates enthusiasm to show he's worth the massive fee, right from the word go.

Playing with the verve of a man inspired he almost gave his side a fourth minute lead then later did just that when Andy Townsend fed the ball in.

Chelsea, once level, grow in stature as Villa, worryingly for Ron Atkinson, do just the opposite. Townsend is now the game's most prominent midfield force, while Fleck is probing away with energy to spare.

It is Fleck's restless endeavours which give Chelsea the lead three minutes later in a dramatic turnaround in fortunes as Villa's normally-so-reliable defence becomes unhinged.

The Scot is the provider for Eddie Newton when he deceives Nigel Spink with a shot of explosive power and accuracy. Refereeing decisions are upsetting Villa players, leading to dissent by Steve Staunton and Earl Barrett who are both shown yellow cards.

Not much is going right for Villa now. Shape has been gone for their formation. So, too, has the confidence required to get back on track.

After 75 minutes the killer blow arrives. A pot shot by Vinnie Jones canons off a defender to Dennis Wise who helps himself to Chelsea's third goal. This uncertain defending leads to further confusion in the ranks though Spink saves heroically from Mick Harford after Shaun Teale loses possession.

Frank McAvennie gets a brief appearance as substitute for limping Cyrille Regis but a difficult 90 minutes has become a lost cause.

Only one win from the opening six games, with two defeats. The script needs re-writing. And quickly.

Saturday 5th September 1992 • Villa Park • 3.00pm

ASTON VILLA 3 CRYSTAL PALACE 0

Half-time 2-0 • Attendance 17,120

Referee Ken REDFERN (Whitley Bay)
Linesmen D.T. COLWELL and J. McGRATH

Claret and Blue Shirts, White Shorts		Goals	Yellow Shirts, Blue Shorts		Goals
1	Nigel SPINK		1	Nigel MARTYN	
2	Earl BARRETT		2	John HUMPHREY †	
3	Steve STAUNTON	41	3	Lee SINNOTT	
4	Shaun TEALE		4	Gareth SOUTHGATE	
5	Paul McGRATH		5	Eric YOUNG	
6	Kevin RICHARDSON		6	Simon OSBORN ‡	
7	Ray HOUGHTON		7	Chris ARMSTRONG	
8	Garry PARKER		8	Geoff THOMAS	
9	Dwight YORKE †	18	9	Mark BRIGHT	
10	Dalian ATKINSON		10	John SALAKO	
11	Stephen FROGGATT	72	11	Eddie McGOLDRICK	

Substitutes			*Substitutes*		
	Frank McAVENNIE †73			Chris COLEMAN †63	
	Ugo EHIOGU			Stuart MASSEY ‡63	
Gk	Les SEALEY		Gk	Paul HEALD	

BEFORE		P	W	D	L	F	A	pts	AFTER		P	W	D	L	F	A	pts
15	Villa	6	1	3	2	6	7	6	11	Villa	7	2	3	2	9	7	9
19	Palace	6	0	4	2	8	10	4	20	Palace	7	0	4	3	8	13	4

FACTFILE

Steve Froggatt scores his first league goal... Frank McAvennie makes his last league appearance for Villa... Villa record their sixth win in the last seven home league meetings with Palace... Mark Bright plays his last game for the Eagles before becoming an Owl. He joins Sheffield Wednesday in a part exchange deal.

Spink keeps
Palace at bay

The fourth home match of the season and not one of the previous three has produced a victory. Not yet a crisis, but supporters are, to put it mildly, a little concerned.

The crowd is a mere 17,120, not the kind of figures required to run financial affairs successfully and the third attendance of below 20,000.

Negotiations for Dean Saunders are dragging out and there are unsubstantiated media hints of friction between manager and chairman over the delay.

In order to remove these doubts and to lift the morale of fans, Ron Atkinson goes out onto the pitch with a microphone to inform fans that he expects the signing to be concluded shortly and that everyone at the club is pulling in the same direction.

In his programme notes the manager refers back to the Chelsea debacle and observes: "The game was there for the taking but we let it slip, losing our shape and our discipline." He's in no mood to see it happen again.

The only team change from that Chelsea defeat is the return of Dwight Yorke in the number nine shirt in place of the injured Cyrille Regis who requires Achilles tendon surgery. Will this shirt be filled by a new player next week? No time to dwell on that. The season's first home win is a desperate immediate priority.

For a while such hopes look dubious and it's a return to last Wednesday night's jitters. Lowly-placed Palace start with an attacking thirst and Nigel Spink has to be at his best in the Holte End goal.

But for him Chris Armstrong and Mark Bright might have scored but better things are ahead. Yorke, back after injury, suddenly gives a tasty reminder of his scoring exploits of 1991-92 with his first goal of the season. A cheeky one, too!

The build up is a delight, and just what Villa need to restore confidence. Garry Parker, fed by Steve Staunton, delays just long enough before passing to Steve Froggatt who measures his pass across the penalty area for Yorke to flick the ball past Nigel Martyn.

Another Spink save from Armstrong defends the lead before Staunton whacks in a 30-yard blockbuster for a 2-0 half-time lead. The Irish international reckons it's his best ever and no-one is arguing.

Palace barely deserve to be trailing at half-time and this feeling is endorsed in the first attack of the second half as Spink turns a drive from England man Geoff Thomas over the crossbar and later saves another from Armstrong.

By this time, however, the result is beyond argument when Froggatt pounces on the rebound as Ray Houghton rattles the bar for a 3-0 scoreline.

Froggatt has decided during the preceding week to withdraw from the England Under-21 squad for a friendly in Spain but has a re-think over the weekend and earns his first cap in Burgos. The Irish Republic would also have liked him to take up their qualification but after initially deciding to put his international career on hold he plumps for England.

At the end, from the terraces there are chants of "Deano... Deano..." Are times a-changing at Villa Park?

Steve Froggatt

Sunday 13th September 1992 • Elland Road • 4.00pm

LEEDS UNITED 1 ASTON VILLA 1

Half-time 0-1 • *Attendance* 27,815

Referee Joe WORRALL (Warrington)

Linesmen D.E. BINSLEY and G.I. GRANDIDGE

White Shirts, White Shorts	Goals	Claret and Blue Shirts, White Shorts	Goals
1 John LUKIC		1 Nigel SPINK	
2 Jon NEWSOME †		2 Earl BARRETT	
3 Scott SELLARS		3 Steve STAUNTON	
4 David BATTY		4 Shaun TEALE	
5 Chris FAIRCLOUGH		5 Paul McGRATH	
6 Chris WHYTE		6 Kevin RICHARDSON	
7 Eric CANTONA		7 Ray HOUGHTON	
8 Gordon STRACHAN		8 Garry PARKER	19
9 Lee CHAPMAN		9 Dean SAUNDERS	
10 Gary McALLISTER		10 Dalian ATKINSON	
11 Gary SPEED		11 Stephen FROGGATT	
Substitutes		*Substitutes*	
Steve HODGE †69	85	Dwight YORKE	
David ROCASTLE		Ugo EHIOGU	
Gk Mervyn DAY		Gk Les SEALEY	

BEFORE		P	W	D	L	F	A	pts	AFTER		P	W	D	L	F	A	pts
11	Villa	7	2	3	2	9	7	9	9	Villa	8	2	4	2	10	8	10
12	Leeds	7	2	3	2	13	12	9	10	Leeds	8	2	4	2	14	13	10

FACTFILE

Dean Saunders makes his Villa debut and has a 'goal' disallowed for offside... Villa make their first live TV appearance in the Premier League... Steve Hodge scores against his former club.

Saunders looks the part

The Dean Saunders signing saga has been successfully completed, as indicated last week by Ron Atkinson. Deano arrives at Elland Road as Villa's record signing at £2.3m, hopefully to complete the team-building jig-saw.

Although he had scored an impressive 23 goals for Liverpool and set a record in European competition, the Welshman appeared not to have been appreciated at Anfield.

There were suggestions that he could not fit in with Ian Rush and that he had never quite settled on Merseyside. He shrugs off the questions.

He's a Villa player now. Judge him on what he does for the claret-and-blues, is all he asks.

Villa fans have given massive approval to the signing which completes an approximate round figure of £20m in buys and sells since Atkinson became manager 15 months ago and David Platt was sold to the Italian club, Bari, for £5.5m.

The return match with Leeds comes less than a month after that closely-fought draw between the clubs at Villa Park and this is to prove another tight and tense confrontation.

Dwight Yorke is the one who has to give way to Deano in an otherwise unchanged team from the Crystal Palace win. Tough on the lad from Tobago, but he's on the bench, close to the action.

Leeds have drifted considerably from the standard which established them as reigning champions.

It is a testing occasion for them. They are defending an unbeaten home record stretching back over seventeen months and 27 games. And in a few days time they start their European Cup programme against German champions Stuttgart.

They are without one of their former Villa men, Tony Dorigo, who pulls out with a stomach bug at short notice, but Steve Hodge is on the bench.

Only Gordon Strachan brings a creative touch to a side who strangely resort to lobbing hopeful balls forward for Eric Cantona or Lee Chapman.

In contrast Villa are working the ball forward from Paul McGrath at the back through an inter-passing midfield, seeking to provide ammunition for Deano to sign in with his opening goal.

As it turns out Saunders is one of the creators this time, and no-one is complaining. Earl Barrett to Ray Houghton, defenders are drawn out of position by Deano's off-the-ball run and Garry Parker is left free to claim the lead.

Earlier Villa have been denied by Leeds' offside tactics but this time they have been caught out.

By now Saunders and Dalian Atkinson are showing signs of feeding off each other just as the manager had planned. The pair have been encouraged to mix socially and share journeys in order to work up a rapport.

Time is running out for Leeds with that home record under severe threat when Hodge, brought on as sub for Newsome mid-way through the half, puts one over on his former club.

Gary McAllister crosses, Cantona, artist to the core, supplies a neat little touch, and Hodge knocks in an 85th minute equaliser, another late dagger thrust into the heart of Villa's defence.

But a draw at Elland Road will do. And, next week, Deano along with Steve Staunton and Ray Houghton will lick their lips in anticipation of meeting Liverpool at Villa Park.

Like the supporters, they can hardly wait.

Saturday 19th September 1992 • Villa Park • 3.00pm

ASTON VILLA 4 LIVERPOOL 2

Half-time 1-1 • *Attendance* 37,863
Referee Philip DON (Hanworth Park, Middlesex)
Linesmen B.L. POLKEY and E.J. WALSH

Claret and Blue Shirts, White Shorts		Goals	Green Shirts, Green Shorts		Goals
1	Nigel SPINK		1	David JAMES	
2	Earl BARRETT		2	Torben PIECHNIK ❑	
3	Steve STAUNTON		3	David BURROWS	
4	Shaun TEALE		4	Steve NICOL	
5	Paul McGRATH		5	Jamie REDKNAPP	
6	Kevin RICHARDSON		6	Mark WRIGHT	
7	Ray HOUGHTON ❑		7	Ronny ROSENTHAL	84
8	Garry PARKER	78	8	Mike MARSH	
9	Dean SAUNDERS	44, 65	9	Don HUTCHISON	
10	Dalian ATKINSON ❑	53	10	Jan MOLBY	
11	Stephen FROGGATT		11	Mark WALTERS	43
	Substitutes			*Substitutes*	
	Dwight YORKE			Nick TANNER	
	Dariusz KUBICKI			Steve HARKNESS	
Gk	Les SEALEY		Gk	Bruce GROBBELAAR	

BEFORE	P	W	D	L	F	A	pts	AFTER	P	W	D	L	F	A	pts
10 Villa	8	2	4	2	10	8	10	7 Villa	9	3	4	2	14	10	13
15 Liverpool	8	2	3	3	9	11	9	17 Liverpool	9	2	3	4	11	15	9

FACTFILE

The 37,863 attendance is the highest in the Premier League so far and produces club record receipts of £313,152... League debuts for Liverpool duo Piechnik and Hutchison... Home debut for Dean Saunders – against his former club... Villa remain unbeaten by Liverpool in the last eight League meetings at Villa Park.

Liverpool played off the park

Suddenly Villa Park is alive to the sound of clicking turnstiles, as supporters react to a combination of circumstances which have filled acres of newspaper column inches.

By kick-off time the biggest attendance of the FA Premier League so far is making the old place hum with the famous atmosphere of earlier successful times.

Villa Park on big-match day is a special place, and 37,863 spectators await the action aglow with the knowledge that this will be a special match.

"Liverpool is still the League's No.1 scalp," insists manager Ron Atkinson, ignoring their recent decline.

Dean Saunders' first home appearance since his £2.3m signing, and against his former club at that. Ex-Anfield colleagues Steve Staunton and Ray Houghton also face their old club, and at a time when Liverpool's defences are down.

Villa are unchanged from Elland Road. Liverpool have their new signing, the Scandinavian Torben Piechnik, at the heart of their defence alongside Mark Wright. Deano's former Derby County colleague has not settled well at Anfield under Graeme Souness either, so he could be in for a tough afternoon.

The match proves ecstatic for everyone connected with Aston Villa, a delight to the neutrals but a particularly horrific nightmare for Souness.

The action is left as something of a blur in people's minds with the goals over-riding all else in the memory except, of course, the miss of the season from Ronny Rosenthal.

When ex-Villa and Rangers winger Mark Walters puts Liverpool ahead two minutes before the break it simply sets-off a chain reaction of explosive moments.

Saunders it is who equalises within a minute from Steve Froggatt's cross for his first Aston Villa goal. It will not be his last. After Dalian Atkinson has benefitted from a mis-cued shot by Parker to apply the finishing touch Villa simply run away with the game, fuelled by pure adrenalin.

A pass by Houghton enables Saunders to knock in his second and Villa's third over goalkeeper David James's legs and Liverpool are two goals down.

That becomes a three-goal deficit when Saunders and Atkinson combine to lay one on for Garry Parker as Wright loses touch. There are only a few minutes left when Ronnie Rosenthal makes it a more respectable 4-2.

The press room line of questioning is predictable. And Souness doesn't like it much. "Do you think it was inevitable that Dean Saunders would score against you, today, Graeme?" one reporter asks.

Exit Souness, without reply. Enter Saunders. "Both my goals went through the 'keeper's legs," he confesses. "I've had a change of luck. All season they have been bouncing off the keeper's legs or the post and coming out. Today they went in."

In vivid contrast, Atkinson's season is truly underway now. He has the high-quality striker he has hunted so relentlessly. His team-building is looking good. Everything has gelled in one dramatic afternoon.

"I'll be happy if Deano scores as many goals for us as he did for Liverpool," he comments breezily before heading off for a quiet, celebratory, and well-deserved drink.

**The Deadly Duo...
Dean Saunders and
Dalian Atkinson in
celebratory mood.**

Wednesday 23rd September 1992 • Manor Ground • 7.45pm

OXFORD UNITED 1 ASTON VILLA 2

Half-time 0-0 • *Attendance* 8,837

Referee Roger WISEMAN (Boreham Wood, Herts)

Linesmen M.A. HAIR and P.A. VOSPER

Yellow Shirts, Blue Shorts		Goals	Claret and Blue Shirts, White Shorts		Goals
1	Paul KEE		1	Nigel SPINK	
2	Gary SMART		2	Earl BARRETT	
3	David COLLINS		3	Steve STAUNTON	
4	Mickey LEWIS		4	Shaun TEALE	72
5	Ceri EVANS		5	Paul McGRATH ❑	52
6	Andrew MELVILLE		6	Kevin RICHARDSON	
7	Jim MAGILTON		7	Ray HOUGHTON	
8	Joey BEAUCHAMP	89	8	Garry PARKER	
9	David PENNEY		9	Dean SAUNDERS	
10	John DURNIN		10	Dalian ATKINSON †	
11	Chris ALLEN		11	Stephen FROGGATT	
	Substitutes			*Substitutes*	
	Nick CUSACK			Dwight YORKE †83	
	Les PHILLIPS		Gk	Les SEALEY	

FACTFILE

Ron Atkinson, Jim Barron, Dean Saunders and Ray Houghton return to their former club. Houghton was a League Cup winner with Oxford in 1986... Paul McGrath's goal is the first from the head of a Villa player this season. He and Shaun Teale open their 92/93 accounts.

Jim Barron, Oxford return

Oxford shown a bit of class

Many supporters fancy Villa's chances of a Wembley run in the League Cup, especially since the team-building jig-saw seems to have been successfully completed.

Ron Atkinson has an outstanding record in sudden-death competitions and never disguises his regard for the thrill of the chase.

Having won the trophy with Sheffield Wednesday, under the Rumbelows sponsorship, and two FA Cups with Manchester United, he knows all about the demands involved.

National focus is still glaring down on Villa since the Dean Saunders signing and expectations for a successful scoring partnership with Dalian Atkinson are high.

Straight after the Liverpool experience, in which Saunders, Steve Staunton and Ray Houghton were hell-bent on 'punishing' the club who sold them, comes the story of rather more sentimental returns.

Atkinson, his No. 2 Jim Barron, Saunders and Houghton are all Oxford old boys. One of the manager's favourite wisecracks is that not many fathers can say that their son went to both Oxford AND Cambridge...!

No-one is surprised to see that an unchanged team has been selected after the four-goal romp of four days earlier nor are there many fears that Villa will leave Manor Ground with a deficit to pull back in the second leg.

Earlier, Atkinson had referred to the fact that his centre backs Paul McGrath and Shaun Teale, powerful strapping men both of them, had not been making a scoring contribution. As in the case of his similar criticisms of his midfielders, the call was to be answered.

It must have been all rather confusing for Oxford whose pre-match briefing by the manager Brian Horton must surely have been on the

obvious dangers likely to eminate from Saunders, Atkinson, Houghton, Parker etc.

By half time they have all been kept relatively quiet even though the gap in quality between Villa individually and collectively, and their First Division opponents is clear for all to see.

The skids go under Oxford seven minutes into the second half. McGrath gets on the end of Parker's superbly-flighted corner and though it bounces off a defender the Irishman is there to knock in the rebound.

"Anything Macca can I can do, too..." thinks Teale, and his chance to prove it arrives with another corner, this one by Richardson after 72 minutes.

The ball falls to the former Bournemouth defender near the edge of the penalty area and his full-blooded blast rebounds off goalkeeper Paul Kee into the corner of the net.

At 2-0 up Villa seem set for the kill as they mostly dictate the flow of the game in search of further goals. Oxford, however, are not lying down in despair. Their own passing football has its moments and Nigel Spink's goal is under siege more than once, especially when a Joey Beauchamp effort hits the Villa keeper's legs.

Despite many promising attacks and close things Villa fail to add to their total and are made to deeply regret it when Beauchamp gives them a taste of their own medicine in front of goal.

David Penney's cross arrows in, Teale blocks the first scoring attempt but Beauchamp gobbles up the rebound McGrath-style for a strike which keeps the tie alive.

"Villa are a top-class side with World-class players," confesses the Oxford manager. "We were a little over-awed..."

Shaun Teale

Saturday 26th September 1992 • Ayresome Park • 3.00pm

MIDDLESBROUGH 2 ASTON VILLA 3

Half-time 0-1 • Attendance 20,905

Referee David ELLERAY (Harrow-on-the-Hill, Middlesex)
Linesmen A.N. BUTLER and J.B. ROBINSON

Red Shirts, White Shorts	Goals	White Shirts, Black Shorts	Goals
1 Ian IRONSIDE		1 Nigel SPINK	
2 Chris MORRIS		2 Earl BARRETT	
3 Jimmy PHILLIPS		3 Steve STAUNTON	
4 Alan KERNAGHAN ❏		4 Shaun TEALE	
5 Derek WHYTE		5 Paul McGRATH	(og 87)
6 Andy PEAKE		6 Kevin RICHARDSON	
7 Bernie SLAVEN	62	7 Ray HOUGHTON	
8 Robbie MUSTOE		8 Garry PARKER ‡	
9 Paul WILKINSON		9 Dean SAUNDERS	22,75
10 Jamie POLLOCK		10 Dalian ATKINSON	72
11 Tommy WRIGHT		11 Stephen FROGGATT †	
Substitutes		*Substitutes*	
Mark PROCTOR		Dwight YORKE †71	
Jon GITTENS		Mark BLAKE ‡87	
Gk Andrew COLLETT		Gk Les SEALEY	

BEFORE	P	W	D	L	F	A	pts	AFTER	P	W	D	L	F	A	pts
7 Villa	9	3	4	2	14	10	13	6 Villa	10	4	4	2	17	12	16
6 Boro	8	4	2	2	17	17	14	7 Boro	9	4	2	3	19	20	14

FACTFILE

*Middlesbrough's first home defeat of the season... and their biggest gate to date...
Villa unbeaten in four games since Deano signing... Les Sealey on first team
squad duty for the last occasion before moving on loan to Birmingham City and
later a permanent transfer to his former club Manchester United.*

Deano and Dalian deliver

Each match is now a different kind of test of the team formation recently established by Villa. They go into their third successive game with an unchanged line-up, the kind of situation managers give blood for.

However, Ayresome Park has not always been Villa's favourite destination. Points are frequently lost here in rather dour, unspectacular games which can upset a visiting team's rhythm.

Also, a new lease of life has been injected into the club by Lennie Lawrence who learned the low-budget managerial business well in constantly keeping Charlton Athletic above the breadline.

Middlesbrough have started the season promisingly and are well in the top half of the table.

Dean Saunders and Dalian Atkinson have not yet, at this very early stage, proved a prolific partnership away from home, having failed to find the net at either Leeds or Oxford.

The attendance of over 20,000 (5,000 above average) creates a competitive atmosphere with Villa having clearly become the sort of big-personality side supporters around the country are prepared to pay to watch.

Six weeks into the first FA Premier League competition, the title race is wide open with surprise names like Norwich City and Coventry City among the early front-runners.

Quickly into their stride, Villa show the large crowd that Boro have a tough one on their hands.

The midfield of Ray Houghton, Garry Parker, Kevin Richardson and Steve Froggatt have that air of 'togetherness' which looks easy when it works but which is actually only produced by hard work on the practice ground.

Deano's first away goal for Villa sees them in at half-time with a 1-0 lead from an entertaining 45 minutes. He and Atkinson are increasing their understanding all the time, as demonstrated when the latter scores Villa's second in the 72nd minute.

The opening is created by Houghton's astuteness from a free kick and is required to restore the lead after Bernie Slaven has equalised.

Another three minutes elapse and Saunders supplies a simple finish to a move which carves open the home defence down the left with Parker and substitute Dwight Yorke both playing an important part.

Chances are being created now with a brand of attacking football rarely seen from visiting sides and two or three more goals are on the cards.

In the event the attacking aggression is at the expense of a shortage of defensive cover and that familiar irritant of conceding a late goal strikes again.

Give Boro their due, they are still looking for goals on the break right to the closing minutes when a mix-up in front of goal sees an Andy Peake shot deflected by Nigel Spink and cannon off McGrath's shins over the line.

Ron Atkinson will not get involved in discussions about his team's prospects of finishing top of the League but Lawrence is happy to say it for him.

"Villa totally and utterly outplayed us," he said unashamedly. "They are championship contenders."

Ron Atkinson, bringing a togetherness to his team

Saturday 3rd October 1992 • Selhurst Park • 3.00pm

WIMBLEDON 2 ASTON VILLA 3

Half-time 1-2 • Attendance 6,849

Referee Stephen LODGE (Barnsley)

Linesmen G. BUTLAND and B.A. WIGGINTON

Blue Shirts, Blue Shorts	Goals	Claret and Blue Shirts, White Shorts	Goals
1 Hans SEGERS		1 Nigel SPINK	
2 Warren BARTON ❑		2 Earl BARRETT ❑	
3 Gary ELKINS		3 Steve STAUNTON	
4 Paul MILLER	35	4 Shaun TEALE	
5 John SCALES		5 Paul McGRATH	
6 Scott FITZGERALD		6 Kevin RICHARDSON	
7 Neil ARDLEY		7 Ray HOUGHTON	
8 Robbie EARLE ❑		8 Garry PARKER	
9 John FASHANU †		9 Dean SAUNDERS	6, 30
10 Lawrie SANCHEZ		10 Dalian ATKINSON	77
11 Andy CLARKE	90	11 Stephen FROGGATT †	
Substitutes		*Substitutes*	
Aidan NEWHOUSE †25		Dwight YORKE †45	
Roger JOSEPH		Bryan SMALL	
Gk Neil SULLIVAN		Gk Mark BOSNICH	

BEFORE		P	W	D	L	F	A	pts	AFTER		P	W	D	L	F	A	pts
6	Villa	10	4	4	2	17	12	16	5	Villa	11	5	4	2	20	14	19
18	Wimbledon	10	2	3	5	12	15	9	21	Wimbledon	11	2	3	6	14	18	9

FACTFILE

Dalian Atkinson's dream goal wins the BBC 'Goal of the Month' competition and is later voted as their 'Goal of the Season'... Mark Bosnich makes his first appearance of the season on the bench... Villa record only their second ever away win over the Dons.

Deadly duo destroy Dons

The fourth away game in five starts, another unchanged team, another examination of Villa's true calibre and a chance to continue climbing the table from the lowly 16th position once occupied.

Since Dean Saunders was signed Ron Atkinson's team has lifted itself from the half-way mark into sixth place in the three league fixtures played to date.

The Dons have made a slow start, only one place above bottom club Nottingham Forest but they are a resilient club with a record of fighting back from adversity.

Losing the use of their own, cramped Plough Lane stadium, and playing to very small crowds as temporary guests at Selhurst Park must be a soul-destroying experience.

Their average attendance is a mere 6,500 and of the 6,849 here today 2,789 are in the Villa enclosure, forty per cent of the total.

The Premier League is still regarded as the most demanding in the World because of its diversity of challenges and the varying unpredictability of the weather and underfoot conditions.

"This one won't be easy," says Ron Atkinson grimly. "We have to be brave enough to keep on playing our way but not brave enough to get our eyebrows split."

After only four games in the claret-and-blue strip Dean Saunders has become a cult figure and we soon see why, after only six minutes to be precise.

Steve Froggatt prises open the rugged Dons defence with a centre which begs to be tucked away and Deano obliges. Unfortunately Froggy receives a whack from Scott Fitzgerald while in the process of delivering and by half-time he's unable to continue.

By then, also, Robbie Earle has been booked for another illegal Wimbledon attempt to stop Villa's leggy and talented young winger.

There is no stopping Deano, though. On the half-hour the Welshman stylishly exchanges passes with Houghton to bury No.2. Wimbledon are struggling now, and Saunders has rattled his third pair of goals in only five starts for Villa. Money well spent, eh?

Just before that second goal Dons have lost John Fashanu with a groin strain. So, with Vinnie Jones a non-starter, there is a distinct lowering of muscle power within the home ranks.

Saunders has helped himself to his couple of little gems but the game's gleaming diamond arrives mid-way through the second half. Atkinson, full of power and acceleration, sprints from his own half past one opponent, and another, and another, before chipping the ball over Hans Segers' head.

"He does it all the time in training," shrugs Big Ron. "I've tried to stop him doing it..." The wisecracking boss is sometimes as much a star turn in the interview room as his players are on the pitch.

Andy Clarke pulls one back on the stroke of full-time but Villa are very good value for their second successive 3-2 win away from home.

Dean Saunders nets his sixth Villa goal to put his side two up at Selhurst Park

Wednesday 7th October • Villa Park • 7.45pm

ASTON VILLA 2 OXFORD UNITED 1

Half-time 1-0 • *Attendance* 19,808
Referee Bob NIXON (West Kirby)
Linesmen R.H. ANDREWS and P.J. GRIGGS

Claret and Blue Shirts, White Shorts		Goals
1	Nigel SPINK	
2	Earl BARRETT	
3	Steve STAUNTON	
4	Shaun TEALE	
5	Ugo EHIOGU	
6	Kevin RICHARDSON	90
7	Ray HOUGHTON	
8	Garry PARKER	
9	Dean SAUNDERS	
10	Dalian ATKINSON	11
11	Dwight YORKE	

Substitutes

Mark BLAKE
Gk Mark BOSNICH

Yellow Shirts, Blue Shorts		Goals
1	Paul REECE	
2	Gary SMART	
3	David COLLINS †	
4	Mickey LEWIS	
5	Ceri EVANS	
6	Andy MELVILLE	
7	Les PHILLIPS	
8	Nick CUSACK	88
9	David PENNEY	
10	John DURNIN	
11	Mike FORD ❏	

Substitutes

Chris ALLEN †80
Darren JACKSON

FACTFILE

Holte End fans take advantage of the £5 reduced price admission fee, hence the larger than expected gate... Oxford's only previous League Cup tie at Villa Park was in the first leg of the 1986 semi-final. Ray Houghton was in the visitors' side that night.

Ray Houghton, a Wembley winner with Oxford in 1986

Below par Villa ease through

Blessed with a 2-1 lead from the first leg at the Manor Ground, Villa have to be everyone's unanimous favourites, though it proves no easy ride.

Ron Atkinson, cautious so far in accepting that his carefully-constructed team is making the progress he demands, has nevertheless publicly declared: "I enjoy watching us play."

Missing from the ranks tonight are Paul McGrath and Steve Froggatt, both injured. Their places are taken by Ugo Ehiogu and Dwight Yorke.

The complications of the current TV deal with switched matches and unpredictable fixture-planning has meant a gap of almost three weeks between home games.

During that period Villa have played three away games, at Oxford, Middlesbrough and Wimbledon, and won them all.

A degree of promising form has emerged in those games but it is not continued in this particular exercise which proves more about its end-product than its means.

"A poor performance, very disappointing," admits Atkinson afterwards. "We weren't switched on in our attitude and some players obviously wanted to play without breaking sweat."

The reason for this, perhaps, was that Dalian Atkinson's 11th minute goal, his third in successive matches and seventh of the season, took the aggregate to 3-1 and virtually took the tie out of Oxford's reach.

Yorke was the provider with a pass which unhinged the Oxford defence for Kevin Richardson's centre to be flicked on by the in-form striker.

An equaliser by Nick Cusack reduced it to 3-2 in the 88th minute but realistically that was

always going to be the limit for the First Division team who were giving it their best shot.

This was confirmed in injury time when a tremendous drive by Richardson from several yards outside the area left trialist 'keeper Gil Reece, from Grimsby, totally stranded.

Strangely, the most exciting part of the occasion came well after the final whistle when Manchester United at Villa Park came out of the hat in the third round-draw.

"The glamour tie of the round," said Villa's manager. You could almost hear him licking his lips.

The tie will virtually fill Villa Park and will be played only ten days before the scheduled Premier League meeting with United at Villa Park.

Two fixtures of massive importance against the club who dismissed him after he had twice won them the FA Cup. Big Ron can hardly wait... but first, a week-end break in the League programme for international calls.

Kevin Richardson - best goal of the tie

Monday 19th October 1992 • Villa Park • 7.45pm

ASTON VILLA 0 BLACKBURN ROVERS 0

Half-time 0-0 • *Attendance* 30,398

Referee Howard KING (Merthyr Tydfil)

Linesmen P.M. ROBERTS and A. STREETS

Claret and Blue Shirts, White Shorts	Goals	Blue and White Halved Shirts, White Shorts	Goals
1 Nigel SPINK		1 Bobby MIMMS	
2 Earl BARRETT		2 David MAY	
3 Steve STAUNTON		3 Alan WRIGHT	
4 Shaun TEALE		4 Tim SHERWOOD	
5 Paul McGRATH		5 Colin HENDRY	
6 Kevin RICHARDSON		6 Kevin MORAN	
7 Ray HOUGHTON		7 Stuart RIPLEY	
8 Garry PARKER		8 Gordon COWANS	
9 Dean SAUNDERS		9 Alan SHEARER	
10 Dalian ATKINSON		10 Mike NEWELL	
11 Steve FROGGATT †		11 Jason WILCOX	

Substitutes	*Substitutes*
Bryan SMALL †45	Nick MARKER
Dwight YORKE	Roy WEGERLE
Gk Mark BOSNICH	Gk Darren COLLIER

BEFORE		P	W	D	L	F	A	pts	AFTER		P	W	D	L	F	A	pts
2	Blackburn	11	7	3	1	24	9	24	2	Blackburn	12	7	4	1	24	9	25
7	Villa	11	5	4	2	20	14	19	4	Villa	12	5	5	2	20	14	20

FACTFILE

£3.6M Shearer and £2.3M Deano are goalless... Draw ends run of five wins on the trot... Gordon Cowans plays his first game against his former club... The game is screened 'live' on Sky Sports... Bryan Small makes his first appearance of the season.

Shoot-out ends as a shut-out

Never mind the match for now. Until kick-off time, just sample the atmosphere. Booming rap music from speakers half the size of a house, dancing girls, huge comic Sumo wrestlers, a jolly-it-up MC who barely needs his microphone, and the ball arriving by air, courtesy of sky divers.

We're left in no doubt that we're into something big. Very big. Kenny Dalglish's Blackburn are setting a scorching pace near the top of the league, backed by their owner, Jack Walker's, seemingly bottomless pocket.

Rovers have in their ranks Alan Shearer for a cool £3.6M. Villa would have liked him when Southampton were forced to part. But Dean Saunders at £2.3M will do very nicely thank you...

Paul McGrath and Steve Froggatt are back after missing the Coca Cola Cup-tie against Oxford United.

Garry Parker is now officially installed as an England 'fringe' player having been called up for Graham Taylor's squad to play Norway in the World Cup qualifier at Wembley last Wednesday.

Because of 'international week' and the change from Saturday to Monday there has been a 12-day gap in competitive fixtures.

And so, build-up over, and action underway, the quality of the football is excellent. Goals would undoubtedly enrich the action but for superb defensive play, especially by Teale at one end and Hendry at the other.

Goalkeepers Spink and Mimms back their defences with some terrific saves. Spink jack-knifes to deny Newell while Mimms contrives to claw up and onto the crossbar, Houghton's 25-yarder which looked to be on its way in.

These two moments were typical of a fine game and Ron Atkinson is gracious in his praise of Blackburn's first-half domination.

Ex-Villa man Gordon Cowans has given tantalising glances of the creativity so revered at Villa Park as Blackburn threaten to take control.

During the interval Atkinson withdraws the injured Froggatt and replaces him with Bryan Small who goes to left back, pushing Staunton forward into midfield.

Rovers have lost the leadership to Norwich but could win it back, if only they can overcome Villa. But Villa could likewise continue their climb and reach third place with a better goals record than Coventry.

Small is an instant hit, effectively shackling the wing runs of Stuart Ripley while Staunton gives more forward drive than the slender Froggatt.

More good football, a few chances, fine defending, a miss or two, and an honourable result.

Kenny Dalglish, not publicly the most forthcoming or articulate of managers, professes himself to be well pleased with 'everything' about the match but picks out the respective displays of the goalkeepers.

This had been billed as the Night of the Big Guns and a shoot-out between Saunders and Shearer. In the event it was the Great Shut-out, with Spink and Mimms in the starring roles.

For Villa a set pattern is continuing to take shape with a team which virtually picks itself.

Nigel Spink - star man

Saturday 24th October 1992 • Boundary Park • 3.00pm

OLDHAM ATHLETIC 1 ASTON VILLA 1

Half-time 1-0 • *Attendance* 13,457

Referee Roger GIFFORD (Mid-Glamorgan)

Linesmen T.A. ATKINSON and R.R. RAWSON

Blue Shirts, Blue Shorts	Goals	Claret and Blue Shirts, White Shorts	Goals
1 Jon HALLWORTH		1 Nigel SPINK	
2 Gunnar HALLE		2 Earl BARRETT	
3 Neil POINTON		3 Steve STAUNTON	
4 Nick HENRY		4 Shaun TEALE	
5 Richard JOBSON		5 Paul McGRATH	
6 Steve REDMOND		6 Kevin RICHARDSON	
7 Ian OLNEY †	19	7 Ray HOUGHTON	
8 Ian MARSHALL		8 Dwight YORKE †	
9 Graeme SHARP		9 Dean SAUNDERS	
10 Mike MILLIGAN		10 Dalian ATKINSON	82
11 Paul BERNARD		11 Bryan SMALL	
Substitutes		*Substitutes*	
Neil McDONALD †71		Dave FARRELL †74	
Neil ADAMS		Mark BLAKE	
Gk John KEELEY		Gk Mark BOSNICH	

BEFORE	P	W	D	L	F	A	pts	AFTER	P	W	D	L	F	A	pts
4 Villa	12	5	5	2	20	14	20	6 Villa	13	5	6	2	21	15	21
13 Oldham	12	3	5	4	20	21	14	14 Oldham	13	3	6	4	21	22	15

FACTFILE

Earl Barrett makes his first return to Oldham since joining Villa in February... Ian Olney plays against his previous club for the first time too, and scores... Garry Parker is missing through injury, Bryan Small comes in at left-back with Steve Staunton moving into midfield... Dave Farrell makes his first-team debut.

Barrett's home and welcome

No prizes for guessing which Villa player has a greater sense of anticipation about this particular game than any other.

Earl Barrett is back at Boundary Park for the first time since his £1.7M move last February, just when Villa are seeking to restore their winning sequence, interrupted by the home draw with Blackburn Rovers last Monday.

Barrett has settled superbly into his right back role despite the fact that he would prefer to play in the centre of the defence.

"The way that Shaun and Paul play together you could not part them," he says with a professional sense of understanding. "I am enjoying playing at right back.

"I've no complaints."

Barrett admits to being slightly apprehensive about the kind of reception he might get having heard stories of other Oldham 'old boys' getting some stick on their return.

He need not have worried. As Villa run onto the field and their names are read out individually there is only applause for Barrett.

"I really appreciated that," he says later.

The game itself proves to be a dogged battle to slog it out for a point as an Oldham team, with ex-Villa striker Ian Olney up front, make it difficult for Villa to play their normal game through midfield.

"As dour and uncompromising as the Lancashire weather," is how the play is decribed locally. This one is a test of character rather than of creative skills, especially after Olney fulfils his little personal dream, in the 19th minute, of netting against his former club.

Chances to square it are few but Villa stick to their task and have the edge in terms of forward play.

Only eight minutes remain when Dean Saunders succeeds in escaping the attentions of Richard Jobson by moving out to the right to supply the decisive cross.

Steve Redmond fails to cut it out allowing Atkinson to connect with a fine header for his seventh goal of the season and his club's ninth game without defeat.

With the 'winger' role Ron Atkinson's obvious selection difficulty, based largely on the loss of Tony Daley after surgery plus Dwight Yorke's fall-off from his peak of last season, the manager includes teenager Dave Farrell into his 14.

The Chelmsley Wood youngster gets a taste of the action as substitute for Yorke, quite a lift from local Sunday football, in the Coronation League, in less than a year!

"Villa are rightly classed as championship contenders," says Joe Royle, the Oldham manager.

Barrett is not disatisfied at leaving his former ground with a useful point in the bag. "There were times last season when, if we went a goal or two down, heads might have gone a little," he said.

"This is not happening now."

Dave Farrell - surprise debut

Wednesday 28th October 1992 • Villa Park • 7.45pm

ASTON VILLA 1 MANCHESTER UNITED 0

Half-time 0-0 • *Attendance* 35,964

Referee Philip DON (Hanworth Park, Middlesex)
Linesmen J. BARLOW and R. THOMAS

Claret and Blue Shirts, White Shorts		Goals	Blue Shirts, Blue Shorts		Goals
1	Nigel SPINK		1	Peter SCHMEICHEL	
2	Earl BARRETT		2	Paul PARKER	
3	Steve STAUNTON		3	Denis IRWIN †	
4	Shaun TEALE		4	Steve BRUCE	
5	Paul McGRATH		5	Darren FERGUSON ❏	
6	Kevin RICHARDSON		6	Gary PALLISTER	
7	Ray HOUGHTON		7	Clayton BLACKMORE	
8	Garry PARKER		8	Paul INCE	
9	Dean SAUNDERS	75	9	Brian McCLAIR	
10	Dalian ATKINSON		10	Mark HUGHES	
11	Dwight YORKE		11	Ryan GIGGS	

Substitutes	*Substitutes*
Bryan SMALL	Andrei KANCHELSKIS †23
Dave FARRELL	Neil WEBB

FACTFILE

Holders United suffer their first League Cup defeat since Ron Atkinson's Sheffield Wednesday beat them in the 1991 Final... It's the Red Devils' first open defeat in 16 games, although they were eliminated from the UEFA Cup on penalties in Moscow.

Steve Bruce holds off Dalian Atkinson

Deano sinks the Cup holders

The pairing with Manchester United, once managed by Ron Atkinson, gives the Villa Park tie a charismatic appeal, as demonstrated by a near-capacity gate.

According to media hype there is no love lost between some elements in the respective clubs.

Atkinson bears no grudges, he says. But a recently-published book by United boss Alex Ferguson, makes controversial references to the Old Trafford situation he inherited from his predecessor.

Paul McGrath, in particular, comes out of this publication in an unfavourable light and, to put it mildly, is not best pleased!

So much for the build-up. What of the match?

United arrive as holders of the trophy in its previous guise, the Rumbelows Cup, Atkinson having won it the previous year as manager of Sheffield Wednesday... by beating Ferguson's Manchester United.

For 75 minutes the tie is as finely-balanced as anticipated with United bedevilled by scoring difficulties which threaten to wreck their season.

Many Villa fans recall a previous great occasion against United when, as a Third Division club on December 23 1970, they removed United, Charlton, Best, Law and all, in the semi-final to reach Wembley.

The atmosphere of that memorable success is re-created as supporters fill the night with sound in urging on their teams.

United had their chances, as did Villa before they finally conjured the winner. But the Old Trafford club, even with the talents of Mark Hughes, Brian McClair and Ryan Giggs to rely on, could not finish them off.

They had scored only six goals in nine games, not the stuff of trophy winners. Villa, in contrast, could always be fancied to tuck away at least one chance, as illustrated by recent achievements.

Welsh cap Hughes wastes one opening in the first minute as the home fans sigh with relief. To concede a goal now would allow the visitors to pack their experienced defence.

A lucky escape, indeed.

Later, when Hughes heads wide a centre from Giggs, United's grip on the trophy is as good as relinquished.

Villa's big moment comes when Kevin Richardson's corner snakes in and Dean Saunders wriggles free from defenders to head in at the far post for his seventh goal in nine games.

Even then, as a torrid tie grips the senses to its final throw, United launch a last-ditch onslaught. McGrath is pressured to head against his own woodwork and Nigel Spink stops possible equalisers from Bruce and Hughes.

"Never in doubt..." Ron Atkinson wrly tells a crowded press conference. But his voice is croaking. And you know he's joking.

It's looking good for a Coca Cola Cup run as another home draw emerges. Ipswich Town are to be the fourth round visitors. Not an 'easy' tie. The East Anglian club are improving as they go along. But Villa will start favourites, especially with Dalian Atkinson's habit of scoring against his former clubs.

Steve Staunton takes on Paul Parker

Sunday 1st November 1992 • Villa Park • 3.00pm

ASTON VILLA 2 QUEEN'S PARK RANGERS 0

Half-time 1-0 • *Attendance* 20,140
Referee Michael PECK (Kendal)
Linesmen E.J. WALSH and B.A. WIGGINTON

Claret and Blue Shirts, White Shorts		Goals	Red and Black Hooped Shirts, Red Shorts		Goals
1	Nigel SPINK		1	Tony ROBERTS	
2	Earl BARRETT		2	David BARDSLEY	
3	Steve STAUNTON		3	Clive WILSON	
4	Shaun TEALE		4	Ray WILKINS	
5	Paul McGRATH		5	Darren PEACOCK	
6	Kevin RICHARDSON		6	Alan McDONALD	
7	Ray HOUGHTON		7	Andrew IMPEY †	
8	Garry PARKER		8	Ian HOLLOWAY	
9	Dean SAUNDERS	43	9	Les FERDINAND	
10	Dalian ATKINSON ‡	79	10	Bradley ALLEN	
11	Dave FARRELL †		11	Simon BARKER	

Substitutes		*Substitutes*
Bryan SMALL †60		Dennis BAILEY †81
Dwight YORKE ‡89		Danny MADDIX
Gk Mark BOSNICH		Gk Jan STEJSKAL

BEFORE		P	W	D	L	F	A	pts	AFTER		P	W	D	L	F	A	pts
3	QPR	13	8	2	3	20	13	23	3	Villa	14	6	6	2	23	15	24
6	Villa	13	5	6	2	21	15	21	4	QPR	14	8	2	4	20	15	23

FACTFILE

Eleven games without defeat as Villa reach their highest position since finishing runners-up in 1989/90... Dave Farrell makes his full league debut in front of a 'live' Sky Sports TV audience... Villa record only their second home win in Rangers last seven visits.

Sky's the limit as Villa go third

Morale is building with every favourable result, and the mid-week Coca Cola Cup victory over Manchester United has sent it soaring to a new high.

The eyes of the dish-owning section of the footballing fraternity are firmly on a Villa team who were 'flavour of the month' in October and kick-off November in front of the Sky cameras.

Atkinson springs a mini-surprise by sending out the virtual 'unknown' winger from Chelmsley Wood, David Farrell (substitute in the two previous games), for his full debut.

Villa kick-off in sixth place, with QPR lying third, so the rewards for victory are self-evident.

The attendance is a surprisingly 'low' 20,140, reflecting the economic climate and the fact that it is the club's fourth home game out of the last five in little more than three weeks.

The gate does, however, also fuel the debate on whether there is too much live TV, plus a touch of confusion about which days of the week fixtures are now played.

Although comparitively few individuals yet possess the necessary receiving dish, many pubs and clubs have them and attract large groups into their establishment and away from the ground.

What those viewers, and the live audience see on this Sunday afternoon is hugely entertaining. Again the decisive factor is the lethal strike partnership forged by Dalian Atkinson and Dean Saunders as they both add to their impressive goals total.

Rangers' defence is completely unhinged by the speed and directness of the first, scored by Deano just before half-time.

Atkinson touches on a long clearance by Nigel Spink, Saunders tears through the left side of the opposition defence, waits his moment to perfection and places the ball clinically beyond approaching goalkeeper Tony Roberts.

"I bet he didn't see anything but the net," enthuses Big Ron. "He didn't see the defender converging in on him, nor the goalkeeper closing him down.

"His eyes were totally focussed on the net..."

The London club had achieved their high League position by virtue of the smooth passing football concentrated around the cultured distribution of veteran Ray Wilkins.

In this stylish fashion QPR contribute to an enthralling contest but with eleven minutes remaining they are left with a lost cause.

Their defender Darren Peacock slips crucially allowing Atkinson to pounce for possession. He could pass to his striker buddy, Deano, who is in a better position to score but chooses to gobble up his ninth of the season.

"...and we haven't seen the best of him yet," insists the manager. "When he really blasts the ball it goes like an Exocet."

Farrell does enough on his full debut to show that, like Steve Froggatt, he has a future in the game, though he needs time to physically mature.

So Villa leap-frog into third place, their most elevated position since Graham Taylor's team finished as runners-up three years ago.

Dean Saunders slips the ball past Tony Roberts, 1-0

Saturday 7th November 1992 • Villa Park • 3.00pm

ASTON VILLA 1 MANCHESTER UNITED 0

Half-time 1-0 • *Attendance* 39,063

Referee David ELLERAY (Middlesex)

Linesmen A.N. BUTLER and M.A. COOPER

Claret and Blue Shirts, White Shorts	Goals	Blue Shirts, Blue Shorts	Goals
1 Nigel SPINK		1 Peter SCHMEICHEL	
2 Earl BARRETT		2 Paul PARKER	
3 Steve STAUNTON		3 Clayton BLACKMORE	
4 Shaun TEALE		4 Steve BRUCE	
5 Paul McGRATH		5 Darren FERGUSON †	
6 Kevin RICHARDSON		6 Gary PALLISTER	
7 Ray HOUGHTON		7 Bryan ROBSON ❑	
8 Garry PARKER ❑		8 Paul INCE ❑	
9 Dean SAUNDERS		9 Lee SHARPE	
10 Dalian ATKINSON	11	10 Mark HUGHES	
11 Bryan SMALL		11 Ryan GIGGS	
Substitutes		*Substitutes*	
Dwight YORKE		Brian McCLAIR †81	
Cyrille REGIS		Andrei KANCHELSKIS	
Gk Mark BOSNICH		Gk Fraser DIGBY	

BEFORE		P	W	D	L	F	A	pts	AFTER		P	W	D	L	F	A	pts
4	Villa	14	6	6	2	23	15	24	3	Villa	15	7	6	2	24	15	27
7	United	14	5	6	3	13	11	21	10	United	15	5	6	4	13	12	21

FACTFILE

The Premier League's largest gate yet... Only Villa's second league win over United in 13 starts... England boss Graham Taylor looks for World Cup selections... Ron Atkinson is presented with the Barclays Manager of the Month award for October prior to kick-off.

Staunton switch is key to success

Villa Park, boiling with anticipation and packed with spectators hungry for sporting drama, is a venue of footballing theatre.

When Manchester United are the visitors memories flick back to previous spectaculars between the two clubs, of which there have been many.

Today, however, a ten-day recall is all that is required. Can Villa repeat the heroics of the Coca Cola Cup success and stay on course for a double?

The history of such close encounters suggests that, over the two games, honours could be shared. Will this be the case? Or does the manager have a trick up his sleeve, ready to conjure a second triumph.

Indeed, he has !

With Tony Daley and Steve Froggatt still not fit enough to take on the wing role, and young Dave Farrell not yet ready for it, Bryan Small is re-introduced.

Not as makeshift front man, but to allow Steve Staunton to move forward, a job he does with aggressive relish.

The selection surprise proves to have dual benefits. Not only is Small a revelation at left back but Staunton's power and drive going forward give the attack an added menace.

The Premier League's biggest gate of the season is quickly caught up in a whirl of action as Staunton takes the ball off England international Paul Ince, in the 11th minute, to deliver it into the path of Atkinson.

Another England cap, Gary Pallister tries, and fails, to block Atkinson's route to goal and as Peter Schmeichel advances, the Villa striker steers it past him.

England boss Graham Taylor, watching from the stand, enjoys 90 minutes of ever-changing action. Villa have several narrow escapes as the brilliant young winger Ryan Giggs displays his talents.

United have Halesowen-born Lee Sharpe back in their side after injury and illness for his first appearance of the season.

After surviving United's determined attempts to equalise Villa sweep out in search of a second goal and Schmeichel brilliantly saves Garry Parker's volley as Deano touches on Staunton's pass.

But one goal is enough. And on the final whistle jubilant home fans noisily celebrate a double success over United, whose goalscoring problem is causing manager Alex Ferguson deep concern.

For Atkinson a quietly-satisfying experience: it was six years ago to the very week since he was fired, unjustly many felt, from the Old Trafford job he loved.

Now the media, after the 12th successive game without defeat, are taking Villa seriously as contenders for honours.

This is Villa's first League win over United for three years as the manager's shrewd team-building policy bears fruit. Many regard United as title favourites despite an inconsistent start and goalscoring problems, but Villa have more than matched them.

Although the talented United side has enjoyed periods of attacking aggression Nigel Spink, who has recently signed a new two-year contract has rarely been unduly troubled.

Dalian Atkinson scores his 10th of the season

Saturday 21st November 1992 • White Hart Lane • 3.00pm

TOTTENHAM HOTSPUR 0 ASTON VILLA 0

Half-time 0-0 • *Attendance* 32,852

Referee Ian BORRETT (Harleston, Norfolk)

Linesmen G.P. BARBER and W.J. NORBURY

White Shirts, Navy Blue Shorts	Goals	Claret and Blue Shirts, White Shorts	Goals
1 Erik THORSTVEDT		1 Nigel SPINK	
2 Justin EDINBURGH		2 Earl BARRETT	
3 Dean AUSTIN		3 Steve STAUNTON	
4 Vinny SAMWAYS		4 Shaun TEALE ❑ †	
5 Gary MABBUTT		5 Paul McGRATH	
6 Neil RUDDOCK ❑		6 Kevin RICHARDSON	
7 David HOWELLS		7 Ray HOUGHTON	
8 Gordon DURIE †		8 Garry PARKER ‡	
9 NAYIM		9 Dean SAUNDERS	
10 Teddy SHERINGHAM		10 Dalian ATKINSON	
11 Paul ALLEN ‡		11 Bryan SMALL	
Substitutes		*Substitutes*	
Nick BARMBY †45		Ugo EHIOGU †71	
Jason CUNDY ‡78		Cyrille REGIS ‡84	
Gk Ian WALKER		Gk Mark BOSNICH	

BEFORE		P	W	D	L	F	A	pts	AFTER		P	W	D	L	F	A	pts
4	Villa	15	7	6	2	24	15	27	3	Villa	16	7	7	2	24	15	28
13	Spurs	15	4	6	5	16	22	18	14	Spurs	16	4	7	5	16	22	19

FACTFILE

It's the first ever goalless draw between these sides at White Hart Lane and the first draw of any kind there since 1954... Shaun Teale misses the last 19 minutes through injury, the first action he's missed since joining the club... Spurs' run of three successive wins is halted...

Goalless, but marvellous

Defending an undefeated run stretching back 12 matches, Villa return to the action following the season's second enforced break due to midweek international calls.

The blank Saturday a week earlier was filled by a short trip to Italy and a friendly game against Fiorentina, but Ron Atkinson has mixed feelings about the country-before-club routine.

"I fully support all the international squads," he points out. "But our three Irish lads who played for the Republic in Seville had a very punishing schedule. They could have done with at least another day to recover."

The Villa manager is watching closely at White Hart Lane for adverse affects in the form of Steve Staunton, Ray Houghton and Paul McGrath plus Dean Saunders who played for Wales in Belgium.

As it transpires he need not have worried, even though Villa are confronted by an in-form Spurs team, themselves unbeaten in six starts.

The absence of goals conceals the quality of a match many regard as being as entertaining as any played throughout a season of escalating standards.

London-based pundits and Spurs players alike are generous in their praise of Villa's football, marking them down as being firmly among the championship contenders.

As one writer had it: "Villa's class and resilience shone through the gloom of London N17 like the beam of a lighthouse.

"..this was marvellous value for anybody's money."

The general view is that, although Gordon Durie snaps a header against Nigel Spink's crossbar just on half-time, and Spurs spurn several chances, Villa's commanding midfield play gives them an 'on points' verdict.

In a second-half spell of inspirational attacking McGrath has two headers blocked on the line while goalkeeper Erik Thorsvedt keeps out Houghton's blockbuster.

Thorsvedt also denies Atkinson as excitement surges around the North London ground.

It would be difficult to envisage a goalless draw of greater entertainment value but there's an apprehensive note on the return journey.

Shaun Teale, booked for a tackle on Durie, is nursing a wound above the eye containing three stitches and, more ominously, a knee injury."

After 71 minutes he had left the field to be replaced by Ugo Ehiogu, ending a run of some 70 matches since his transfer from Bournmouth, tough and reliable in the heart of the defence.

How soon would he be back? Not long if the gaffer has his way... "He's John Wayne, he's got true grit," says Atkinson.

But our hero limps painfully off the coach... and next Saturday league leaders Norwich are due at Villa Park.

Although the team pattern has fallen neatly into place with a quality of ground-level passing to match any team in the country, there remains a slight lack of power from the centre of midfield.

Atkinson may, however have an ace up his sleeve. The previous week when at Birmingham Airport the Villa party on its way to Florence has met up with the Pisa party in their Anglo-Italian Cup travels.

In a brief airport meeting Pisa's Danish international midfielder Henrik Larsen has made it known to the Villa manager that he would love a move to Villa Park.

Atkinson admired Larsen when he was in Sweden as a TV analyst for Denmark's European Championship, especially his two-goal semi-final display.

A future Villa signing? Who knows...

Saturday 28th November 1992 • Villa Park • 3.00pm

ASTON VILLA 2 NORWICH CITY 3

Half-time 1-2 • *Attendance* 28,837

Referee Alf BUKSH (London)

Linesmen J. LEECH and B.A. WIGGINTON

Claret and Blue Shirts, White Shorts		Goals	Yellow Shirts, Green Shorts		Goals
1	Nigel SPINK		1	Bryan GUNN	
2	Earl BARRETT		2	Ian CULVERHOUSE	
3	Steve STAUNTON		3	Mark BOWEN	
4	Ugo EHIOGU †		4	Ian BUTTERWORTH	
5	Paul McGRATH		5	John POLSTON	
6	Kevin RICHARDSON		6	Daryl SUTCH	49
7	Ray HOUGHTON	44	7	Ian CROOK	
8	Garry PARKER	46	8	Darren BECKFORD †	31
9	Dean SAUNDERS		9	Mark ROBINS	
10	Dalian ATKINSON		10	Ruel FOX	
11	Bryan SMALL		11	David PHILLIPS	18
	Substitutes			*Substitutes*	
	Cyrille REGIS †83			Chris SUTTON †74 ❑	
	Dariusz KUBICKI			Gary MEGSON	
Gk	Mark BOSNICH		Gk	Mark WALTON	

BEFORE	P	W	D	L	F	A	pts	AFTER	P	W	D	L	F	A	pts
1 Norwich	16	10	3	3	29	28	33	1 Norwich	17	11	3	3	32	30	36
4 Villa	16	7	7	2	24	15	28	4 Villa	17	7	7	3	26	18	28

FACTFILE

Villa are beaten for first time since September 2nd... Ray Houghton scores his first goal for the club... Injured Shaun Teale is missing after 70 successive starts... Ugo Ehiogu starts his first League game of the season... Norwich continue their impressive record of having scored in every League game this season.

Canaries extend lead at the top

A week of intense anticipation builds up to the Premier League's match of the day and questions are being asked about Norwich City's capacity to maintain their table-topping place.

Popular theory has it that Norwich, lacking the financial muscle of the major clubs, will run out of steam.

One person who does not subscribe to that view is Ron Atkinson. "OK, so in the last few years it has been one of the giants who have lasted the course best," he reasoned.

"But you only have to remember Derby County and Nottingham Forest to appreciate that slightly smaller clubs, like Norwich, can pull it off."

Ron is not being unduly pessimistic about Villa's role in the Championship chase. But the Villa boss has a problem. He's putting a brave face on the fact that Shaun Teale was found to have damage to a medial ligament and will be out for an unspecified period. But Big Ron knows, and the fans know, that the tigerish Teale, with his mean defensive play, will be missed. Teale's stock-in-trade is to keep the ball out of the net at any cost. A priceless asset.

In the event Atkinson's warning on Norwich is driven home in unpalatable fashion.

The Carrow Road club's growing reputation for the quality of their passing football was confirmed by a victory which took them eight points clear of Villa (fourth) and five points ahead of Blackburn (second).

Atkinson ignores the chance to blame Teale's absence for the ending of a 13-match unbeaten sequence. He doesn't have to. The connection is obvious. But it's only part of the story.

True, Teale had played in every game under Atkinson's rule. He and Paul McGrath have become virtually telepathic. Losing him would

inevitably unsettle the defence, which is why the Villa boss decides on a straight swop for Ugo Ehiogu. He could switch Earl Barrett into his favourite role and recall Dariusz Kubicki at right back. But that means two changes.

Hackney-born of Nigerian parents, the England under-21 defender goes in with the reassuring tribute from his manager that he was 'better at the same age (20) than McGrath'.

Norwich have done their homework well. Rookie manager Mike Walker and his assistant, former Villa favourite John Deehan, shrewdly use Ian Culverhouse as a sweeper to counteract the speed of Dalian Atkinson and Dean Saunders. The dashing front pair are close-marked by Ian Butterworth and John Polston.

In half-an-hour, sheer calamity. Villa are two down to David Phillips and Darren Beckford. Defensive mistakes are being made. And not only by Ehiogu.

Things HAVE to improve. For a while they do. Just before half-time, Ray Houghton scores his first goal for the club in 19 starts, a 20-yard shot which, perhaps, 'keeper Bryan Gunn might have stopped.

Inspired by the experience, Houghton chips forward for Garry Parker to equalise at the start of the second half with a crisp half-volley.

At last the storyline Villa fans had in mind before the kick-off is taking shape. Though not for long. Ruel Fox, as stealthy and cunning as his name suggests, combines with the highly-promising Daryl Sutch, to reclaim a Norwich lead which they never relinquish.

Villa are left needing a new impetus if they are to be restored as genuine title contenders. But they have found a friend in the man from The Times.

The experienced and knowledgeable David Miller writes in Monday's paper that the match was... "the finest English league match I can recall in some years, played at breathtaking pace in broad sweeps back and forth across Villa Park's perfect surface."

Wednesday 2nd December 1992 • Villa Park • 7.45pm

ASTON VILLA 2 IPSWICH TOWN 2

Half-time 0-0 • *Attendance* 21,545

Referee John MARTIN (Alton, Hampshire)

Linesmen D.W. MANSFIELD and P.J. ROBINSON

Claret and Blue Shirts, White Shorts	Goals	White Shirts, Blue Shorts	Goals
1 Nigel SPINK		1 Clive BAKER	
2 Earl BARRETT		2 Phil WHELAN	
3 Steve STAUNTON		3 Neil THOMPSON	
4 Dariusz KUBICKI		4 Mick STOCKWELL	
5 Paul McGRATH		5 John WARK	
6 Kevin RICHARDSON		6 David LINIGHAN	
7 Ray HOUGHTON ‡		7 Gavin JOHNSON	
8 Garry PARKER †		8 Paul GODDARD †	
9 Dean SAUNDERS	77	9 Steve WHITTON	
10 Dalian ATKINSON	65	10 Jason DOZZELL	
11 Bryan SMALL		11 Chris KIWOMYA	74, 83
Substitutes		*Substitutes*	
Neil COX †77		Eddie YOUDS †84	
Cyrille REGIS ‡84		Vlado BOZINOSKI	

FACTFILE

Dariusz Kubicki and Neil Cox make their first appearances of the season... Dalian Atkinson scores against his former club again, he netted at Portman Road on the opening day of the new season... The eventual winners will be at home to Sheffield Wednesday.

Deano scores Villa's second

It's the curse of East Anglia!

East Anglia has suddenly assumed a new and menacing dimension in terms of Villa's possible fortunes this season. Norwich's victory last Saturday has inevitably left its scars on morale by undermining the Premier League title challenge.

Now Ipswich will learn from Carrow Road's five-man defensive plan and mount similar tactics an an attempt to block the route to Wembley.

One consolation is that the Villa Park pitch cover, plus the repair work carried out both to the surface and to the drainage, has produced a magnificent playing surface.

As other games fall to the recent excessive and seemingly never-ending deluge, Villa's tie goes on in conditions which amaze everyone.

Fears that Ipswich will defend in numbers and Ron Atkinson's pre-match warning that Villa will have to learn how to overcome 'blanket defences', are confirmed as Ipswich pack their half of the field.

This time Earl Barrett has been switched into the injured Shaun Teale's central defensive role, after Ugo Ehiogu's difficulties against Norwich, with Dariusz Kubicki recalled at right back.

By half-time Villa have run themselves into a rare old muddle with their midfield work having lost its accuracy and only Dean Saunders' energetic and speedy mobility raising hopes of a breakthrough.

"We might have done better if we had turned up in the first half..." groaned the

Dariusz Kubicki

manager in his post-match interview, adding a less printable condemnation.

To be fair to Ipswich they employ their pre-determined tactics almost to perfection with 35-year-old John Wark an experienced defensive sweeper. It takes 64 minutes, mostly on the retreat, before they are prised apart, predictably by Saunders' restless roaming and sharp eye for a weakness.

The Welsh cap darts down the right, measures his centre to the far post with defenders still scrambling to pick up their men, and Dalian Atkinson is on the end of it for a far post header.

"After two games without either Deano or myself scoring it has been something of a drought by previous standards," says the former Ipswich player.

"But I have a good record of scoring against previous clubs, at Sheffield Wednesday last season and at Ipswich in the first match of this season."

Saunders adds a second goal during an eventful, error-ridden last half-hour, but by this time Chris Kiwomya has celebrated his 23rd birthday by equalising for Ipswich.

Villa's second goal, bringing the strike partnership's total to 20, is set up for him by a fine through ball from his 'other half' and superbly placed wide of goalkeeper Clive Baker.

Surely there is no way back for Ipswich this time? But, indeed, there is.

Nigel Spink races out to fly-kick a clearance in his goal area but it strikes Mick Stockwell and rebounds to the grateful Kiwomya who buries it in the goal deserted by Spink.

Only one defeat in the past 15 matches, a superb record and no cause to be downhearted. And yet... it hasn't been the best five days of the season so far. Ipswich richly deserve their Portman Road replay, an occasion given additional flavour by the immediate quarter-final draw which pairs the winners at home to Sheffield Wednesday.

Saturday 5th December 1992 • Hillsborough • 3.00pm

SHEFFIELD WEDNESDAY 1 ASTON VILLA 2

Half-time 1-1 • *Attendance* 29,964

Referee Robert HART (Darlington)

Linesmen J. McGRATH and M.R. WARREN

Blue and White Striped Shirts, Black Shorts		Goals	Claret and Blue Shirts, White Shorts		Goals
1	Chris WOODS		1	Mark BOSNICH	
2	Roland NILSSON		2	Earl BARRETT	
3	Nigel WORTHINGTON		3	Steve STAUNTON ❏	
4	Carlton PALMER		4	Neil COX	
5	Viv ANDERSON		5	Paul McGRATH	
6	Paul WARHURST		6	Kevin RICHARDSON	
7	John HARKES †		7	Dwight YORKE	
8	Chris WADDLE		8	Garry PARKER	
9	David HIRST		9	Dean SAUNDERS	
10	Mark BRIGHT	26	10	Dalian ATKINSON	19, 67
11	John SHERIDAN ‡		11	Bryan SMALL	

Substitutes			*Substitutes*		
	Chris BART-WILLIAMS †77			Matthias BREITKREUTZ	
	Gordon WATSON ‡80			Cyrille REGIS	
Gk	Kevin PRESSMAN		Gk	Michael OAKES	

BEFORE		P	W	D	L	F	A	pts	AFTER		P	W	D	L	F	A	pts
4	Villa	17	7	7	3	26	18	28	3	Villa	18	8	7	3	28	19	31
15	Wednesday	17	4	8	5	19	20	20	16	Wednesday	18	4	8	6	20	22	20

FACTFILE

Mark Bosnich comes in for Nigel Spink, injured against Ipswich on Wednesday, to make his first appearance of the season... Neil Cox starts his first game of the season... Dalian Atkinson keeps up his record of scoring against his former clubs, his second goal wins the BBC 'Goal of the Month' award.

A happy return for the Atkinsons

Ron Atkinson's second return to the club he left 18 months ago amid deep controversy raised the pre-match hype but the Villa manager was more concerned about lingering injury problems.

A large squad sets off, unusually for such a short trip, on the Friday so that Nigel Spink, Ray Houghton and two or three unnamed casualties can have regular overnight treatment from physiotherapist Jim Walker.

In the event both Spink and Houghton are ruled out, thus allowing the young Aussie Mark Bosnich to test his calibre in goal and Dwight Yorke to make a welcome return.

Steve Staunton partners Paul McGrath and Bryan Small plays at left back. Neil Cox comes in at right back to the exclusion of the Pole, Dariusz Kubicki, with Earl Barrett in midfield.

There are, of course, TWO Atkinsons making their return to Hillsborough against the team now managed by Trevor Francis who has seen a challenging start in the league fall away a little.

England boss Graham Taylor is in the stand to watch a game of cut-and-thrust with the ball kept largely on the ground and Wednesday threatening to take command with some lethal-looking attacking form.

The difference between two attractive sides is Dalian Atkinson, sold from Hillsborough to the Spanish club Real Sociedad by his namesake when he was in charge there and then re-purchased when he arrived at Villa Park in the summer of '91.

Dalian has this habit of scoring against his former clubs (twice against Ipswich and also on his previous appearance at Hillsborough) and he has no interntion of letting it slide.

Despite Wednesday having their tails up after beating QPR 4-0 in mid-week in the Coca Cola Cup, it takes Atkinson only 20 minutes to consolidate that record of his, though it is a break-away strike as the home side push forward ominously.

Villa had watched the video of Wednesday's mid-week Coca Cola Cup win and their feelings were succinctly summed up by manager Atkinson when he told the media before the game: "Watching it frightened me to death..."

An illustration of what he means arrives within eight minutes of Villa taking the lead, Chris Waddle and David Hirst opening up Villa's defence for Mark Bright to deliver the equaliser.

Now the heat is really on with Bosnich having to show his mettle with a confident save from John Sheridan's 20-yard pile-driver and Villa still under the cosh too often for comfort.

By half time it looks a case of being happy if they can cling to a draw but such caution is not in the manager's make up. He has clearly delivered a far more positive interval rallying call, namely to 'go for it...'.

The outcome is more challenge and impetus from midfield which re-directs the flow of the game and steps up the service to the inexhaustible Dean Saunders, roaming and probing non-stop up front.

Viv Anderson and Paul Warhurst in the centre of the Wednesday defence are now being pulled about more and more as Villa shake off the memory of the mid-week slip against Ipswich and roll out their most impressive passing football.

The justified reward is a second goal for Dalian Atkinson when he takes out Anderson, swivels, picks his spot and hits the target with an angled shot which England goalkeeper Chris Woods can't get near.

Villa's 3,000+ travellers rise to a goal which deserves the status of match-winner... and so it proves.

Saturday 12th December 1992 • Villa Park • 3.00pm

ASTON VILLA 2 NOTTINGHAM FOREST 1

Half-time 1-1 • *Attendance* 29,015

Referee Joe WORRALL (Warrington)

Linesmen A. BLACK and C. JONES

Claret and Blue Shirts, White Shorts		Goals	White Shirts, Black Shorts		Goals
1	Nigel SPINK		1	Steve CROSSLEY	
2	Earl BARRETT		2	Brian LAWS	
3	Steve STAUNTON		3	Stuart PEARCE	
4	Shaun TEALE		4	Steve CHETTLE	
5	Paul McGRATH	46	5	Carl TILER	
6	Kevin RICHARDSON		6	Roy KEANE	9
7	Ray HOUGHTON		7	Neil WEBB	
8	Garry PARKER		8	Scot GEMMILL	
9	Dean SAUNDERS		9	Nigel CLOUGH	
10	Cyrille REGIS	33	10	Lee GLOVER †	
11	Neil COX		11	Kingsley BLACK	

Substitutes		*Substitutes*
Dwight YORKE		'Toddi' ORLYGSSON †78
Matthias BREITKREUTZ		Gary BANNISTER
Gk Michael OAKES		Gk Andrew MARRIOTT

BEFORE		P	W	D	L	F	A	pts	AFTER		P	W	D	L	F	A	pts
4	Villa	18	8	7	3	28	19	31	2	Villa	19	9	7	3	30	20	34
22	Forest	18	3	5	10	17	28	14	22	Forest	19	3	5	11	18	30	14

FACTFILE

Cyrille Regis is a late replacement for the injured Dalian Atkinson... Regis and Paul McGrath each score their first goals of the season... Villa move into second place, their highest position so far... Forest left further adrift at the bottom after wins by Palace and Wimbledon... Mark Bosnich is suspended.

Experience wins the day

Ron Atkinson is steadfastly sticking to his view that the bookies are 'barmy' to install Aston Villa as Championship favourites though he does make one concession to his team's chances.

"Nottingham Forest have a player who could make us favourites to win everything," he says. Ron Keane, the Irish Republic international who cost Brian Clough a mere £15,000 from Cobh Ramblers, is the phenomenon he has in mind.

"He is the best player of that kind I have seen since Bryan Robson emerged," adds Big Ron who does not hand out such tributes lightly.

Forest arrive at Villa Park in the unprecedented position under Clough's 18-year reign at City Ground of bottom place.

As always they have been widely applauded for the quality of their passing football. Indeed, no-one admires them more than the Villa manager, whose playing principles are similar. But Forest have had their problems.

England central defender Des Walker and striker Teddy Sheringham were sold and neither has been adequately replaced.

In the circumstances Villa kick-off as firm favourites, though Dalian Atkinson has succumbed to injury, posing a possible goalscoring problem.

The good news is that Shaun Teale is now back in central defence after his injury, with Steve Staunton restored to the left back berth. Also, compared to the team which won at Hillsborough, Nigel Spink and Ray Houghton are back in place of Mark Bosnich and Dwight Yorke, though Neil Cox is still at right back with Earl Barrett retained in midfield.

There is no doubt the significance in this... the job of 'keeping an eye' on Keane.

Predictably this game proves to be another demonstration of football skills to delight the purist with both sides making their contribution.

Atkinson's fears over the versatile Keane, a midfield player who started the season as Walker's defensive replacement and who is a deadly finisher, prove soundly-based.

In only 10 minutes Keane escapes Barrett and executes one of his familiar forward surges from midfield in which his power and single-mindedness are quite awesome, lobbing Spink for a Forest lead.

Villa badly need a touch of inspiration and it arrives neatly wrapped up in mature experience. Regis, taking on the striker role vacated by Dalian Atkinson, equalises in the 34th minute by shrewdly chipping Mark Crossley when he spots the 'keeper has allowed himself to be stranded too far forward.

Forest's defence is finding the mercurial Dean Saunders, with his engine ticking over tirelessly, an increasingly difficult character to pin down since he can attack from almost any point of the compass. The Welsh cap looks the most likely one to get Villa's nose in front but, in the opening minute of the second half, another member of the thirty-something 'club' conjures the winning moment.

Paul McGrath, widely acknowledged as one of the best defenders in World football, had scored only twice in his previous 139 league games. But his 46th minute header, in a packed goalmouth deceives Crossley and gives Villa three more points.

After that the action flows freely with enough entertainment to satisfy the most demanding of the 29,015 spectators but, the odd scare apart, Villa are worthy of the 2-1 scoreline.

'Macca', as he is known in the dressing room, thus joins Big Cyrille in the headlines which scream out the Golden Oldie angle.

Golden? You bet.

Oldies? You must be joking...

Tuesday 15th December 1992 • Portman Road • 7.30pm

IPSWICH TOWN 1 ASTON VILLA 0

Half-time 0-0 • *Attendance* 19,196

Referee Michael JAMES (Horsham, West Sussex)

Linesmen B.J. FOREMAN and R.L. TYE

Blue Shirts with White Sleeves, White Shorts		Goals	Claret and Blue Shirts, Blue Shorts		Goals
1	Clive BAKER		1	Nigel SPINK	
2	Phil WHELAN		2	Earl BARRETT	
3	Neil THOMPSON		3	Steve STAUNTON	
4	Mick STOCKWELL		4	Shaun TEALE	
5	John WARK		5	Paul McGRATH	
6	David LINIGHAN		6	Kevin RICHARDSON	
7	Gavin JOHNSON		7	Ray HOUGHTON	
8	Paul GODDARD †		8	Garry PARKER ‡	
9	Steve WHITTON		9	Dean SAUNDERS	
10	Jason DOZZELL		10	Cyrille REGIS †	
11	Chris KIWOMYA	57	11	Neil COX	
	Substitutes			*Substitutes*	
	Geraint WILLIAMS †81			Dwight YORKE †12	
	Bontcho GUENTCHEV			Matthias BREITKREUTZ ‡71	

FACTFILE

Chris Kiwomya takes his tally to six goals in the competition this season... Matthias Breitkreutz makes his League Cup debut... Ron Atkinson suffers his first defeat in the competition since 1989, Villa having lost on the away goals rule last season.

Chris Kiwomya – six goals in the Coca Cola Cup.

Kiwomya kills off cup hopes

On the heels of the fine home win over Nottingham Forest last Saturday, Villa ought to be in just the right confident frame of mind for Portman Road. But, as kick-off time arrives, something is missing...

Failure to dispose of Ipswich, when the chance was on at the first time of asking has produced a touch of uncertainty.

Manager Ron Atkinson's reputation in the League Cup has, perhaps, raised public anticipation a shade too high.

Whatever the cause, the Coca Cola Cup replay proves one of the season's least memorable occasions.

In the build-up to the game against his former club, Dalian Atkinson has been the subject of some unsual publicity because of an experiment with a piece of space-age technology.

Atkinson is plagued with an injury to his abdominal regions which kept him out of the Forest game and disrupted his flourishing strike partnership with Dean Saunders.

For several hours a day he has been seated in an oxygen unit, shaped like an old-fashioned bubble car, and designed to speed up the healing process. Unfortunately the forward-looking scheme does not have the necessary results.

In Dalian's absence manager Atkinson sticks with the line-up that beat Forest, with Cyrille Regis up front and Neil Cox keeping the No.11 shirt to the exclusion of Dwight Yorke, who is on the bench.

Ipswich have been beaten only twice in 23 previous league and cup games and are especially resilient at home. Their style of closing the opposition down in midfield and defence before supplying the lightning Chris Kiwomya with ammunition is a troublesome one.

Kiwomya has been out with 'flu, but unlike his mate from the ranks of the Ipswich youth squad, Atkinson, he is fit in time.

With a quarter-final place against Sheffield Wednesday as the prize more is expected of Villa than they actually produce on the night against opponents who give nothing away.

There is hope in the opening half-hour or so but it leads to nothing and Villa suffer unwanted early disruption as Regis, a scorer against Forest three days earlier, limps off to be replaced by Yorke.

Ipswich's lead arrives after 57 minutes in a move described by Ipswich team manager Mick McGiven as 'the only bit of quality attacking in the game'.

A fine intercepting tackle by Cox on Jason Dozzell leads to a corner from which Neil Thompson's kick is headed on by Dozell for Kiwomya's flicked header to beat the diving Nigel Spink.

This was Kiwomya's eleventh goal of the season and his sixth in this competition as Villa fail to raise the necessary collective will to reply.

They manage to muster just one chance to hit back, within two minutes of Ipswich taking the lead, but it comes to nothing.

Aided by Dwight Yorke's decoy run on the hour, Saunders bursts through on the left with only goalkeeper Clive Baker blocking his way. The Welsh cap has an excellent scoring chance but shoots weakly at the 'keeper.

This proves the last chance and out go Villa with no tangible excuses.

Cyrille Regis - suffered an early injury

Saturday 19th December 1992 • Maine Road • 3.00pm

MANCHESTER CITY 1 ASTON VILLA 1

Half-time 0-1 • *Attendance* 23,525

Referee Raymond BIGGER (Harleston, Norfolk)

Linesmen A.N. BUTLER and A.J. HILL

Sky Blue Shirts, White Shorts	Goals	Claret and Blue Shirts, White Shorts	Goals
1 Tony COTON		1 Nigel SPINK	
2 Ian BRIGHTWELL		2 Earl BARRETT	
3 Terry PHELAN ❏		3 Steve STAUNTON	
4 Steve McMAHON		4 Shaun TEALE	
5 Keith CURLE ❏		5 Paul McGRATH	
6 Andy HILL		6 Kevin RICHARDSON	
7 David WHITE		7 Ray HOUGHTON	
8 Peter REID †		8 Garry PARKER	34
9 Niall QUINN		9 Dean SAUNDERS	
10 Garry FLITCROFT	59	10 Dalian ATKINSON †	
11 Rick HOLDEN		11 Dwight YORKE	
Substitutes		*Substitutes*	
Mike SHERON †58		Matthias BREITKREUTZ †61	
Fitzroy SIMPSON		Neil COX	
Gk Martyn MARGETSON		Gk Mark BOSNICH	

BEFORE	P	W	D	L	F	A	pts	AFTER	P	W	D	L	F	A	pts
2 Villa	19	9	7	3	30	20	34	2 Villa	20	9	8	3	31	21	35
11 City	19	7	4	8	26	22	25	11 City	20	7	5	8	27	23	26

FACTFILE

Substitute Matthias Breitkreutz gets his first taste of the Premier League... Garry Parker's volley earns him third place in the BBC 'Goal of the Month' competition, home fans are convinced the ref should have blown for offside... City recover after three successive defeats.

Parker packs a powerful punch

The start of a Festive period programme of three matches in nine days, two of them away, which marks the half-way stage in the title race and begins to reduce its serious contenders.

Dalian Atkinson is back though not, it transpires, for the entire game, while with Yorke continuing in midfield, Earl Barrett is restored to right back.

Manchester City are caught on an afternoon when they are under pressure to end a run of three successive defeats after an earlier sequence of four wins on the trot.

The highlight of a fairly-even game, which City afterwards felt with some cause that they might have won, is the goal by Garry Parker which gives Villa a 34th minute lead.

When a centre by Ray Houghton is cleared the former Forest player who has progressed to the verge of the England squad, strikes with a goal which could rate among the best of the season.

Leaping into the air he connects right-footed with a scissor-kick volley which scorches out of goalkeeper Tony Coton's reach into the left-hand corner of the net.

Parker's goal is one of those rabbit-out-of-a-hat stunners which momentarily leaves spectators silent with appreciation or dismay, depending on their colours.

The home club's 'dismay' turned to outrage backed by a claim that Dalian Atkinson had moved into an offside position before Parker connected with his shot. This, they reckoned, was confirmed by TV slow-motion replays, a technological aid which was not, of course, available to the referee and linesman making their instant, on-the-spot decision.

To be fair to City they enjoyed a good share of the attacking play and the chances created,

especially after Dalian Atkinson left the field with a recurrence of his muscle injury, to be replaced by substitute Matthias Breitkreutz on the hour.

Dean Saunders' relative shortage of goals is something of a disappointment considering the amount of his unselfish running and endlish probing for the merest whiff of a chance.

This, allied to the loss after an hour of his up-front partner and off-the-field pal, Dalian, has tended to undermine the team's flow and consistency.

Dwight Yorke has made a promising contribution in terms of ball control and creative running if not on the scoresheet while Barrett looks more 'at home' back in his defensive role.

Now, as the nation prepares for its annual festivities, Villa players are on a programme of professional restraint in preparation for Highfield Road on Boxing Day.

Second place in the table is maintained over the pre-Christmas weekend as Manchester United are held to a 1-1 draw at Stamford Bridge to remain fourth.

Norwich, without a fixture until Monday 21st, enjoy the luxury of staying top, now with a game in hand. That spare game soon disappears in the East Anglian derby when ever-improving Ipswich win 2-0 at Carrow Road.

Garry Parker volleys Villa in front

Saturday 26th December 1992 • Highfield Road • 12 noon

COVENTRY CITY 3 ASTON VILLA 0

Half-time 0-0 • *Attendance* 24,245

Referee Roger DILKES (Manchester)

Linesmen P.M. ROBERTS and J.B. ROBINSON

Sky Blue Shirts, Sky Blue Shorts	Goals	Claret and Blue Shirts, White Shorts	Goals
1 Jonathan GOULD		1 Nigel SPINK	
2 Brian BORROWS		2 Earl BARRETT	
3 Phil BABB		3 Steve STAUNTON	
4 Peter ATHERTON ❑		4 Shaun TEALE	
5 Kenny SANSOM		5 Paul McGRATH	
6 John WILLIAMS		6 Kevin RICHARDSON ❑	
7 Lloyd McGRATH		7 Ray HOUGHTON	
8 Lee HURST		8 Garry PARKER ‡	
9 Robert ROSARIO	60	9 Dean SAUNDERS	
10 Mick QUINN ❑ ‡	52, 55	10 Cyrille REGIS †	
11 Kevin GALLACHER †		11 Bryan SMALL	

Substitutes		*Substitutes*	
Peter NDLOVU †82		Stefan BEINLICH †67	
Andy PEARCE ‡89		Neil COX ‡84	
Gk Steve OGRIZOVIC		Gk Mark BOSNICH	

BEFORE	P	W	D	L	F	A	pts	AFTER	P	W	D	L	F	A	pts
2 Villa	20	9	8	3	31	21	35	4 Villa	21	9	8	4	31	24	35
8 Coventry	20	7	8	5	30	27	29	7 Coventry	21	8	8	5	33	27	32

FACTFILE

Villa's heaviest defeat since Ron Atkinson took over... Villa's fifth successive defeat at Highfield Road... Coventry's biggest gate of the season, so far, and the largest for a Villa visit to Coventry since the championship season of 1980-81... Substitute Stefan Beinlich makes his first League appearance of the season

Shot down at high noon

Noon on Boxing Day, high noon it transpires, with Aston Villa on the wrong end of the West Midland shoot-out. Only 4,500 Villa fans are able to make the short, morning-after jaunt along the A45 or sundry roads into Coventry. Several thousand ticket-less ones are denied the chance to see the festive local derby.

They proved to be the lucky ones. A Coventry side who had hammered five goals past Liverpool a week earlier were perilously close to inflicting a similar scoreline on Villa.

Were it possible to do so Villa would like to draw a veil across this one, the most embarrassing experience since the arrival of Ron Atkinson had corrected the inadequacies of the Joe Venglos year. "We never turned up..." was Big Ron's scathing summing up after his team fails to compete at the necessary level to avoid Sky Blues' three goals in eight minutes of the second half.

Excuses, there are none. True, Dalian Atkinson is out after limping off at Maine Road. So, too, is Dwight Yorke. But their replacements are more than adequate, Bryan Small returning at left back to allow Steve Staunton to move into midfield and Cyrille Regis in Dalian's place back at his former ground.

There has been an increasing threat hanging over Villa's desire to at least take a point from this difficult occasion. This threat is provided by striker Mick

Stefan Beinlich - given a chance as late substitute

Quinn, Coventry boss Bobby Gould's inspired capture from Newcastle United.

In five previous appearances for Sky Blues Quinn has bagged a remarkable eight goals. After adding two more in four minutes of the second half he could appropriately be re-named Micky Finn, such is the hang-over he leaves Villa to nurse.

First a volley past Nigel Spink as Rosario nods on, then a simple side-footer as Rosario is again the supplier. To complete Villa's acute discomfort it is Quinn this time feeding his tall, powerful fellow striker for the third.

Adding to the Xmas-wrecking feeling of total inadequacy is the knowledge that manager Bobby Gould's son, Jonathan, has had a trouble-free ride in the home goal.

Losing to a Coventry team in such a mood of destructive confidence is no disgrace in itself. The manner of the defeat is the feature which sends those 4,500 home with cold turkey very much on their mind.

A grim-faced Ron Atkinson now has to rally his demoralised troops for Bank Holiday Monday's visit of Arsenal. A near capacity gate is expected to see if Villa, having dropped from second to fourth in the Highfield Road debacle, can get the Championship Show back on the road again.

Only in retrospect, as Coventry inflict further heavy defeats on shattered visitors, does Villa's experience appear slightly less horrific.

But another hint of a problem is emerging. Dean Saunders has not scored for five games, a positive goal drought for him. With Dalian Atkinson out injured a record of only one goal in the past three games is becoming a worry.

Monday 28th December 1992 • Villa Park • 7.30pm

ASTON VILLA 1 ARSENAL 0

Half-time 1-0 • *Attendance* 35,170

Referee Martin BODENHAM (Looe, Cornwall)
Linesmen I.A. MADGE and D.C. RICHARDS

Claret and Blue Shirts, White Shorts	Goals	Yellow Shirts, Blue Shorts	Goals
1 Nigel SPINK		1 David SEAMAN	
2 Earl BARRETT		2 Pål LYDERSEN	
3 Steve STAUNTON		3 Nigel WINTERBURN	
4 Shaun TEALE		4 David HILLIER ‡	
5 Paul McGRATH		5 Steve BOULD	
6 Kevin RICHARDSON		6 Andy LINIGHAN ❑	
7 Ray HOUGHTON		7 David O'LEARY	
8 Garry PARKER		8 Ian WRIGHT	
9 Dean SAUNDERS	pen 44	9 Alan SMITH	
10 Dwight YORKE		10 Kevin CAMPBELL	
11 Steve FROGGATT †		11 Ray PARLOUR †	

Substitutes	*Substitutes*
Neil COX †74	Mark FLATTS †45
Stefan BEINLICH	Anders LIMPAR ‡66
Gk Mark BOSNICH	Gk Allan MILLER

BEFORE		P	W	D	L	F	A	pts	AFTER		P	W	D	L	F	A	pts
4	Villa	21	9	8	4	31	24	35	3	Villa	22	10	8	4	32	24	38
8	Arsenal	21	9	4	8	23	21	31	9	Arsenal	22	9	4	9	23	22	31

FACTFILE

A penalty at last, the first in a Villa game this season... Deano takes his Villa goals tally into double figures... Steve Froggatt returns after missing 12 games through injury... It's Villa's first League win in an evening match since Ron Atkinson took over a season and a half ago!

Villa end the year with style

The Bank Holiday game, screened live by BSkyB, arrives with Villa in dire need of a lift after a six-game spell of confused fortunes. If honours are on the agenda, more stability is needed for the second half of the season.

League defeats by Norwich and Coventry plus the Coca-Cola Cup exit are threatening to see 1992 out in slightly disappointing fashion despite the high league position.

As an attacking force there has clearly been a need for a more orthodox winger. The long-term absence of Tony Daley and the spasmodic fitness of Steve Froggatt has certainly been an adverse factor.

Against this background the good news is that Froggatt is fit to return against the Gunners who, after setting off as strong championship contenders, have already lost eight games in a dangerous drift down the table.

An atmosphere of tangible excitement is in the air. Villa Park is packed with folks looking to end the old year with a memorable footballing experience.

As it turns out, the claret-and-blue contingent are not to be disappointed as the Highfield Road 'hangover' is cured. Comparisons with that debacle are inevitable. And long before a Dean Saunders penalty on the stroke of half-time provides the lead, all-round improvements are strong and obvious.

Once again the Welshman is full of energetic mobility across the width of the field, to the constant discomfort of the visiting defence.

Dwight Yorke is working well with him while the midfield, anxious to jettison the apathy of Highfield Road, are well in charge of their area of the field. Considering his lay-off Froggatt is playing his part well, too.

Because of this David Seaman is infinitely the busier goalkeeper throughout, saving his side several times, mainly by advancing quickly and bravely to narrow Villa shooting angles before making his saves.

Deano is a particular 'victim' of the England squad 'keeper's courage and expertise especially on one occasion just before the break when he darts clear and looking certain to score until Seaman dashes out to deny him.

The penalty arrives seconds before the break when Yorke, penetrating menacingly into the Arsenal box, is sent sprawling by a David O'Leary tackle which is so high that few could dispute the referee's decision.

This time Saunders cuts out Seaman with the pace and precision of his shot for his tenth goal in Villa colours.

Arsenal alter their second half defensive strategy, changing from a sweeper system to a 'flat' back four and Villa continue to dominate.

Strangely, for all the home attacks and the frequent saves by Seaman, Arsenal are perilously close to sneaking a draw in the closing seconds of injury time. Ian Wright, whose danger had been severely restricted by the defensive work of Paul McGrath and Shaun Teale, suddenly strikes with a fierce on-target shot. Fleetingly the trauma of an equaliser is on the cards.

Over to you, Nigel Spink. For most of the 90 minutes the home 'keeper has admired his opposite number's demonstration of their mutual arts. But now it is Spink's turn and he proves his calibre by diving bodily into what many regarded as the best save of the match.

"That was only the second time this season we have been comprehensively beaten," confessed George Graham, the Arsenal manager.

"I thought we were by far second best." As for Ron Atkinson, asked live on Sky to outline the difference between this and the display on Boxing day, he replies with characteristic humour: "Well, this time we turned up..."

So the 1992 programme rings out on a high. Now for 1993, and the FA Cup.

Saturday 2nd January 1993 • Villa Park • 3.00pm

ASTON VILLA 1 BRISTOL ROVERS 1

Half-time 1-0 • *Attendance 27,048*
Referee Bob NIXON (West Kirby, Wirral)
Linesmen A.J. HILL and A.C. WILLIAMS

Claret and Blue Shirts, White Shorts	Goals	Blue and White Quartered Shirts, Blue Shorts	Goals
1 Nigel SPINK		1 Gavin KELLY ❑	
2 Earl BARRETT		2 Ian ALEXANDER	
3 Steve STAUNTON †		3 Andy TILLSON	
4 Shaun TEALE		4 Steve YATES	
5 Paul McGRATH		5 Paul HARDYMAN	
6 Kevin RICHARDSON		6 Richard EVANS	
7 Ray HOUGHTON		7 Marcus BROWNING	72
8 Garry PARKER		8 Marcus STEWART †	
9 Dean SAUNDERS		9 John TAYLOR	
10 Dwight YORKE ‡74		10 Carl SAUNDERS	
11 Steve FROGGATT		11 Gary WADDOCK	
Substitutes		*Substitutes*	
Neil COX †17	38	David MEHEW †64	
Cyrille REGIS ‡74		Geoff TWENTYMAN	

FACTFILE
Gavin Kelly is the Rovers hero, saving a 51st minute penalty from Dean Saunders... Neil Cox, an early substitute for the injured Steve Staunton, scores his first goal in the Villa first team... Cox's goal turns out to be the only one from a Villa sub all season.

Penalty! Dwight Yorke is sent tumbling

Missed chances embarrass Villa

This is, without doubt, the most disappointing result of the season and an occasion which gives the tabloid headline writers a field day.

"Big Mal Shoots From the Lip," is typical of the lines which taunt Villa as Rovers' caretaker boss Malcolm Allison revels in his return to the national spotlight.

During the build-up Ron Atkinson strove in vain to switch the emphasis away from the high-profile image of himself and his rival boss.

Meanwhile his opposite number, thrust unexpectedly back into the limelight on the resignation of manager Dennis Rofe a few weeks earlier, was stirring up the orgy of publicity with undisguised glee. So, while Allison was enjoying this experience of re-living by-gone days, when he was manager of Manchester City, Atkinson urgently needed his players to shoot for the net.

A trigger-happy response with a barrage of goals would have been the most satisfying response. Irritatingly, it is not to be.

Villa set off as though they intend to bury the lower division visitors in the opening half hour. Until then Rovers are mainly sat in their own half, defending in numbers and getting accustomed to the experience of playing in a 'big atmosphere' stadium.

The only problem for Villa in the opening spell is when Steve Staunton goes down with concussion caused by an elbow in the face. After lengthy treatment he is replaced in the 17th minute by Neil Cox. The change brings a touch of disruption for a while and late in the half Rovers ominously begin to play with more style and composure.

As the first half comes to a close substitute Cox fires Villa into the lead as Dwight Yorke helps on Steve Froggatt's corner from the right.

Anticipation of Premier League Villa making home advantage and higher status tell in the second half is now high. TOO high, it transpires. This unhappy afternoon emerges as a tie Dean Saunders will look back on with regrets.

Six minutes into the second half Yorke is pulled down for a clear penalty. Before Saunders can attempt to repeat his success in the previous match the Rovers goalkeeper Gavin Kelly complains at such length about the position of the ball on the spot that he is booked for time wasting.

Deano, perhaps unsettled by the delay, fires his shot too close to the 'keeper who guesses correctly and saves. Allison and his men would surely have been out of it at 2-0. But now they're off the hook.

Nothing goes right from now on. Marcus Browning equalises in the 72nd minute and six minutes from time Saunders jabs an excellent chance of the winner, from inside the six-yards box, against an upright.

Next day, more irritation for Villa when what should have been an undisputed fourth round home draw arrives in the shape of a visit from either Wimbledon or Everton.

But, due to those missed chances, there is first the need for a tricky replay at Twerton Park. More in hope than expectation a request is made from Villa Park to switch the venue back to Birmingham from Rovers' tiny temporary home.

"No deal," say the First Division club. Allison is happy to keep shooting from the lip.

A first goal for Neil Cox

Saturday 9th January 1993 • Anfield • 3.00pm

LIVERPOOL 1 ASTON VILLA 2

Half-time 1-0 • *Attendance* 40,826

Referee Keith HACKETT (Sheffield)

Linesmen R. PEARSON and T.J. STEVENS

Red Shirts, Red Shorts	Goals	White Shirts, Blue Shorts	Goals
1 Mike HOOPER		1 Nigel SPINK	
2 Mike MARSH		2 Earl BARRETT	
3 Rob JONES		3 Steve STAUNTON	
4 Paul STEWART		4 Shaun TEALE ❑	
5 Torben PIECHNIK		5 Paul McGRATH	
6 Stig BJORNEBYE		6 Kevin RICHARDSON	
7 Steve McMANAMAN		7 Ray HOUGHTON	
8 Jamie REDKNAPP ‡		8 Garry PARKER	54
9 Ronny ROSENTHAL †		9 Dean SAUNDERS	65
10 John BARNES	41	10 Dalian ATKINSON †	
11 Michael THOMAS		11 Dwight YORKE	
Substitutes		*Substitutes*	
12 Mark WALTERS †70		12 Steve FROGGATT †45 ‡	
14 Don HUTCHISON †78		14 Neil COX ‡87	
Gk David JAMES		Gk Mark BOSNICH	

BEFORE		P	W	D	L	F	A	pts	AFTER		P	W	D	L	F	A	pts
3	Villa	22	10	8	4	32	24	38	2	Villa	23	11	8	4	34	25	41
11	Liverpool	21	8	5	8	35	33	29	11	Liverpool	22	8	5	9	36	35	29

FACTFILE

Villa's first win at Anfield since November 1977 and the first League 'double' over the Reds for 40 years... Dean Saunders scores his third goal against Liverpool since leaving them four months ago... Dalian Atkinson, playing only his second game in seven, is injured again.

Double delight for Villa

Liverpool's image of near-invincibility is crumbling. With the second half of the Premier League campaign underway Graeme Souness is looking more towards mid-table respectability than the old annual championship challenge.

Anfield is not quite the forbidding venue of days gone by when teams were psychologically beaten before they even came face to face with the residents of the famous Kop.

Wounded tigers can, however, be even more menacing than the healthy variety and Villa approach with caution. No manager holds the famous soccer temple in greater reverence than Ron Atkinson, Liverpool born and a deep Anfield devotee.

It's the day of 'going back' for the ex-Anfield trio, Steve Staunton, Ray Houghton and Dean Saunders who were part of the memorable 4-2 victory over their former team-mates at Villa Park on September 19.

The chance of the club's first double over Liverpool for 40 years, thus beckons temptingly. As Andy Colquhoun put it in the Birmingham Post to describe the last time Villa beat Liverpool twice: "Ron Atkinson was in short trousers getting over the shock of the ending of 'Dick Barton: Special Agent' on the wireless while Doug Ellis was a million short of his first million..."

There will rarely be a better chance of repeating that double feat of four decades earlier. Ian Rush and Steve Nicol have succumbed to training injuries while the likes of Ronnie Whelan, Jan Molby and Mark Wright are also missing.

But Liverpool are still Liverpool. And Deano reckons they have eleven players in the treatment room who are still capable of winning the title. That's an exaggeration. But only just.

Although Liverpool are a goal up at half-time through John Barnes the danger signs have been flashing in their defence right from the start. Scandinavian centre backs Piechnik and Bjornebye are uncomfortable as Saunders and Dalian Atkinson make deep penetrating runs, fed by a midfield in which Houghton is examining every inch of the pitch he knows so well.

The interval is not a happy period for Villa. By now Atkinson has to be sidelined yet again with a groin strain, allowing Steve Froggatt to be called in. That, plus a goal deficit which now looks almost monumental.

Character is clearly more in demand even than quality, and Big Ron's boys dig deep to produce it to order.

Garry Parker rockets the equaliser from the edge of the penalty area as Kevin Richardson's headed-on pass falls sweetly for him.

That was nine minutes into the half. Another eleven minutes and Deano punishes his former club for the third time since they sold him.

Piechnik is just a shade indecisive in allowing the Welsh cap to bury a left-footer at the feet of a silent Kop. Yet more stress for Graham Souness who has had more than his share.

Defensive determination around an agile and alert Nigel Spink is the final ingredient to complete another famous victory. "I'll be having a couple of lemonades," said Deano. Ray Houghton, too. It's his 31st birthday.

Cheers...

Ray Houghton, plenty to celebrate

Sunday 17th January 1993 • Villa Park • 4.00pm

ASTON VILLA 5 MIDDLESBROUGH 1

Half-time 3-0 • *Attendance* 19,977

Referee Keith COOPER (Pontypridd)

Linesmen R.H. ANDREWS and M.J. HOLOHAN

Claret and Blue Shirts, White Shorts	Goals	White Shirts, Black Shorts	Goals
1 Nigel SPINK		1 Stephen PEARS	
2 Earl BARRETT		2 Nicky MOHAN	
3 Steve STAUNTON		3 Jimmy PHILLIPS	
4 Shaun TEALE	68	4 Derek WHYTE ‡	
5 Paul McGRATH ‡	31	5 Jon GITTENS	
6 Kevin RICHARDSON		6 Willie FALCONER	
7 Ray HOUGHTON		7 Graham KAVANAGH †	
8 Garry PARKER	25	8 Andy PEAKE	
9 Dean SAUNDERS	58	9 Paul WILKINSON	
10 Dwight YORKE	44	10 Tommy WRIGHT	
11 Steve FROGGATT †		11 John HENDRIE	
Substitutes		*Substitutes*	
12 Stefan BEINLICH †71		12 Craig HIGNETT †45	82
14 Neil COX ‡81		14 Jamie POLLOCK ‡67	
Gk Mark BOSNICH		Gk Ian IRONSIDE	

BEFORE		P	W	D	L	F	A	pts	AFTER		P	W	D	L	F	A	pts
4	Villa	23	11	8	4	34	25	41	1	Villa	24	12	8	4	39	26	44
17	'Boro	23	6	9	8	33	34	27	17	'Boro	24	6	9	9	34	39	27

FACTFILE

Villa top the table for the first time this season and score five at home for the first time in three years... Villa are now unbeaten in five live TV appearances this season... Five different Villa players score in a home League game for the first time since April 1978.

Middlesbrough are paralysed

A tempting place at the top of the Premier League beckons as the prize for victory in this latest live BSkyB TV transmission, though Manchester United can take over tomorrow if they win at Loftus Road.

After the previous win, at Liverpool, and the current high-riding league position, a better gate than the one of fewer than 20,000 might have been expected.

As a result of the disappointing turn-out pre-match crowd atmosphere is cool, but the players are demonstrably not affected by it. And things quickly warm up as the action rolls.

'Boro are simply no match for Villa as the ball is repeatedly swept forward through defence and midfield to eager forwards ready to make the break.

Dalian Atkinson has not recovered from his Old Trafford injury but Dwight Yorke has his old touch back and Steve Froggatt is supplying the necessary attacking width.

Gradually, and to 'Boro's increasing discomfort, the best Villa all-round team performance of the season so far takes shape.

As it builds in the second half Ron Atkinson offers the best compliment at his command... he stays firmly in his stand seat throughout the game, abandoning his usual custom of moving to the pitch-side dug-out to sort out any emerging team problems.

Today there ARE no such problems...

Not only are the midfield an ever-effective supply unit but the full backs Earl Barrett and Steve Staunton constantly provide an alternative back up down each flank.

The strike which starts the five-goal romp comes from Garry Parker after 25 minutes of home ascendancy. Staunton's pass sets him up but the former-Forest midfield player hestitates

briefly, fearing an off-side verdict.

Quickly reassured he drives his shot for goal and finds his target, helped by a defensive deflection. Paul McGrath makes it two, forcing Froggatt's centre over the line after pressuring goalkeeper Stephen Pears to lose possession.

Yorke's impressive work is rewarded just before the half-time whistle as he dives to head in as Saunders' shot rebounds off the bar.

In the second half Saunders joins the fun by using his searing pace to pursue a long goal clearance by Nigel Spink and deposit No.4 out of Pears' way.

By now 'Boro can only pray for the final whistle to put them out of their misery. Before it arrives defender Shaun Teale knocks one in from close range to complete Villa's journey to the top with a nice little booster for their goal difference.

Villa are now the Premier League's top scorers but United's goal difference is superior by just three goals, the fraction which gives them the edge 24 hours later when they beat Queen's Park Rangers.

Yorke captures the sponsors' Man of the Match and earns himself a place in the third round FA Cup replay with Bristol Rovers at Twerton Park on Wednesday.

"I can't remember when I've enjoyed a performance more," beams Ron Atkinson. "Probably never at Villa Park. We could have had a lot more goals. We paralysed them."

Lennie Lawrence, the 'Boro boss does not disagree. "I'm glad the League is not full of Aston Villa's," he confesses. I will be amazed if they are not first or second at the end of the season."

Celebrations after Parker's opener

Wednesday 20th January 1993 • Twerton Park, Bath • 8.00pm

BRISTOL ROVERS 0 ASTON VILLA 3

Half-time 0-1 • *Attendance* 8,880

Referee Martin BODENHAM (Looe, Cornwall)
Linesmen J.H. GRIFFITHS and G.K. RODERICK

Blue and White Quartered Shirts, White Shorts	Goals	Claret and Blue Shirts, Blue Shorts	Goals
1 Gavin KELLY		1 Nigel SPINK	
2 Richard EVANS †		2 Earl BARRETT	
3 Billy CLARK ■		3 Steve STAUNTON	
4 Steve YATES		4 Shaun TEALE	
5 Paul HARDYMAN		5 Paul McGRATH	
6 Vaughan JONES		6 Kevin RICHARDSON	
7 Marcus BROWNING		7 Ray HOUGHTON	83
8 Marcus STEWART		8 Garry PARKER †	
9 John TAYLOR		9 Dean SAUNDERS	23, 75
10 Carl SAUNDERS		10 Dwight YORKE ‡	
11 Gary WADDOCK		11 Neil COX	
Substitutes		*Substitutes*	
Geoff TWENTYMAN †30		Steve FROGGATT †84	
Lee ARCHER		Cyrille REGIS ‡84	

FACTFILE

Villa's first appearance at Twerton Park... Ray Houghton's penalty miss is Villa's fourth successive miss in the competition following Dean Saunders' in the first game with Rovers and two from Dwight Yorke at Derby last season... Another live BSkyB appearance.

Malcolm Allison's team were well beaten this time

Class tells at the end of the day

On the eve of the Cup replay there is a squad boost for Villa when Henrik Larsen, the Danish international, is signed from the Italian club, Pisa, on loan until the end of the season.

After lengthy negotiations the chance meeting between Larsen and Ron Atkinson at Birmingham Airport all those weeks earlier bears fruit.

As he prepares for the chance to put right the failures of the first meeting at Villa Park, the Villa manager continues his wise policy of declining to be drawn into the so-called 'War of Words' with Allison.

Reaching the fourth round and maintaining a challenge at the top of the league is all that interests Atkinson as he makes it clear that Larsen will be thrust into the squad as soon as he is match-fit after a few games in the reserves.

The replay has been put back a week because of heavy rain which has waterlogged Twerton Park. Even on the eve of this second attempt the surface is suspect but an overnight improvement delivers playable conditions.

The return of Dalian Atkinson had been anticipated but, once again, frustration reigns as an unchanged team is named. "I can't say how long he will be out because we are not sure of the extent of the injury," the manager confesses.

No qualms, however, about Dwight Yorke continuing as Dean Saunders' up-front partner. "Maybe his time has now come," declares Big Ron. "After last season's high it must have been disappointing not to be a regular but maybe the Cup is 'his' competition. He scored a lot of goals in the competition in '91-'92."

Soon it is clear that, for all Big Mal's verbal bravado, there will be no repeat shocks.

Deano is in terrific form, motoring all over the punishing surface. To counteract Villa's quality-in-depth, Rovers have only the old-fashioned virtues of commitment and desire. They are not going to be enough, especially when defender Billy Clark is sent off for deliberate hands soon after Villa go a goal up.

Clark's on-the-line handling offence has also produced a penalty and, perhaps with Kelly's save from Saunders' spot kick in the first game in mind, Ray Houghton is the one to take it this time. The Irish international attempts to place his shot low to Kelly's right but the 'keeper is again equal to it with a diving save.

The first of Deano's two goals arrived from Steve Staunton's corner to the near post. Yorke flicked on and the Welsh international headed in at the far post.

But for missed chances by Villa Rovers would have been buried but Nigel Spink, who made just one save, from Marcus Browning, is rarely threatened and 15 minutes from time another Staunton dead-ball kick finds Deano waiting to head in again.

Ray Houghton rounds it all off nicely as the ball is played around by Villa in a passing move which defied tired Rovers legs and left the Irish Republic international clear to place his finish past goalkeeper Gavin Kelly.

"I wasn't pleased with the 20 we missed but their goalkeeper played very well," said Atkinson.

Kevin Richardson and Garry Parker have kept things ticking over very well in midfield and, in the centre of defence, Paul McGrath and Shaun Teale have been rock-solid as ever.

The First Division club's supporters have enjoyed their break from relegation battling and Villa's visit to their tiny, borrowed Bath-based ground. But now it's all over. And Allison goes back to one of his favourite pastimes, pouring controversial words into the tabloids.

For Villa, it is on to the Fourth Round, and a mere three days to prepare for the visit of Wimbledon to Villa Park on Saturday.

Saturday 23rd January 1993 • Villa Park • 3.00pm

ASTON VILLA 1 WIMBLEDON 1

Half-time 1-1 • *Attendance* 21,088
Referee Ken REDFERN (Whitley Bay)
Linesmen F.R.K. MARTIN and P.E. TOWNSEND

Claret and Blue Shirts, White Shorts		Goals	White Shirts, Black Shorts		Goals
1	Nigel SPINK		1	Hans SEGERS ❑	
2	Earl BARRETT		2	Roger JOSEPH	
3	Steve STAUNTON		3	Gary ELKINS	35
4	Shaun TEALE		4	Vinnie JONES ❑	
5	Paul McGRATH		5	John SCALES	
6	Kevin RICHARDSON		6	Dean BLACKWELL	
7	Ray HOUGHTON		7	Neil ARDLEY	
8	Garry PARKER		8	Robbie EARLE	
9	Dean SAUNDERS		9	John FASHANU	
10	Dwight YORKE	3	10	Lawrie SANCHEZ	
11	Steve FROGGATT		11	Steve COTTERILL †	
	Substitutes			*Substitutes*	
	Neil COX			Dean HOLDSWORTH †22	
	Stefan BEINLICH			Andy CLARKE	

Villa have now drawn each of their last four home FA Cup ties, two of them against Wimbledon... Dwight Yorke takes his FA Cup goals total to six... The fifth round draw gives the eventual winners an away tie at Tottenham.

FACTFILE

A yellow card for Hans Segers

Dons deny Cup progress again

Those who believe that, for potentially successful clubs, too many important fixtures are packed into too short a time, are given plenty of ammunition for their argument by Villa's crowded week. With barely enough time to recover from Wednesday night's exploits on a heavy Twerton Road pitch players have to contemplate the rigours of a visit by Wimbledon.

The team is unchanged but for the return of Steve Froggatt in place of Neil Cox at No.11. The young winger has a knee condition which, while not preventing him playing, restricts his training in between games.

"We have to be careful how much work we give him," explains the manager, thus explaining the player's slightly erratic appearance record this season.

Three fixtures in six days, between Sunday and Saturday, inevitably throws a strain on players who have too little recovery period between. The absence of Dalian Atkinson continues so Stefan Beinlich is substitute striker. Cox gets the other place on the bench.

To put it discreetly, Wimbledon are not a popular draw. They have dismissed Villa from the FA Cup twice in the previous four years in matches which have not endeared themselves to the onlookers.

Before the tie is very old a similar pattern emerges. No-one is surprised when, in the second half, the notorious Vinnie Jones commits a blatant foul on Garry Parker and is booked amid scenes of unpleasantness which do nothing for the enjoyment of the afternoon.

Even his indulgent manager, Joe Kinnear, admits that the challenge is 'stupid'. At the age of 28 there is not much chance of Jones reforming now, though his influence on games is, at best, so frequently a sour one.

Opposition supporters inevitably object to his belligerent style and Villa's are no exception. The Dons play in their usual way, concentrating more on the destruction of their opponents' creative skills than in attempting quality football on their own account.

Villa have made a highly promising start. Although Dwight Yorke has missed a chance by shooting wide in the opening seconds he redeems himself in the third minute by getting on the end of Ray Houghton's centre to score with a header which he steers out of Hans Segers' reach.

From then on it is largely a game of stoppages with little coherent flow as Wimbledon apply themselves to their negative style of closing down all Villa attempts to play a passing game.

The visitors' cause is given the impetus it needs in the 35th minute in the shape of an unexpected and slightly fortunate equaliser.

A long-range free kick is touched to left-side defender Gary Elkins whose shot bounces off the far post, against goalkeeper Nigel Spink, and rebounds into the net.

Now Wimbeldon can defend with even greater gusto knowing that a replay is within their grasp.

The second half sees Villa mostly in the Wimbledon half attempting to break down a side who will demonstrably be happy to settle for a replay at Selhurst Park.

"We are not everyone's cup of tea," said Kinnear with a flair for understatement.

"They make things difficult," observed Ron Atkinson, showing commendable restraint.

Dwight Yorke gave Villa an early boost

Wednesday 27th January 1993 • Villa Park • 7.45pm

ASTON VILLA 3 SHEFFIELD UNITED 1

Half-time 0-0 • *Attendance* 20,266

Referee Keith BURGE (Tonypandy)

Linesmen K.J. HAWKES and J. LEECH

Claret and Blue Shirts, White Shorts	Goals	White Shirts, Black Shorts	Goals
1 Nigel SPINK		1 Alan KELLY	
2 Earl BARRETT		2 Kevin GAGE	
3 Steve STAUNTON		3 David BARNES	
4 Shaun TEALE		4 Jamie HOYLAND	
5 Paul McGRATH	54	5 Brian GAYLE	
6 Kevin RICHARDSON	90	6 Paul BEESLEY ❑	
7 Matthias BREITKREUTZ ‡		7 Franz CARR ❑ ‡	
8 Garry PARKER		8 Charlie HARTFIELD †	
9 Dean SAUNDERS	58	9 Chris KAMARA ❑	
10 Dwight YORKE †		10 Brian DEANE	74
11 Bryan SMALL		11 Glyn HODGES	
Substitutes		*Substitutes*	
Stefan BEINLICH †75		Alan CORK †61	
Neil COX ‡80		Carl BRADSHAW ‡82	
Gk Michael OAKES		Gk Mel REES	

BEFORE	P	W	D	L	F	A	pts	AFTER	P	W	D	L	F	A	pts
2 Villa	24	12	8	4	39	26	44	2 Villa	25	13	8	4	42	27	47
19 United	23	6	7	10	22	29	25	19 United	24	6	7	11	23	32	25

FACTFILE

Villa become the first English club to field two Germans in a League game... Matthias Breitkreutz starts his first League game of the season... Villa complete the 'double' over the Blades for the first time since season 1954/55, when they won both games 3-1.

Bassett's Blades are blunted

Villa Park attendances have been thrown into focus by a set pattern which has emerged. Despite the team's battle for supremacy in the ever-changing championship race, some gates are disappointing.

In round figures League gates number either 28,000 and more, or 20,000 and less with none in-between, depending on the name of the opposition.

Sheffield United fall into the bracket of the 'less attractive' and in consequence only 20,266 are present for the club's latest attempt to hit the top.

Leadership could be achieved by a Villa victory unless Manchester United also win their home fixture with Nottingham Forest.

Dalian Atkinson continues to be unfit and this time he is joined by Ray Houghton. The strength of the squad is now undergoing a searching test but Ron Atkinson is quietly satisfied with the progress of many young players, including the German pair.

Matthias Breitkreutz is the one to claim Houghton's No. 7 shirt, Bryan Small replaces Steve Froggatt, while Henrik Larsen continues his daunting programme under the watchful eye of fitness expert Roger Spry.

Breitkreutz has already survived all this with honours and is ready to play his part at first team level. By the time he is replaced by Neil Cox ten minutes before the end he leaves to a warm ovation from supporters who have appreciated his skill and commitment.

The first half is rated as one of Villa's poorest of the season as United close them down, often with all eleven players packed into their back-third of the field.

Villa are being drawn into the trap, allowing their style to become too cramped instead of creating more space for themselves. "We did have a little 'discussion' about how we might play in the second half..." said Ron Atkinson, with heavy irony.

One suspected that sparks had been flying in the home dressing room. If so they ignited the fireworks.

A 54th minute scrambled goal by Paul McGrath, when fed by a beautifully-struck free kick by Breitkreutz which pierces across goal as Steve Staunton 'dummies' defenders, opens the way for a superbly-entertaining second half.

Only the alert agility of goalkeeper Alan Kelly and several close shaves, restricts Villa to a two-goal winning margin as flowing football is rounded off with a thirst for goals.

An acrobatic scissor kick by Dean Saunders produces the second as McGrath nods on a right wing corner at the Holte End. Deano's stunner deflects off Chris Kamara on the line... but don't talk about 'own goals' to the Welsh hit man!

Villa's concentration on attack is such that United are presented with the chance of hitting them on the break. Glynn Hodges makes a rather casual-looking run down the left before measuring a centre of deadly accuracy to the far post where the England-bidding Brian Deane jabs United back in with the whiff of a chance.

It is, however, only a whiff, as Villa return to rampaging forward play. Another quickfire break by Saunders who rounds the 'keeper but then appears to be tripped. Penalty? None given. And no time to dwell on it.

In the dying seconds Richardson is released by a lovely pass from Neil Cox. The ground is awash with feverish excitement, such has been the quality and menace of the attacking play.

The Villa skipper, the calmest man in the ground, advances, picks both his spot and moment and buries Goal No.3. "The second half saw some of our best football of the season," added Atkinson. That half-time 'discussion', or rollicking maybe, has worked.

Saturday 30th January 1993 • The Dell • 3.00pm

SOUTHAMPTON 2 ASTON VILLA 0

Half-time 1-0 • *Attendance* 19,087

Referee Philip WRIGHT (Northwich)

Linesmen W.M. JORDAN and S.G. TOMLIN

Red and White Striped Shirts, Black Shorts	Goals		Claret and Blue Shirts, White Shorts	Goals
1 Tim FLOWERS			1 Nigel SPINK	
2 Jason DODD			2 Earl BARRETT	
3 Micky ADAMS			3 Steve STAUNTON	
4 Terry HURLOCK			4 Shaun TEALE	
5 Richard HALL			5 Paul McGRATH	
6 Kevin MOORE			6 Kevin RICHARDSON ❏	
7 Matthew LE TISSIER ❏			7 Matthias BREITKREUTZ †	
8 Nicky BANGER	40		8 Garry PARKER	
9 Iain DOWIE	64		9 Dean SAUNDERS	
10 Neil MADDISON			10 Dwight YORKE	
11 Francis BENALI			11 Bryan SMALL ‡	
Substitutes			*Substitutes*	
Jeff KENNA			Neil COX †69	
Lee POWELL			Stefan BEINLICH ‡70	
Gk Ian ANDREWS			Gk Michael OAKES	

BEFORE	P	W	D	L	F	A	pts	AFTER	P	W	D	L	F	A	pts
2 Villa	25	13	8	4	42	27	47	3 Villa	26	13	8	5	42	29	47
16 Soton	25	6	9	10	25	30	27	16 Soton	26	7	9	10	27	30	30

FACTFILE

The crowd of 19,087, included some 3,000 Villa fans, is Southampton's biggest since the opening day of the season... It's ten games without success for Villa at The Dell... Villa complete a busy opening month of the new year with four wins and two draws from seven games.

Battling Saints have the edge

An ominous fixture for Villa. The Dell is never a comfortable venue for teams who prefer to engage in an exchange of passing skills and need a yard or two of space to parade them.

Saints' boss Ian Branfoot is not dissimilar to the Dave Bassetts and Bobby Goulds in requiring his teams to win the physical battles first and to close down every spare yard of available space.

After that they go for the shortest, least complicated route to the penalty area where Matthew Le Tissier is quite likely to appear ready to execute his lethal finishing skills.

Southampton have been an example to many of the medium-sized clubs in the way they have survived for so many years in the top flight.

Le Tissier is the only one of their many home-produced stars who have not been sold for financial reasons, yet they have always found adequate replacements.

This season, for instance, they have been without the new England striker Alan Shearer, sold to Blackburn Rovers for a record £3.6M.

The morning newspapers point out that Villa are top of the Premier League's unofficial fair play league, with only a dozen bookings and no dismissals. In contrast Southampton have not been saints. Their disciplinary record is the poorest in the division.

A pattern is set very early on when, as Villa strive to get the ball moving around at ground level, the tenacious and physically aggressive Terry Hurlock and Neil Maddison lead their team-mates into a relentless and intimidating hunt for possession.

For a while Villa'a football produces a fleeting chance or two. Garry Parker, Steve Staunton and Matthias Breitkreutz combine to set up Dean Saunders on the edge of the box but Tim Flowers takes it safely.

The German then opens up the home defence with a fine through pass to Dwight Yorke and it is panic stations in front of goal until Parker's shot is blocked.

Failure to force the lead from this early superiority proves expensive five minutes before the break.

There's a skirmish between Kevin Richardson and Le Tissier. The Southampton player has been at the receiving end of a double tackle by the Villa skipper and Earl Barrett. He reacts by lashing out. A free-for-all is threatened.

When its all sorted out Richardson and Le Tissier have been shown yellow cards. The free kick goes to Southampton and leads to Nicky Banger's left-footed drive sending his side into the dressing room a goal up at half-time.

As it transpires there is no way back for Villa. "Southampton played very well in the second half," concedes Ron Atkinson who adds, with his particular brand of mocking criticism: "We did well in the warm-up."

In the second half there is a tantalising chance that Deano might square it but his long-range shot on the turn lifts and clears the bar.

By now Saints are in control, with Le Tissier's skills concentrated more on attacking from midfield then joining the two main strikers.

In the 64th minute Villa go 2-0 down. A mis-hit pass from Kevin Moore loops over Bryan Small to Iain Dowie who makes very good use of the good fortune by finishing clinically from a narrow angle.

With both subs on Villa make a rather forlorn late attempt to claw their way back. Saunders just misses the target with one stinging drive, Stefan Beinlich, a lively replacement for Small, sends an overhead kick just over the bar.

January has been a seven-match slog for Villa. Things are tough near the top. And getting tougher...

Wednesday 3rd February 1993 • Selhurst Park • 8.00pm

WIMBLEDON 0 ASTON VILLA 0

After extra time • Wimbledon win 6-5 on penalties
Half-time 0-0 • Attendance 8,048

Referee Ken REDFERN (Whitley Bay)
Linesmen R.J. HARRIS and W.M. JORDAN

Blue Shirts, Blue Shorts		Goals	Claret and Blue Shirts, White Shorts		Goals
1	Hans SEGERS		1	Mark BOSNICH	
2	Roger JOSEPH		2	Earl BARRETT	
3	Brian McALLISTER		3	Steve STAUNTON	
4	Vinnie JONES ❑		4	Shaun TEALE	
5	John SCALES		5	Paul McGRATH	
6	Dean BLACKWELL		6	Kevin RICHARDSON	
7	Neil ARDLEY		7	Ray HOUGHTON	
8	Robbie EARLE		8	Garry PARKER	
9	John FASHANU ❑		9	Dean SAUNDERS	
10	Dean HOLDSWORTH		10	Dwight YORKE	
11	Andy CLARKE †		11	Neil COX	

Substitutes		*Substitutes*	
	Gerald DOBBS †77		Cyrille REGIS
	Lawrie SANCHEZ		Stefan BEINLICH

PENALTY SHOOT-OUT

1	John FASHANU	✔	1-0	1	Garry PARKER	✔	1-1
2	Neil ARDLEY	✔	2-1	2	Dean SAUNDERS	✔	2-2
3	Brian McALLISTER	✔	3-2	3	Steve STAUNTON	✔	3-3
4	Vinnie JONES	✔	4-3	4	Neil COX	✘	4-3
5	Dean HOLDSWORTH	✘	4-3	5	Dwight YORKE	✔	4-4
6	Gerald DOBBS	✔	5-4	6	Shaun TEALE	✔	5-5
7	Roger JOSEPH	✔	6-5	7	Kevin RICHARDSON	✘	6-5

FACTFILE

FA Cup elimination at the hands of Wimbledon for the third time in five years... Nigel Spink is ill, Mark Bosnich gets a late call-up... It's 10.38pm when Kevin Richardson misses the vital penalty... Dons go on to face Tottenham.

Shot down in shoot-out

The FA Cup trail is proving a gruelling and unyielding one for Villa, mixed in as it is, with the highly-charged competition for places among the FA Premier League's leading bunch.

After two demanding games against Bristol Rovers and the fourth round slog with Wimbledon the replay arrives on the heels of a slightly demoralising defeat in the League at The Dell.

For the trip to Selhurst Park Ray Houghton is back again, to the exclusion of Matthias Breitkreutz whose status in the squad has been significantly improved during the Irish Republic cap's absence.

With only two substitutes allowed in the Cup, it is two strikers who get the vote in Stefan Beinlich and Cyrille Regis.

Unlike the Cup rules of the past, there has to be a winner and loser tonight.

If the teams are still level after 90 minutes then there will be penalty shoot-out, dreaded by the players, derided by most pundits, but relished by onlookers, especially the neutrals.

In the hours leading up to the kick-off a well-kept selection secret emerges. Nigel Spink has been unwell during the week and can't make it. Another chance for the young Aussie international Mark Bosnich on a night when goalkeepers could well be thrust into the national limelight. Bosnich has, himself, only just recovered from a shoulder injury. Otherwise young Michael Oakes would have received a call-up.

Few are surprised when, after normal time and extra-time, there is still a stalemate. The initiative has swung back and forth. Early on it seemed that Villa's greater control might put them into the driving seat.

Dean Saunders might have scored in the first half of normal time. Dwight Yorke later failed to accept a scoring chance. But Wimbledon are nothing if not resilient and defiant. Gradually their forthright methods put Villa under siege and Bosnich has to be as alert and competent as the more experienced Hans Segers.

The promising Aussie is particularly impressive in extra time with a number of confident interventions but the penalty decider becomes inevitable.

Have Villa staged a practice-ground rehearsal? "No point," insists manager Atkinson. "The shoot-out is all about nerve. You can't re-create the atmosphere in training."

John Fashanu takes the first for the Dons. No nerves. No chance for Bosnich. Garry Parker shows his bottle by netting the equaliser.

Then it's Neil Ardley and Dean Saunders cancelling each other out. Brian McAllister and Steve Staunton follow suit. No problem.

In the fourth of Wimbledon's five shots, before a 'sudden death' situation takes over, Vinnie Jones bulges the Villa net. Who next for Villa? Paul McGrath... Earl Barrett... Dwight Yorke... Shaun Teale?

In fact it is the least likely of all, the inexperienced Neil Cox, who steps up. And misses.

Now Dean Holdsworth can send the Dons through at 5-3. But, as tension clutches muscles and limbs, he misses, too.

This unexpected reprieve is gratefully accepted by Yorke who makes it 4-4. No more second chances now. Next one to make a mistake pulls the plug on his team's Cup ambitions.

Gerald Dobbs, knocks one in. Teale squares it at 5-5. Roger Joseph blasts his shot past past Bosnich, so Kevin Richardson is the next one on the spot. He must feel like Bernhard Langer in the famous final Ryder Cup putt at Kiawah Island in 1991.

Langer's putt missed the hole. Richardson's shot cleared the bar. There are no words to adequately describe how he felt.

The closest he could get was 'gutted'...

Saturday 6th February 1993 • Villa Park • 3.00pm

ASTON VILLA 2 IPSWICH TOWN 0

Half-time 2-0 • *Attendance* 25,395

Referee Paul DURKIN (Portland, Dorset)

Linesmen R.J. HARRIS and I.A. MADGE

Claret and Blue Shirts, White Shorts	Goals	Blue Shirts with White Sleeves, Blue Shorts	Goals
1 Mark BOSNICH		1 Clive BAKER	
2 Earl BARRETT		2 Phil WHELAN	
3 Steve STAUNTON		3 Neil THOMPSON	
4 Shaun TEALE		4 Mick STOCKWELL ❑	
5 Paul McGRATH		5 John WARK	
6 Kevin RICHARDSON		6 David LINIGHAN †	
7 Ray HOUGHTON		7 Geraint WILLIAMS ❑	
8 Garry PARKER		8 Bontcho GUENTCHEV	
9 Dean SAUNDERS	42	9 Steve WHITTON	
10 Dwight YORKE ‡	32	10 Jason DOZZELL	
11 Steve FROGGATT †		11 Chris KIWOMYA	

Substitutes		*Substitutes*	
Neil COX †80		Gavin JOHNSON †45	
Stefan BEINLICH ‡86		Frank YALLOP	
Gk Michael OAKES		Gk Craig FORREST	

BEFORE	P	W	D	L	F	A	pts	AFTER	P	W	D	L	F	A	pts
3 Villa	26	13	8	5	42	29	47	2 Villa	27	14	8	5	44	29	50
4 Ipswich	26	10	12	4	36	29	42	5 Ipswich	27	10	12	5	36	31	42

FACTFILE

Dwight Yorke's goal is chosen as the BBC's 'Goal of the Month' for February, Dean Saunders' is third... It's Villa's first win over Ipswich in four meetings this season, but is the fifth successive home League win against the East Anglians... Mark Bosnich keeps a clean sheet in his home League debut for the club.

Villa bounce back with style

It's not been a good week. Beaten in the League at Southampton last Saturday, shot out of the Cup on penalties by Wimbledon on Wednesday and now it's Ipswich, a recent bogey team.

This is the fourth fixture of the season against the East Anglian side, who currently lie fourth and who removed Villa from the Coca Cola Cup.

Anything but a win today will be a serious setback, especially if Manchester United beat Sheffield United. Pressure is the name of the game just now and Villa have to withstand it, or slide.

Still no Dalian Atkinson available while Henrik Larsen has not been too impressive in the reserves. The one interesting item of team news is that Steve Froggatt is back to add width on the left flank.

An attendance of 25,395 is not as high as the club would like for a fixture between two clubs in the top four but at least that 'gate gap' between 20,000 and 28,000 is breached.

The 'Match of the Day' cameras are at Villa Park to continue the team's growing reputation as a big attraction on the small screen.

By the end of January an assured TV income of £1.1M, £300,000 up on the whole of last season, had been achieved. This includes the basic £750,000 all Premier League clubs will receive from a total £37.5M to be shared among the clubs in the TV contract. With £815,000 merit money for the Champions and similar graded figures for the other leading clubs, there is a total of up to £2.5M to be played for over and above normal club income.

High stakes... and soon it is clear that Villa are heading for a high-octane performance. No chance this time of being closed down by Ipswich as they have been previously.

Full backs Earl Barrett and Steve Staunton go raiding down the flanks, Garry Parker's distribution is finely-tuned and considered, Dean Saunders is all go and Froggatt is happy about his return.

When the goals arrive, in a ten-minute spell before the break, they guarantee nationwide appreciation when screened later for Saturday night consumption.

Froggatt slips a quick ball down the left to Parker, whose pass to Steve Staunton wrong foots the Ipswich back line.

The Irish Republic cap's centre to the far post is so superbly-placed and so begging to be translated into a goal that the stand spectators are on their feet applauding even before Dwight Yorke arrives on the end of it with a diving header.

Some goal! And a matching moment of individual brilliance still to come.

Three minutes before half time. Deano is up to 40 yards out when Ray Houghton feeds him with a pass from the centre circle.

No danger for Ipswich, or so their goalkeeper mistakenly believes. Clive Baker is forward from his line awaiting events when the little Welshman demonstrates the speed of his football brain and reflexes.

With a volley Pele would have been proud of he loops the ball over Baker's head and under the bar. Pure magic... and Villa Park erupts to acknowledge it.

The second half sees more brilliant attacking football from Villa, some good counter-attacks from Ipswich, with Chris Kiwomya his usual lurking threat, and Bosnich again proving an able deputy for Nigel Spink.

This, however, is a match to be remembered for the quality of its two goals. "Villa showed what attacking football is about," said Ipswich manager Mick McGiven. "It was no fluke by Saunders. He saw the 'keeper off his line and killed us off with the quality of his finish.

"It was worth the admission money on its own."

Wednesday 10th February 1993 • Selhurst Park • 8.00pm

CRYSTAL PALACE 1 ASTON VILLA 0

Half-time 1-0 • Attendance 12,270

Referee Ken REDFERN

Linesmen G. BUTLAND and A. SCHNEIDER

Red and Blue Striped Shirts, White Shorts		Goals	White Shirts, Blue Shorts		Goals
1	Nigel MARTYN		1	Mark BOSNICH	
2	Bobby BOWRY	8	2	Earl BARRETT	
3	Richard SHAW †		3	Steve STAUNTON	
4	Chris COLEMAN ‡		4	Shaun TEALE	
5	Eric YOUNG		5	Paul McGRATH	
6	Andy THORN		6	Kevin RICHARDSON	
7	Simon OSBORN		7	Ray HOUGHTON	
8	Geoff THOMAS		8	Garry PARKER †	
9	Chris ARMSTRONG		9	Dean SAUNDERS	
10	Simon RODGER		10	Dwight YORKE	
11	Eddie McGOLDRICK		11	Steve FROGGATT	

Substitutes

John HUMPHREY †71

Paul WILLIAMS ‡82

Gk Andy WOODMAN

Substitutes

Stefan BEINLICH †78

Neil COX

Gk Nigel SPINK

BEFORE	P	W	D	L	F	A	pts	AFTER	P	W	D	L	F	A	pts
2 Villa	27	14	8	5	44	29	50	2 Villa	28	14	8	6	44	30	50
18 Palace	27	7	9	11	34	44	30	17 Palace	28	8	9	11	35	44	33

FACTFILE

Villa return to Selhurst Park just seven days after the heartbreaking penalty shoot-out with Wimbledon and again come home deflated... Ron Atkinson's side have scored just two goals in seven away games with Palace... The Eagles' Bobby Bowry scores his first senior goal.

One that got away...

If Aston Villa narrowly miss out on winning the championship, then this second trip to Selhurst Park in a week will be recalled by supporters as one of the great 'if only...' occasions of the campaign.

Two days earlier a small but significant gap had appeared through which Ron Atkinson's team could surge into the lead, provided they could get all three points.

Manchester United had been held to a 0-0 draw by reigning champions, Leeds, at Elland Road on the Monday night.

Consequently when Villa approached this mid-week fixture against a team struggling at the other end of the table, it was in the knowledge that they could go ahead of title favourites United by two clear points.

The team is unchanged from the one which beat Ipswich, Mark Bosnich being retained in goal despite Nigel Spink's return to fitness. The young Australian has pleased Ron Atkinson with his agility and expertise and deserves his extended opportunity.

Young players are very much in the boss's mind as part of his squad. He has made it clear that he has no plans for the rest of the season to sign new players.

Evidence of his confidence in his Young Lions comes with the inclusion in the party which arrives in London of 18-year old Graham Fenton, a hungry striker who has repeatedly impressed for the youths and reserves. Fenton is not in the fourteen but he is clearly now on the fringe.

In all, eight players of 21 or less have been used this season in a nicely rounded balance of imported and home-grown players.

Of the 14-man squad at Selhurst Park, nine are Atkinson signings and two others are youngsters he has blooded. The exceptions are Paul McGrath, Dwight Yorke and Spink.

Hopes and expectations of a table-topping place to be admired in tomorrow's newspapers are very high but, it transpires, extremely brief.

In just eight minutes a threatening ball is nodded away from near the goal by Shaun Teale. It bounces nicely, a yard or two inside the 18-yards line for 18-year-old Bobby Bowry.

Little-known outside of the Palace circle, he was a parks player only 12-months earlier but the shot he conjures would have graced any World Cup Final.

A jumbled mass of players are between Bowry and the goal but he finds a space, thunders his shot through it into the roof of the net, and leaves Bosnich to watch its unstoppable flight over his right shoulder.

Eighty-two minutes sounds plenty of time to erase the lead, but not as events turn out. Steve Coppell's well-drilled team get players behind the ball in large numbers, meanly soaking up space.

Villa's possession football pleases the eye and works the ball again and again into the Palace area, frequently by means of quality centres by Steve Froggatt, but clear chances are rare.

Palace get legs or bodies in the way of several scoring attempts and Nigel Martyn confirms his international potential when he has to.

With Villa's increasing requirement to press forward comes a degree of concern at the back with Chris Armstrong, who was a menacing threat at Villa Park in September, again a free-running dangerman.

Bosnich is needed to show his worth with a stop or two and Villa battle into a full five minutes of injury time pressuring Palace in search of, at least, an equaliser. Sadly, it is not going to be granted.

"I can't criticise the team," says Atkinson. "They were always positive and worked very, very hard. We'll just have to dismiss it."

Saturday 13th February 1993 • Stamford Bridge • 3.00pm

CHELSEA 0 ASTON VILLA 1

Half-time 0-1 • Attendance 20,081

Referee Michael PECK (Kendal)

Linesmen M.R. SIMS and M. STOBBART

Blue Shirts, Blue Shorts	Goals	Claret and Blue Shirts, White Shorts	Goals
1 Kevin HITCHCOCK		1 Mark BOSNICH	
2 Gareth HALL		2 Earl BARRETT	
3 Frank SINCLAIR		3 Steve STAUNTON	
4 Andy TOWNSEND ❑		4 Shaun TEALE	
5 David LEE		5 Paul McGRATH	
6 Mal DONAGHY ‡		6 Kevin RICHARDSON	
7 David HOPKIN †		7 Ray HOUGHTON	21
8 Robert FLECK		8 Garry PARKER ‡	
9 Mick HARFORD		9 Dean SAUNDERS ❑	
10 Eddie NEWTON		10 Dalian ATKINSON †	
11 Dennis WISE		11 Steve FROGGATT	
Substitutes		*Substitutes*	
Graham STUART †57		Dwight YORKE †60	
John SPENCER ‡66		Neil COX ‡82	
Gk Dave BEASANT		Gk Nigel SPINK	

BEFORE		P	W	D	L	F	A	pts	AFTER		P	W	D	L	F	A	pts
2	Villa	28	14	8	6	44	30	50	1	Villa	29	15	8	6	45	30	53
11	Chelsea	28	9	10	9	32	35	37	11	Chelsea	29	9	10	10	32	36	37

FACTFILE

With only three Premier League games taking place Villa grab their second chance of the week to go top, but the chasing pack all have games in hand... Dalian Atkinson returns, but fails to last... This proves to be Ian Porterfield's last game, the Chelsea manager is sacked days later and replaced by David Webb.

Not pretty, but Villa go top

Time to recall Dalian Atkinson to the front-line of the championship battle for only his third start in the last sixteen.

After two away defeats in the league his presence is needed to provide an extra goalscoring possibility. One statistic brought to light since the Palace defeat in mid-week has surprised Ron Atkinson, and troubled him just a touch.

Only three players have scored away goals in the League. "That's amazing considering we have scored more goals overall in the Premier than any other club," he concedes.

Dalian is one of that trio. Deano and Garry Parker are the other two. Saunders enthusiastically welcomes back his scoring buddy who confides: "People keep telling me that I have got to play through the pain of my stomach muscle strain to get fully fit.

"I can still feel it but I'll give it a go. But I shall not be looking for anything special at Stamford Bridge, just to get through the 90 minutes."

In the event he doesn't. Nor does he score, though he does play a valuable part in the decisive goal by Ray Houghton. Outjumping his marker he nods on for Houghton to chase it, and Villa's cause is helped by defenders bumping into each other and leaving goalkeeper Kevin Hitchcock without cover.

So, now, four players have scored away from home, but the satisfaction gleaned from that fact evaporates a little on the hour when Atkinson leaves the field again.

Football is a contrary and contradictory activity as its followers discover again and again. In the previous two away games, against Southampton and Palace, Villa's approach play has been immaculate yet their scoresheet has remained blank.

At Stamford Bridge it is a fragmented performance, not always pleasing to the eye, often not the stuff of potential champions, but a precious one-goal lead has to be preserved. Looking good is a poor priority compared to that.

Chelsea attack a good deal with Irish Republic international Andy Townsend a handful in midfield and Dennis Wise, back after injury, dangerous down their left flank.

Ron Atkinson has pondered with the thought of playing Earl Barrett in midfield to police Townsend. "I like Earl in midfield," he explains. "But then, again, I like him at right back..." Which is where he remains.

The manager has cause to applaud his decision as Wise threatens to run riot but is frustrated again and again by the former Oldham defender.

Paul McGrath and Shaun Teale are solid as ever in the centre of the defence and behind them Mark Bosnich completes his third shut-out in four games, the Cup penalty shoot-out apart.

The Australian plays impressively throughout and makes one extraordinary save curving upwards and backwards to deny John Spencer.

"It was our least attractive performance of the season," admits the manager. "But we fought hard and after some sloppy defending had given us a goal we hung on well.

Ray Houghton eases the away goals worry

Saturday 20th February 1993 • Villa Park • 3.00pm

ASTON VILLA 2 EVERTON 1

Half-time 2-1 • *Attendance 32,913*

Referee Tony WARD (London)

Linesmen B.L. POLKEY and E.J. WALSH

Claret and Blue Shirts, White Shorts		Goals	White Shirts, Blue Shorts		Goals
1	Mark BOSNICH		1	Jason KEARTON	
2	Earl BARRETT	18	2	Matthew JACKSON	
3	Steve STAUNTON		3	Kenny SANSOM	
4	Shaun TEALE ❑		4	Ian SNODIN ❑	
5	Paul McGRATH		5	Dave WATSON	
6	Kevin RICHARDSON		6	Gary ABLETT	
7	Ray HOUGHTON		7	Robert WARZYCHA †	
8	Neil COX ❑	11	8	Peter BEARDSLEY	pen 24
9	Dean SAUNDERS ❑		9	Tony COTTEE ❑	
10	Dwight YORKE		10	Maurice JOHNSTON ‡	
11	Stefan BEINLICH		11	Barry HORNE	

Substitutes

Cyrille REGIS

Bryan SMALL

Gk Nigel SPINK

Substitutes

Stuart BARLOW †51

Predrag RADOSAVLJEVIC ‡75

Gk Stephen REEVES

BEFORE	P	W	D	L	F	A	pts	AFTER	P	W	D	L	F	A	pts
1 Villa	29	15	8	6	45	30	53	1 Villa	30	16	8	6	47	31	56
18 Everton	28	9	5	14	30	37	32	18 Everton	29	9	5	15	31	39	32

FACTFILE

Earl Barrett scores his first goal for the club... Neil Cox nets his first in the Premier League... Stefan Beinlich makes his full debut... For the first time in an English game both goalkeepers are Australian... There's also a Pole, a Yugoslav, a Tobagan and a German on the field. Plus the Irish, Welsh and Scotsmen!

Cox and Barrett - the deadly duo

During the luxury of a period without a mid-week fixture the talk has been more about Villa Park attendances than the intense struggle for supremacy at the top of the League.

As a result of articles in Aston Villa News & Record, spotlighting the curious difference between the better and the poorer gates, a campaign to improve things is underway.

In the build-up to Everton's visit a £10,000 newspaper and radio advertising project is launched, fronted by Ron Atkinson calling for a return of good, old-fashioned 'Villa-Mania'.

As a goodwill gesture three beds will be donated to the children's ward of Good Hope Hospital if the crowd reaches 30,000. The response is a figure of just below 33,000 on another crucial day when Villa need to win to stay on top.

On the fitness front all is not well. In addition to the Dalian Atkinson stomach strain which will simply not go away, Garry Parker is out with bruised ribs, Steve Froggatt is also out (unwell) and 'two or three others' are carrying minor injuries.

On the eve of the match it is revealed by the manager that his namesake will definitely require stomach surgery 'if not sooner, then later' while Parker and Shaun Teale also require end-of-season operations, for hernias, and Froggatt for a very minor knee disorder.

Neil Cox is brought in at right back in order to move Earl Barrett forward into Parker's place. The German Stefan Beinlich plays on the left side of midfield with Dwight Yorke alongside Dean Saunders. Everton arrive as a struggling side and never succeed in improving that image during a game which Villa are always going to win. One unusual feature of the occasion is that both teams have an Australian in goal with

Jason Kearton deputising for suspended Neville Southall and Mark Bosnich keeping out Nigel Spink.

England boss Graham Taylor is watching in the aftermath of last Wednesday's 6-0 Wembley win over San Marino when his World Cup plans looked anything but firmly in place.

Barrett is being widely quoted as a player who ought now to be coming into the former Villa boss's international reckoning and he certainly does himself no harm.

With only eighteen minutes gone Barrett collects a loose ball on the right-hand edge of the box, turns and aims a right-footed cross-shot wide of Kearton for his first-ever Villa goal.

Previous scoring efforts in claret-and-blue colours have suggested that Earl's many impressive talents exclude the art of finishing so he welcomes his successful strike with visible delight!

Barrett's midfield presence brings added ball-winning prowess to the department though his distribution does not match Parker's.

However, five minutes earlier he has delivered a telling pass to Cox for the opening goal, demonstrating Big Ron's oft-repeated theory that there is enough varied talent in the team to present a range of selection options.

Everton reduce the lead with a 24th minute penalty by Peter Beardsley, though many disagree with referee Tony Ward's decision. Sansom's 'fall' is widely judged to have been a 'dive' but Howard Kendall's average team rarely threatens to inflict further damage on Villa's title push.

The one black mark against Villa is that their smooth and pleasing forward play fails to produce more goals. Both Manchester United and Norwich have won so the position at the top remains unchanged.

That apart it is another good day. Villa have remained on top, watched by a far more satisfactory attendance. And the hospital is to get four new beds rather than three.

Saturday 27th February 1993 • Villa Park • 3.15pm (delayed)

ASTON VILLA 1 WIMBLEDON 0

Half-time 0-0 • Attendance 34,496

Referee Steve LODGE (Barnsley)
Linesmen A. BLACK and P. REJER

Claret and Blue Shirts, White Shorts	Goals	Blue Shirts, Blue Shorts	Goals
1 Mark BOSNICH		1 Hans SEGERS	
2 Earl BARRETT		2 Roger JOSEPH	
3 Steve STAUNTON		3 Gary ELKINS	
4 Shaun TEALE		4 Vinnie JONES	
5 Paul McGRATH		5 John SCALES	
6 Kevin RICHARDSON		6 Brian McALLISTER	
7 Ray HOUGHTON		7 Neil ARDLEY	
8 Neil COX		8 Robbie EARLE	
9 Dean SAUNDERS		9 John FASHANU	
10 Dwight YORKE	79	10 Steve COTTERILL	
11 Cyrille REGIS		11 Gerald DOBBS †	
Substitutes		*Substitutes*	
Stefan BEINLICH		Andy CLARKE †80	
Bryan SMALL		Dean BLACKWELL	
Gk Nigel SPINK		Gk Neil SULLIVAN	

BEFORE	P	W	D	L	F	A	pts	AFTER	P	W	D	L	F	A	pts
1 Villa	30	16	8	6	47	31	56	1 Villa	31	17	8	6	48	31	59
13 Wimbledon	29	9	9	11	35	36	36	16 Wimbledon	30	9	9	12	35	37	36

FACTFILE

Seventh home league win on the trot... Villa complete a first ever league 'double' over Wimbledon... Dwight Yorke scores for the third successive home meeting with the Dons... Stomach surgery for Dalian Atkinson... Mid-week offer of £150,000 for Chelsea's Mick Harford is rejected.

Fiver-fans are the winners

Any club in a championship-challenging position would regard the visit of Wimbledon as a necessary evil, an occasion for damage limitation rather than for exhibition of style.

That's precisely how Ron Atkinson sees it, though he is careful, in his programme notes, to assure supporters that, despite a miserable Cup record against them, the Dons are 'not our bogey side'.

No need for negative vibes, though there IS cause for apprehension. Wimbledon are on a roll while Villa's run of six straight home league wins is beginning to tempt the fates.

One problem for teams entertaining Wimbledon is that a percentage of home supporters tend to take the afternoon off, thus downgrading the atmosphere around the stadium.

All credit to the club management, they have thought of that one in advance, and done something about it. Following the healthy turn-out for the Everton game last Saturday, cut-priced football is on offer for standing fans.

Admission price at the Holte End has been cut from £9 to a recession-busting fiver, with an offer to terrace season ticket holders to bring a guest for a pound. Not all such ideas bring their reward, but this one does.

Such is the demand for table-topping football at 'Winter Sales' prices that the rush causes the kick-off to be delayed for fifteen minutes and even then many are locked out.

On-the-field preparations have been equally sound despite injury problems. Dalian Atkinson underwent surgery on his stomach injury the previous day and Garry Parker has not yet recovered from his rib injury.

Those extra fans at the Holte End are not rewarded with the kind of fluid, open play which has become a Villa Park feature but nor are they subjected to the danger of a near-disastrous defeat.

Wimbledon, on their best behaviour, are largely contained by a defence marshalled magnificently by that smoothest of smooth operators, Paul McGrath.

Fears of a physical free-for-all are not realised. Even Vinnie Jones, booed whenever in possession, seems anxious to show that he's a lovely, well-meaning chap at heart.

Villa take it cautiously. First-half form reflects a determination not to lose this one while, after the break, their increasing forward thrusts are always tinged with restraint.

With only eleven minutes left, and a hint of anxiety coming through, Steve Staunton's corner from the left is only partially cleared and Dwight Yorke delights in the chance to fire a cross-shot away from Hans Segers.

Now those fiver-fans have a tangible return on their investment and their appreciation reverberates around the ground.

"If I were giving a star-rating it would be to the crowd," Big Ron tells the massed media afterwards.

"It wasn't just the size of the crowd that helped, it was the way they just got louder and louder and lifted the team."

Matchwinner Dwight Yorke

Wednesday 10th March 1993 • Villa Park • 8.00pm

ASTON VILLA 0 TOTTENHAM HOTSPUR 0

Half-time 0-0 • Attendance 37,727

Referee Keith HACKETT (Sheffield)

Linesmen J. LEECH and B.T. MILLERSHIP

Claret and Blue Shirts, White Shorts	Goals	White Shirts, Navy Blue Shorts	Goals
1 Mark BOSNICH		1 Erik THORSTVEDT	
2 Earl BARRETT		2 Dean AUSTIN	
3 Steve STAUNTON		3 Justin EDINBURGH	
4 Shaun TEALE		4 Vinny SAMWAYS	
5 Paul McGRATH		5 Gary MABBUTT	
6 Kevin RICHARDSON		6 Neil RUDDOCK	
7 Ray HOUGHTON		7 Steve SEDGLEY ❑	
8 Garry PARKER		8 NAYIM	
9 Dean SAUNDERS		9 Darren ANDERTON	
10 Dwight YORKE		10 Teddy SHERINGHAM	
11 Tony DALEY †		11 Andy GRAY †	
Substitutes		*Substitutes*	
Cyrille REGIS †85		Andy TURNER †73	
Neil COX		Pat VAN DEN HAUWE	
Gk Nigel SPINK		Gk Ian WALKER	

BEFORE	P	W	D	L	F	A	pts	AFTER	P	W	D	L	F	A	pts
2 Villa	31	17	8	6	48	31	59	2 Villa	32	17	9	6	48	31	60
9 Spurs	31	12	8	11	39	47	44	9 Spurs	32	12	9	11	39	47	45

FACTFILE

Honours even in 100th League meeting between the sides. Full record reads Villa won 36, Spurs won 43, Draws 21... Spurs earn their third successive goalless draw at Villa Park. The teams also drew 0-0 at White Hart Lane in November... Tony Daley returns to first team action after a seven month absence.

Spurs get what they come for

Until now Championship talk has been muted, even among supporters, most of them afraid to even dare hope that Ron Atkinson might create such a miracle in two short seasons.

Most Villa fans have been agreeing with the bookmakers that Manchester United are clear favourites to erase the agony of last season when they allowed Leeds United to overtake them at the finishing post.

Suddenly, however, the mood changes. Glory be, United have lost the previous evening at Oldham. The unexpected opportunity to go two points clear with the same number of matches played, has arrived.

Yes, Villa CAN win the title and tonight might even emerge as favourites for it...

The scheduled 7.45 kick-off is delayed for 15 minutes as Holte End queues stretch in each direction. The good old days are returning and when the gates are closed and the match kicks off 15 minutes late more than a thousand fans have been locked out.

"We started a bit edgily," Atkinson admits afterwards. "But maybe that was because we had no match last Saturday."

That 'edginess' gradually evaporates as Garry Parker's distribution from midfield allied to Ray Houghton's restless running pushes Spurs into their most ultra-defensive mode.

England winger Tony Daley is back after months out to repair cruciate ligament damage. He stretches the opposition with his bursts on either side but his final ball inevitably reflects his shortage of match-play.

With old campaigner Gary Mabbutt marshalling a well-contructed offside trap Villa have to rely more and more on trying to work their way through by means of intricate passing moves.

As they get increasingly on top the fates, it seems, are evilly plotting against them. If there is any such thing as luck, then it deserts Aston Villa on this night when they deserve much more. Unbelievably referee Keith Hackett refuses a penalty when Neil Ruddock cuts Dwight Yorke off across the thighs as he chases a dangerous through ball from Parker. TV slow-motion replays confirm it as an indisputable foul tackle yards off the ball.

Dean Saunders, meanwhile, is the chief culprit of fate's dirty tricks campaign. He sees Justin Edinburgh given a disputed verdict as he clears a Deano effort 'off' the line when it looks suspiciously like 'over' it. Another shot by the Welsh international beats the 'keeper and hits the post. Yet another similar strike in the second half suffers the same fate.

Parker has created several openings, Yorke has looked subtle in his stealthy footwork and Cyrille Regis has replaced Daley in a forlorn last throw of the dice five minutes from time.

So what have Spurs been doing in attack all this time? Nothing worth recording, that's what.

"On another night Dean Saunders might have had a hat-trick," says Big Ron trying to appear matter-of-fact but looking homicidal around the eyes.

"They came to defend and that's all." Mark Bosnich, in fact, never had a meaningful shot to save. "I could have played in goal for us tonight." For once, he wasn't joking.

When the dust has cleared there is an ironical twist in the tail. Not only have Villa lost the chance to go top, but Norwich have won and shortened the gap. It's a three-horse race again!

Tony Daley - he's back

Sunday 14th March 1993 • Old Trafford• 1.00pm

MANCHESTER UNITED 1 ASTON VILLA 1

Half-time 0-0 • Attendance 36,163

Referee Allan GUNN (South Chailey, Sussex)
Linesmen W.J. NATTRASS and P.M. ROBERTS

Red Shirts, White Shorts	Goals	White Shirts, Black Shorts	Goals
1 Peter SCHMEICHEL		1 Mark BOSNICH	
2 Paul PARKER		2 Earl BARRETT	
3 Denis IRWIN		3 Steve STAUNTON	54
4 Steve BRUCE		4 Shaun TEALE ❑	
5 Lee SHARPE		5 Paul McGRATH	
6 Gary PALLISTER		6 Kevin RICHARDSON	
7 Eric CANTONA		7 Ray HOUGHTON	
8 Paul INCE		8 Garry PARKER †	
9 Brian McCLAIR		9 Dean SAUNDERS	
10 Mark HUGHES	57	10 Dwight YORKE	
11 Ryan GIGGS		11 Bryan SMALL	

Substitutes	*Substitutes*
Bryan ROBSON	Tony DALEY †66
Andrei KANCHELSKIS	Neil COX
Gk Les SEALEY	Gk Nigel SPINK

BEFORE		P	W	D	L	F	A	pts	AFTER		P	W	D	L	F	A	pts
1	United	32	17	9	6	49	35	60	1	United	33	17	10	6	50	36	61
2	Villa	32	17	9	6	48	31	60	2	Villa	33	17	10	6	49	32	61

FACTFILE *It's a Sunday spectacular for satellite viewers, and a happy return to Old Trafford for Mark Bosnich, Paul McGrath and Big Ron... The three Villa-United meetings this season have attracted a total attendance of over 111,000... Steve Staunton's goal comes third in the BBC 'Goal of the Month' competition.*

Brilliant Bosnich denies United

This is, or so the pundits say, the most crucial FA Premier League fixture played so far.

Awaited with hushed expectancy by the supporters of both clubs, hyped up unmercifully by the media, the fixture at Old Trafford is in danger of being upstaged by its own image.

BSkyB have a real scoop on their hands, especially as Manchester United restrict visiting supporters to just 639. Back in the Holte Suite at Villa Park, hundreds of Villa fans watch the championship head-to-head on a giant screen.

In pubs and clubs around the region a similar scenario is repeated while, at those Villa homes blessed with satellite TV, the whiff of Spring in the air is not, on this occasion, marked by the re-appearance of rusty lawn mowers!

Ron Atkinson makes one concession to the possible pitfalls of the visit to the home of the current leaders and title favourites. He calls up Bryan Small for the daunting task of policing either Ryan Giggs or Lee Sharpe. This allows Steve Staunton to push forward to add power to a midfield department which was short of drive in the mid-week draw with Spurs.

Such occasions can be an anti-climax, but not, emphatically, this one. United, with Bryan Robson in reserve on the bench, attempt to impose their will on Villa with an aggressive start.

Villa are on the defensive a great deal, though it is of necessity not by design. Whenever they can they attack with conviction, Dean Saunders motoring willingly across the width of the front line.

Goalkeeper Mark Bosnich, as one of the Old Trafford 'old boys' on the Villa staff, has been part of the pre-match publicity machine but he quickly proves that his nerves have not been over-stretched when he dives to the post to block Eric Cantona's 12-yards volley. A magnificent and crucial save.

This is but one of several such heroic interventions by the young Australian whose reputation grows by the game.

Deano is just off-target with one shot and Ray Houghton follows suit, when he should have scored, while at the other end there are penalty appeals after last-ditch tackles by Small on McClair and Earl Barrett on Lee Sharpe.

The action is full-speed and non-stop and though United are the more threatening it is Villa who stun the home crowd with a 53rd minute lead.

The merest hint of a chance on the left-hand side of the penalty area is created by Kevin Richardson and Small for Staunton. United's defence looks to be in place in front of Peter Schmeichel but the Irish international's inspirational drive curves into the top corner of the net.

A brilliant goal and a lead to savour but few feel it is the end of the story, and those who do are quickly proved wrong. United, finding yet another attacking gear, go all-out for the equaliser and it takes them but four minutes to achieve.

Denis Irwin's centre from the right is headed back by Cantona and the ball falls just right for Mark Hughes to connect with a powerful header.

Villa are by no means disatisfied with their draw. Nor, indeed, are Norwich City who beat Oldham yesterday and now lie only two points behind the top two who are level on points.

"Beforehand I thought it would be crap because of the build-up and all the hype but it wasn't," said Atkinson.

"It was a superb game. We were well worth a point."

Nine games to go now, with both Villa and United facing a trip to Carrow Road...

Saturday 20th March 1993 • Villa Park • 3.00pm

ASTON VILLA 2 SHEFFIELD WEDNESDAY 0

Half-time 1-0 • Attendance 38,024

Referee Roger MILFORD (Bristol)
Linesmen K.J. HAWKES and A.J. MARTIN

Claret and Blue Shirts, White Shorts		Goals		Blue and White Striped Shirts, Black Shorts		Goals
1	Mark BOSNICH			1	Chris WOODS	
2	Earl BARRETT			2	Roland NILSSON	
3	Steve STAUNTON			3	Nigel WORTHINGTON	
4	Shaun TEALE			4	Carlton PALMER	
5	Paul McGRATH			5	Simon STEWART †	
6	Kevin RICHARDSON			6	Viv ANDERSON	
7	Ray HOUGHTON			7	Danny WILSON	
8	Garry PARKER			8	Chris WADDLE	
9	Dean SAUNDERS			9	Paul WARHURST	
10	Dwight YORKE	3, 56		10	Mark BRIGHT	
11	Cyrille REGIS			11	John SHERIDAN	
	Substitutes				*Substitutes*	
	Neil COX				Graham HYDE †57	
	Bryan SMALL				Nigel JEMSON	
Gk	Nigel SPINK			Gk	Kevin PRESSMAN	

BEFORE		P	W	D	L	F	A	pts	AFTER		P	W	D	L	F	A	pts
3	Villa	33	17	10	6	49	32	61	1	Villa	34	18	10	6	51	32	64
4	Wednesday	31	13	10	8	41	34	49	4	Wednesday	32	13	10	9	41	36	49

FACTFILE

Villa back on top as bookies favourites... Ron Atkinson's former club hit by a goal of creative perfection... Cyrille Regis back in winning tactical ploy... Wednesday weary in fifth game in 13 days... Another League double for Villa... Dwight Yorke's opener wins the BBB 'Goal of the Month' competition.

VILLA MOVE BACK INTO POLE POSITION

Wednesday are mesmerised

Sheffield Wednesday, Ron Atkinson's former club, arrive at Villa Park at the end of a demanding week of chasing their dual cup-winning dream.

Manager Trevor Francis's squad bristle with confidence having reached Wembley in the Coca Cola Cup while also qualifying for an all-Sheffield FA Cup semi-final at Wembley.

On top of all this the season's goal-scoring phenomenon, Paul Warhust, has been named in Graham Taylor's England squad.

In the Premier League the pattern is changing, shifting, developing in kaleidoscopic fashion as Villa, United and Norwich constantly swop places.

The morning has produced an inviting gap for Villa to attempt to pierce with United drawing 1-1 at Maine Road, though fourth-placed Wednesday could join the race if they escape with the three points today.

Championship fever has now broken out in epidemic proportions as the realisation dawns that Villa emphatically do not see themselves as potential runners-up. They want European football, sure. But preferably as champions.

United are now looking anxiously over their shoulder, just as they did last season when Leeds were breathing down their necks.

Cyrille Regis has been recalled into attack for only his second start since September and this, like so many of the manager's previous strategical moves, works to perfection.

The first of two goals by Dwight Yorke, a mere three minutes into the game, is created with such sublime passing skills that the entire footballing nation will savour its perfection on BBC Match of the Day later tonight.

As the ball is lovingly caressed into the path of Yorke every outfield player except Shaun Teale is involved, making the pristine Villa Park surface, effectively, a temporary exclusion zone for the visiting players.

As ten inter-changing moves by-pass opponents in dazzling style to supply Yorke with a tap-in from close range fans talk of 'like Liverpool at their best' and 'Don Revie's Leeds'.

"I played in my favourite position behind the front two (Regis and Dean Saunders) and I enjoyed it," says Yorke afterwards.

He did, too, though his second goal was never going to match the sheer majesty of the first. A mistake by Roland Nilsson is capitalised on by the stealthy West Indian and fired past Chris Woods.

The England 'keeper has had an outstanding game, as has the deceptively dangerous Chris Waddle described pre-match by Atkinson as in 'mesmeric form' but team performance-wise this is another claret-and-blue day.

There are no bookings, no problems, a full-house, and some wonderful football. If there is such thing as championship-chasing pressure it certainly hasn't screwed itself into Villa limbs yet.

Norwich are beaten by Wimbledon, Villa go top, the bookies make them favourites and Big Ron declares once again: "We won't bottle it."

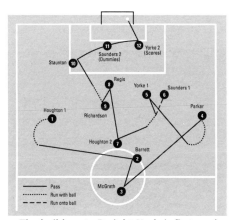

The build-up to Dwight Yorke's first goal

Wednesday 24th March 1993 • Carrow Road • 7.45pm

NORWICH CITY 1 ASTON VILLA 0

Half-time 0-0 • *Attendance* 19,528

Referee Robert HART (Darlington)

Linesmen W.J. NORBURY and A. SCHNEIDER

Yellow Shirts, Green Shorts	Goals	Claret and Blue Shirts, White Shorts	Goals
1 Bryan GUNN		1 Mark BOSNICH	
2 Ian CULVERHOUSE		2 Earl BARRETT	
3 Mark BOWEN		3 Steve STAUNTON	
4 Chris SUTTON		4 Shaun TEALE	
5 John POLSTON	82	5 Paul McGRATH	
6 Gary MEGSON		6 Kevin RICHARDSON	
7 Ian CROOK		7 Ray HOUGHTON	
8 Jeremy GOSS		8 Garry PARKER †	
9 Mark ROBINS †		9 Dean SAUNDERS	
10 Ruel FOX		10 Dwight YORKE	
11 David PHILLIPS		11 Cyrille REGIS	
Substitutes		*Substitutes*	
Lee POWER †82		Tony DALEY †82	
Colin WOODTHORPE		Bryan SMALL	
Gk Mark WALTON		Gk Nigel SPINK	

BEFORE		P	W	D	L	F	A	pts	AFTER		P	W	D	L	F	A	pts
1	Villa	34	18	10	6	51	32	64	1	Norwich	36	19	8	9	50	49	65
3	Norwich	35	18	8	9	49	49	62	2	Villa	35	18	10	7	51	33	64

FACTFILE

Norwich become the only team to complete a league double over Villa this season... United draw as Villa lose, and Canaries go top... Villa have won only two of nine mid-week league matches this season... Only nine goals scored in the last eleven league and cup games.

Parker miss proves so costly

Neither Aston Villa nor Manchester United would be likely to admit it in public but this is the trip they must both fear most.

The nightmare scenario for each of them is that while the major focus is constantly on their results in what is widely regarded as a two-club shoot-out, Norwich might nip through on the blind side.

Numerically the fixture is an important one for Mark Bosnich because, being his tenth full appearance in the league, he would now qualify for a championship medal should the last eight results go favourably for Villa.

"Whatever happens here tonight, or in Manchester United's home game with Arsenal, nothing changes much," said Ron Atkinson in a pre-match nerve-calming exercise.

"All three of us will still be in the pot afterwards. And you can forget Mike Walker's comments about being out of it after losing to Wimbledon.

"That was sheer kidology. If they beat us and then United they will be on top as favourites."

True, true. But defeat for Norwich would reduce them to outsiders and elevate Villa to their strongest position yet. An appetizing prospect, but one not to be realised.

Everyone predicted a game of footballing excellence similar to the 3-2 Norwich win at Villa Park and so it proves.

Both sides move the ball around scientifically on the smooth Carrow Road surface with Villa marginally the better side.˙

Bosnich's goal survives the odd threatening moment as Norwich break quickly and dangerously but by mid-way through the second half a very satisfactory 0-0 draw looks on the cards.

Good scoring chances wasted bedevil all teams throughout any season but Villa are left agonising one which proves particularly expensive.

Ray Houghton's pinpoints a forward pass to Garry Parker taking up a menacing position on the left of the Norwich goal.

Parker gets control, rounds the approaching Bryan Gunn but with the target stretched ahead of him, screws his shot off the outside of the post. A dreadful waste but, at least, it's still 0-0.

With news of a similar scoreline eminating from Old Trafford, Villa fans will happily settle for that. With only ten minutes left that still remains the odds-on outcome.

Then, calamity.

A centre from Ian Crook deceives Shaun Teale and Gary Megson is granted an unchallenged header. Bosnich, with only four goals conceded in those previous nine league games, plunges to the foot of the post. The 'keeper from Oz brilliantly blocks Megson's effort but can't hold on to it.

In that fleeting, split second when a clearance is required there is no defender close enough. In moves John Polston to fire his first goal of the season.

Too little time now to pull it back and the points go to the Canaries. Not a disaster, but it ensures a subdued and lengthy journey home for the official party and supporters.

"We played some magnificent football and, in all fairness, so did Norwich but I thought we were the better side from start to finish," said Atkinson.

"The way we look at it we are one point off the pace with a game in hand. We would have settled for that at the start of the season."

The blow of defeat is softened by the home draw for United who have taken only three point from the last 12. English football's most fascinating and exciting championship race in years takes another intriguing turn.

Sunday 4th April 1993 • The City Ground • 3.00pm

NOTTINGHAM FOREST 0   ASTON VILLA 1

Half-time 0-0 • Attendance 26,742
Referee Keith BURGE (Tonypandy, Mid-Glamorgan)
Linesmen P.M. ROBERTS and J.B. ROBINSON

Red Shirts, White Shorts	Goals	White Shirts, Black Shorts	Goals
1 Mark CROSSLEY		1 Mark BOSNICH	
2 Gary CHARLES		2 Earl BARRETT	
3 Steve CHETTLE		3 Steve STAUNTON	
4 Steve STONE		4 Shaun TEALE ❏	
5 Carl TILER		5 Paul McGRATH	63
6 Roy KEANE		6 Kevin RICHARDSON	
7 Kingsley BLACK		7 Ray HOUGHTON	
8 Gary BANNISTER		8 Garry PARKER	
9 Nigel CLOUGH ❏		9 Dean SAUNDERS	
10 Robert ROSARIO †		10 Dalian ATKINSON	
11 Ian WOAN		11 Dwight YORKE †	

Substitutes	*Substitutes*
Gary CROSBY †45	Tony DALEY †76
'Toddi' ORLYGSSON	Neil COX
Gk Andrew MARRIOTT	Gk Nigel SPINK

BEFORE		P	W	D	L	F	A	pts	AFTER		P	W	D	L	F	A	pts
2	Villa	35	18	10	7	51	33	64	1	Villa	36	19	10	7	52	33	67
21	Forest	34	9	9	16	33	47	36	21	Forest	35	9	9	17	33	48	36

FACTFILE

The 100th Villa-Forest League meeting brings Villa's first City Ground success in ten years and a 'double' for 93/93... Dalian Atkinson returns as Villa go top. "I thought he was electric," says Big Ron... Paul McGrath celebrates, with a goal, his PFA Player's Player award... Forest's biggest gate of the season to date.

This is one for the purists...

National focus has briefly switched away from the enthralling, ever-changing league scene as the historic weekend of two FA Cup semi-finals at Wembley takes centre stage.

Also, in direct contrast to the stride-for-stride drama of the Premier League, this proved to be the occasion when the Grand National never even got underway!

Come Sunday afternoon, however, the Aintree furore had died down a shade, Arsenal and Sheffield Wednesday are to meet in not one, but two, Wembley Finals and City Ground, Nottingham is now the place to be.

Brian Clough welcomes Villa with a programme note expressing his wish that Villa will become champions because he admires both Ron Atkinson's, and his team's, sense of style. Or words to that effect.

No-one is kidded by the sentiment, though it's clearly a genuine one. Forest need the points to help their relegation-fighting cause. Goodwill ends on this side of the touchline.

Villa are strengthened by the return of Dalian Atkinson, now fully recovered from his stomach surgery but without any reserve-match fitness build-up.

The previous meeting, at Villa Park on December 12, when Villa won 2-1, was a mini-classic, and no-one is surprised as this takes shape as another one for the purists.

The previous weekend's Premier League break for international calls has not affected rhythm. Nor has the involvement of Steve Staunton, Ray Houghton, Paul McGrath and Dean Saunders in the World Cup qualifiers.

Dalian's presence is felt immediately as he attempts to release Deano for a forward surge as a cut-and-thrust contest swings along entertainingly.

Fans are frequently relieved to have such an accomplished back four out there as Forest's passing style threatens to create openings, with Ian Woan, Kingsley Black and Roy Keane particularly dangerous.

Atkinson provides another lift as he powers past Steve Chettle to feed Houghton who forces a corner from which Staunton almost scores direct, just as he did for the Irish Republic a few days earlier against Northern Ireland in Dublin.

The game is an enjoyable hour old when the moment fans have been waiting for arrives. And it proves an ecstatic celebration for Paul McGrath, named PFA Player of the Year a few days earlier.

Another probing corner by Staunton is met by McGrath, timing his run to perfection, who thumps his header well out of Mark Crossley's reach.

As supporters rejoice in their packed enclosure Forest are left with the massive task of lifting their morale in the final 26 minutes.

With England forward Nigel Clough playing as emergency sweeper they strive for an equaliser. Happily the solid Villa back-line shows no sign of cracking, though Mark Bosnich is required to make a save or two.

At the height of Forest's fight-back Shaun Teale is booked for an offence which will bring him a one-match automatic ban, Villa's first disciplinary blemish of the season.

Villa hold on for a narrow but significant win. "It was kind of Brian Clough to say he wanted us to win the championship," said Ron Atkinson. "I hope just as much that they stay up."

Most of the football-loving public would agree with him, but any Grand National wagers now returned by bookies to the punters would be safer placed on Villa's cause than Forest's.

Tomorrow night Norwich entertain Manchester United in a fixture which can seriously help Villa's cause.

Pass the tranquilisers...

Saturday 10th April 1993 • Villa Park • 3.00pm

ASTON VILLA 0 COVENTRY CITY 0

Half-time 0-0 • *Attendance* 38,543

Referee Allan GUNN (South Chailey, Sussex)

Linesmen P.D. HARDING and B.L. POLKEY

Claret and Blue Shirts, White Shorts	Goals	Sky Blue Shirts, Sky Blue Shorts	Goals
1 Mark BOSNICH		1 Jonathan GOULD	
2 Earl BARRETT		2 Brian BORROWS	
3 Steve STAUNTON		3 Phil BABB	
4 Shaun TEALE		4 Peter ATHERTON	
5 Paul McGRATH		5 Micky GYNN	
6 Kevin RICHARDSON		6 David RENNIE	
7 Ray HOUGHTON		7 Lloyd McGRATH	
8 Garry PARKER		8 Lee HURST	
9 Dean SAUNDERS		9 Mick QUINN	
10 Dalian ATKINSON		10 Roy WEGERLE †	
11 Dwight YORKE †		11 John WILLIAMS	
Substitutes		*Substitutes*	
Tony DALEY †83		Leigh JENKINSON †67	
Bryan SMALL		Dave BUSST	
Gk Nigel SPINK		Gk Steve OGRIZOVIC	

BEFORE	P	W	D	L	F	A	pts	AFTER	P	W	D	L	F	A	pts
1 Villa	36	19	10	7	52	33	67	2 Villa	37	19	11	7	52	33	68
8 Coventry	37	13	11	13	48	47	50	9 Coventry	38	13	12	13	48	47	51

FACTFILE

The two dropped points prove costly as Manchester United beat Sheffield Wednesday 2-1 at Old Trafford to take top spot. United's winner comes in the sixth minute of injury time! ... Coventry still can't win at Villa Park. They've now played 19 League games there, lost 11, drawn 8, won 0.

Early misses cost Villa dearly

A sunny Easter Saturday, another near-capacity attendance breathes charisma into Villa Park, hopes and expectations are high with only six matches to go in the championship race.

Since Manchester United's emphatic win at Carrow Road last Monday the public at large regard Norwich as out of it, psychologically if not mathematically.

'A two-horse race' is what they're calling it with Manchester United favourites and Villa needing a successful holiday period to keep their noses in front.

Supporters have recent memories of how the Sky Blues effectively wrecked Villa's Christmas spirit with that resounding 3-0 win at Highfield Road on Boxing Day.

"They didn't simply turn us over," recalled Ron Atkinson. "They murdered us. Now we would like to think it is our turn."

Goalscoring has been a problem, no point in disguising that self-evident factor, though with Dalian Atkinson back alongside Dean Saunders, maybe a late boost in that department is on the cards.

It should have been, too. In the opening seconds Jonathan Gould, son of manager Bobby, blocks a Deano shot and then Atkinson misses the target from a good position.

The scene is set for an afternoon

Mark Bosnich

of frustration as Villa control the attacking play and Coventry live dangerously, absorbing all the pressure and keeping out everything Villa can offer.

In truth Sky Blues are blocking most Villa raids before they can threaten goal too seriously, though Gould is on the mark again as Shaun Teale drills in a possible winner.

Suddenly a wave of euphoria swells around the ground as transistor radios convey the news that Sheffield Wednesday have taken the lead at Old Trafford. A Villa goal would lift morale to the skies but scoring attempts are either off-target or crowded out. Paul McGrath is, as always, inspirational both in his defensive play and his forward forays.

Coventry do threaten on the odd occasion but Teale is defiant as ever in the centre of midfield and Mark Bosnich makes an important save or two.

Come the final whistle, the loss of two home points is bearable but not good news, though the bad news arrives late. Two goals by Steve Bruce in SIX MINUTES of stoppage time at Old Trafford has established United on top.

Saunders has gone ten games on the trot without a goal. Dalian Atkinson, held back by his lengthy injury problem, has not scored since early December.

Only ten goals have been scored in the last dozen League games and Villa have failed to score in nine of their 37 league fixtures. This, however, is counter-balanced by the fact that no goals have been conceded in 14 of those league games.

Just one goal today would have kept Villa in the driving seat. It is as close as that. Big Ron, understandably, struggles to swallow his disappointment afterwards and when, in the press conference, a journalist asks a question he regards as 'banal' there is a brief altercation.

The tension can be attributed to a tantalising shortage of goals but with five games to go the issue is still wide open.

Monday 12th April 1993 • Highbury • 3.00pm

ARSENAL 0 ASTON VILLA 1

Half-time 0-0 • Attendance 27,125

Referee Gerald ASHBY (Worcester)

Linesmen M.E. ALEXANDER and D.C. RICHARDS

Red Shirts with White Sleeves, White Shorts	Goals	White Shirts, Black Shorts	Goals
1 David SEAMAN		1 Mark BOSNICH	
2 Lee DIXON		2 Earl BARRETT	
3 Nigel WINTERBURN		3 Steve STAUNTON	
4 Ian SELLEY		4 Shaun TEALE	
5 Martin KEOWN		5 Paul McGRATH	
6 Tony ADAMS		6 Kevin RICHARDSON ❏	
7 Steve MORROW		7 Ray HOUGHTON	
8 Ian WRIGHT ❏ ‡		8 Neil COX	
9 Alan SMITH		9 Dean SAUNDERS	
10 Paul MERSON		10 Dalian ATKINSON	
11 Kevin CAMPBELL †		11 Tony DALEY †	69

Substitutes		Substitutes	
Ray PARLOUR †69		Bryan SMALL †75	
Andy LINIGHAN ‡83		Dwight YORKE	
Gk Allan MILLER		Gk Nigel SPINK	

BEFORE		P	W	D	L	F	A	pts	AFTER		P	W	D	L	F	A	pts
2	Villa	37	19	11	7	52	33	68	2	Villa	38	20	11	7	53	33	71
11	Arsenal	35	14	8	13	35	32	50	11	Arsenal	36	14	8	14	35	33	50

FACTFILE

Tony Daley's first goal in more than a year... Villa stay in touch with Man United who win at Coventry... Mark Bosnich's ninth shut-out in 13 games... Another double for Villa, the second over the Gunners in four seasons... Daley's goal is Villa's 6,300th in league football.

A rare Daley header wins it

Villa now look to neighbours Coventry City to deliver a Bank Holiday body-blow to Manchester United at Highfield Road as they take on in-form Arsenal at Highbury.

Changes have been made in midfield and attack, strategic moves in an attempt to carve a result out of a difficult situation.

Garry Parker is replaced in midfield by Earl Barrett with Neil Cox at right back, while Tony Daley gets his first start since the 0-0 draw with Spurs at home, six games earlier.

England winger Daley, who has been on the bench four times since his return from injury, replaces Dwight Yorke who is now himself on the bench.

This is Villa's 47th game of a high-pressure season and their second in three days, again on a sunny Spring afternoon. Traditionally such fixtures can be played with an air of 'let's get the job done' rather than with consummate style or high passion.

This is rather like that as Villa wisely go for the result more than to win friends in North London.

"We picked a team to be a little industrious because we felt we needed that against Arsenal's pressure game," explained Ron Atkinson.

Defensively Villa are superb while work rate is encouragingly high in midfield but no-one would claim this as one of their season's classics.

Arsenal, themselves not at their peak, have the attacking edge but Mark Bosnich is in superb shape as he keeps his ninth clean sheet in 13 games since he replaced Nigel Spink for the FA Cup replay against Wimbledon at Selhurst Park.

"I thought Spink would be back after one game," confessed Atkinson. "But Bosnich has been working on the principle that if he keeps a clean sheet he can't be left out."

Even Spink himself could not argue with such blinding logic from a fellow 'keeper.

The goalless, unentertaining slog is 68 minutes towards what increasingly looks like a 0-0 draw when a new Tale of the Unexpected is written into a season of surprises.

World Cups run their course and half-way through again in the time it takes Tony Daley to score with his rather quaintly-shaven head, six years to be precise.

It is 12 months since he scored a goal of any sort but Atkinson has brought him in to add 'a cutting edge' to a side more intent on building a road-block. The selection proves to be inspired.

When Ray Houghton feeds in an ideally-flighted centre from the right, Daley nips into the perfect spot in a crowded goalmouth to nod the ball away from David Seaman.

Gunners, on this occasion, are not an explosive force as both Atkinson and Cox are close to giving Villa a wider victory margin.

Near the end Dean Saunders blazes the ball over the top from a position where, earlier in the season, he would have buried his chance.

"I felt disappointed for Deano," said Atkinson. "He worked himself barmy. You have to remember that but for the work of Atkinson and Saunders earlier in the season we wouldn't be where we are now."

'Where we are now' is still a strong and healthy second place in the league, one point behind United who have won a tight game at Coventry through a Denis Irwin long shot.

A shot by Roy Wegerle has, it seems, hit the inside of the United post, rolled along the goal-line and escaped to safety. Had it rolled the other way Villa would have been back on top.

Has there ever been a neck-and-neck Championship race quite like this one?

Sunday 18th April 1993 • Villa Park • 2.30pm

ASTON VILLA 3 MANCHESTER CITY 1

Half-time 0-1 • Attendance 33,108
Referee Philip DON (Middlesex)
Linesmen D.T. COLDWELL and E.J. WALSH

Claret and Blue Shirts, White Shorts		Goals
1	Mark BOSNICH	
2	Earl BARRETT	
3	Steve STAUNTON	
4	Neil COX	
5	Paul McGRATH	
6	Kevin RICHARDSON	
7	Ray HOUGHTON	89
8	Garry PARKER †	pen 67
9	Dean SAUNDERS	47
10	Dalian ATKINSON	
11	Tony DALEY	

Substitutes

Bryan SMALL †77
Dwight YORKE
Gk Nigel SPINK

White Shirts, Light Blue Shorts		Goals
1	Tony COTON	
2	Ray RANSON	
3	Terry PHELAN	
4	Peter REID	
5	Keith CURLE	
6	Michel VONK	
7	David WHITE	
8	Fitzroy SIMPSON	
9	Niall QUINN	34
10	Garry FLITCROFT	
11	Rick HOLDEN †	

Substitutes

David BRIGHTWELL †76
Kare INGEBRIGTSEN
Gk Martyn MARGETSON

BEFORE		P	W	D	L	F	A	pts
2	Villa	38	20	11	7	53	33	71
10	Man City	37	14	10	13	51	42	52

AFTER		P	W	D	L	F	A	pts
2	Villa	39	21	11	7	56	34	74
10	Man City	38	14	10	14	52	45	52

FACTFILE

Dean scores his first goal in twelve games (1,085 minutes play)... Garry Parker scores his ninth of the season - a personal best... Shaun Teale serves a one-match ban, Earl Barrett moves across to partner Paul McGrath... The game is shown live on Sky Sports.

Deano ends his goal drought

Another Sunday game, live on Sky, and this one takes the Villa players into unchartered territory in terms of putting their nerves through a shredding machine.

Modern TV exposure has brought a new dimension to the demands of championship conflict, unfair demands some might feel.

Previously, before dates and kick-off times were subject to so much change, rival title-chasers knew nothing of the opposition's situation until they reached the dressing room.

But Villa kick-off in the knowledge that only a win will do, United having beaten an irresolute Chelsea the day before to take a lead of four points and goal difference.

In a phsychological step to ease the pressure from strikers Dean Saunders and Dalian Atkinson, manager Ron Atkinson has taken the unprecedented step of naming them both for all four remaining games 'as long as they stay fit'.

But changes are necessary. With Shaun Teale suspended Earl Barrett, in the England squad for the World Cup qualifier against Holland, moves into the centre.

Neil Cox is at right back, Tony Daley is on the left wing, while Garry Parker is recalled to midfield.

Visiting Manchester City fans find themselves in a peculier position in wanting their team to win while hoping United falter!

A banner displayed by one group wishes Villa well from 'The City of Manchester' a rather inflammatory message which the police remove in the second half when passions mount.

As the play gets patchily underway the Villa indicators are not good. Early on Deano, without a goal in eleven games, ought to ease the tension but his shot lacks conviction.

Anyone hoping that City will play as poorly as Chelsea had done against United is in for a disappointment. Their offside trap, pulled well forward, not only traps breakaway forwards consistently but also cramps the amount of space available for Villa's passing style.

Barrett does not settle easily back in his favourite role having long since become, perhaps, the best right back in the league. There is unease in Villa's defensive ranks when City move forward.

This is confirmed when, in 34 minutes, Terry Phelan's sizzler of a left wing centre is headed in by Niall Quinn. Lovely cross, stunning header. But... ought Mark Bosnich at least to have made a challenge? Likewise Barrett? McGrath?

By half time Villa look a losing team. Fans are verbally handing the title to United. Around the ground spirits are low. In the dressing room the manager's blood pressure is high.

Kevin Richardson makes some captain's observations about where improvement might be expected. "They were well directed," said manager Atkinson afterwards having himself lifted the dressing room ceiling an inch or two.

"The best way forward is to raise the tempo a little," he told them, though in more emphatic terms! "The boss slaughtered us..." was Dean Saunders' version.

Daley's first impact on the game is in the 47th minute. A well-struck cross from the left deflects off Ray Ranson, veers to Tony Coton's left and Saunders leaps to head from a few feet. A DEANO GOAL. At last...

Twenty minutes of Villa domination later and Keith Curle's upflung hand connects with Saunders' centre. Parker's penalty is not well struck. It is low and close to the feet of Coton who dives over it.

Seconds from time Ray Houghton runs onto a pass from Steve Staunton, now in midfield, to chip Coton for a stylish sign off.

So the deficit goes back to one point and the action moves enticingly to next Wednesday.

Wednesday 21st April 1993 • Ewood Park • 7.45pm

BLACKBURN ROVERS 3 ASTON VILLA 0

Half-time 3-0 • *Attendance* 15,127
Referee Joe WORRALL (Warrington)
Linesmen R.H. ANDREWS and G.I. GRANDIDGE

ARTE ET LABORE

Blue and White Halved Shirts, White Shorts	Goals	Claret and Blue Shirts, Blue Shorts	Goals
1 Bobby MIMMS		1 Mark BOSNICH	
2 David MAY		2 Earl BARRETT	
3 Graham LE SAUX		3 Steve STAUNTON	
4 Tim SHERWOOD		4 Shaun TEALE ❑	
5 Colin HENDRY		5 Paul McGRATH	
6 Kevin MORAN		6 Kevin RICHARDSON	
7 Stuart RIPLEY		7 Ray HOUGHTON	
8 Gordon COWANS		8 Bryan SMALL †	
9 Kevin GALLACHER	14	9 Dean SAUNDERS	
10 Mike NEWELL	10, 40	10 Dalian ATKINSON	
11 Jason WILCOX		11 Tony DALEY	

Substitutes

Nick MARKER

Mark ATKINS

Gk Frank TAILA

Substitutes

Dwight YORKE †61

Neil COX

Gk Nigel SPINK

BEFORE		P	W	D	L	F	A	pts	AFTER		P	W	D	L	F	A	pts
2	Villa	39	21	11	7	56	34	74	2	Villa	40	21	11	8	56	37	74
4	Blackburn	38	17	11	10	61	42	62	4	Blackburn	39	18	11	10	64	42	65

FACTFILE

United need only two points from two games for the title... Villa are left needing wins over Oldham and QPR while United must slip... A Villa Park audience is frustrated as they watch the closed-circuit TV play-back... Mark Bosnich concedes more than one goal in a game for the first time in his 17th appearance.

Villa thrashed... United win

Aston Villa's equivalent of golf's Amen Corner has arrived, with hazards lurking at every turn and one slip spelling possible disaster.

Spirits and expectations were raised by the second half revival against Manchester City last Sunday but, with matches running out, three victories out of three is the only realistic route left.

If United also win their three fixtures however, the extra point they have in the bank, plus superior goal difference will be decisive.

Villa's 7.45pm kick-off at Ewood Park is 15 minutes earlier than Manchester United's at Crystal Palace and a nation of football lovers is tuned in to what many sense is c-r-u-n-c-h night for Villa, if not for United.

"We can only attempt to stay in touch with the red-hot favourites," points out Ron Atkinson. "I guess the neutrals will expect United to win and us to lose but we have had a nasty habit of staying in there.

"We'll see..."

In the event those neutral views, gloomy ones for Villa, are proved accurate as things go wrong virtually from the word 'go'.

Before Kenny Dalglish's team can settle Villa have an excellent chance to go ahead. A ball bounces temptingly for Dalian Atkinson, five yards out and almost level with the goalpost. An inviting space yawns for him to aim at.

Disappointingly, his indecisive jab, as he gets on the end of Ray Houghton's cross from the right, rebounds off the post

Dalian Atkinson

and a large crowd back at Villa Park assembled for the close-circuit play-back from Ewood Park, groans in dismay.

Such misses have been frustrating for Villa on several occasions and this proves the last chance they have of getting their noses in front.

Although Shaun Teale is back after suspension, Villa's defence is not at its best. Bryan Small has been included at left back enabling Steve Staunton to move forward to provide power from midfield to the exclusion of Garry Parker.

In the event Small has a bad time against the quick and incisive Stuart Ripley whose work stretches Villa again and again.

In only ten minutes he draws defenders to cover Small, crosses into an over-exposed goalmouth and Mike Newell strikes his shot firmly past Mark Bosnich.

Another chance, a more difficult one, falls to Atkinson whose reflex-action response sends the ball over the bar. Again punishment is waiting. Bosnich plunges to block another shot from the excellent Newell but as defenders hesitate, the predatory Kevin Gallacher moves in to put Villa two down.

In London, United are just about to kick-off, in very good heart, no doubt. News travels fast...

By half-time Newell has thrashed in a brilliant third goal with Villa totally unhinged and the cause is a lost one.

"We have made things very difficult for ourselves tonight," Atkinson tells the media in massive understatement. There is a blank week-end ahead due to England's World Cup qualifier against Holland. It feels suspiciously like wound-licking time...

Sunday 2nd May 1993 • Villa Park • 4.00pm

ASTON VILLA 0 OLDHAM ATHLETIC 1

Half-time 0-1 • Attendance 37,247

Referee David ALLISON (Lancaster)
Linesmen K.J. HAWKES and P. NEWALL

Claret and Blue Shirts, White Shorts	Goals	Blue Shirts, Blue Shorts	Goals
1 Mark BOSNICH		1 Paul GERRARD	
2 Earl BARRETT		2 Gunnar HALLE	
3 Steve STAUNTON		3 Neil POINTON	
4 Shaun TEALE		4 Nick HENRY	29
5 Paul McGRATH		5 Richard JOBSON ❑	
6 Kevin RICHARDSON		6 Craig FLEMING	
7 Ray HOUGHTON		7 Steve REDMOND	
8 Garry PARKER †		8 Darren BECKFORD	
9 Dean SAUNDERS		9 Ian OLNEY	
10 Dalian ATKINSON		10 Mike MILLIGAN	
11 Dwight YORKE		11 Paul BERNARD	
Substitutes		*Substitutes*	
Tony DALEY †60		Andy RITCHIE	
Neil COX		Neil ADAMS	
Gk Nigel SPINK		Gk John KEELEY	

BEFORE		P	W	D	L	F	A	pts	AFTER		P	W	D	L	F	A	pts
2	Villa	40	21	11	8	56	37	74	2	Villa	41	21	11	9	56	38	74
21	Oldham	39	10	10	19	55	69	40	20	Oldham	40	11	10	19	56	69	43

FACTFILE

This is Villa's 3,700th league game... Defeat hands Manchester United the championship... Villa lose two successive games for the first time this season... It's also a first defeat in nine 'live' TV appearances in 92/93... The average Villa Park gate for the season is 29,594, the highest since 1980/81.

Another defeat ends the race

Villa Park's fourth Sunday fixture of the season is one with a sudden-death factor which is drummed up with the usual sense of breathless anticipation by Sky TV.

With only one more subsequent game to go and the championship count-down heavily in Manchester United's favour Villa need to shake off their recent uncertainties if the season is to stay alive.

To avoid the prize being served up on a plate at Old Trafford without United even having to seek points against Blackburn Rovers tomorrow, Oldham must be overcome.

"We want to make United play on a razor's edge, not with party hats and balloons," said Ron Atkinson in a typically colourful rallying call to his players.

A worthy sentiment, but Oldham need the points as an escape route from the bottom three. And it shows.

Once again Villa Park is packed virtually to its corners as mixed emotions reverberate around the stadium. In the event Oldham's hunger for survival outstrips Villa's fragile belief that the star prize can actually be landed.

Recent form has been too mixed to be encouraging. A record of only four wins in the last nine games while United have been winning has swung the odds heavily away from Villa. The most telling statistic is that Villa have failed to score in four of those games and the trend is not going to be broken this time.

So much seems to hinge on the restless running and ceaseless probing of Dean Saunders, whose scoring knack has deserted him. Like Dalian Atkinson alongside him he is not currently 'deadly' in front of goal.

With the half-hour mark approaching Gunnar Halle's header rebounds off Darren Beckford's shins and it falls perfectly for Nick Henry to strike his chance firmly out of Mark Bosnich's reach.

Shortly afterwards Deano sees his 30-yard free-kick rebound from the corner of the woodwork and a left-foot volley cleared off the line. There is little else to suggest that the championship race will go neck-and-neck right to the finishing line as once seemed likely.

Those who believe that 'luck', or lack of it, plays a part, will point to the fact that Villa hit the woodwork for the sixth successive match. Others might call this a symptom of inaccurate finishing...

Still Saunders probes on in an excellent display which contains everything, except the commodity he most wants, goals.

Elsewhere in the overall performance there is less to applaud. Neither Atkinson nor Dwight Yorke provide a threat up front while the midfield, so creative and confident in mid-season, is outrun and too easily denied possession.

Tony Daley is brought on to replace Garry Parker but with no tangible improvement and manager Atkinson is left to confess: "I was disappointed with our performance. I thought we let our crowd down.

"This was easily our worst home display."

Rather worryingly, as the championship party kicks off in Manchester, second place is still not quite decided though the doubt exists a mere 24 hours.

In a May Day, Bank Holiday Monday celebration at Old Trafford, Blackburn Rovers are decisively beaten 3-1 before the first FA Premier League trophy is presented to the winners.

Villa have to settle for runners-up place and a return to Europe as UEFA Cup representatives.

"We haven't scored enough goals during the run-in," concludes manager Atkinson. "We must have hit the woodwork 155 times. They (United) may win it by a street in the end which wouldn't be a fair reflection of how it's gone."

Sunday 9th May 1993 • Loftus Road • 2.00pm

QUEEN'S PARK RANGERS 2 ASTON VILLA 1

Half-time 0-1 • *Attendance* 18,904
Referee Paul DURKIN (Portland, Dorset)
Linesmen G.T. BUTLAND and A.P. D'URSO

Blue and White Hooped Shirts, White Shorts	Goals	Claret and Blue Shirts, White Shorts	Goals
1 Tony ROBERTS		1 Mark BOSNICH	
2 David BARDSLEY		2 Earl BARRETT ❑	
3 Clive WILSON		3 Steve STAUNTON ‡	
4 Ray WILKINS		4 Shaun TEALE	
5 Darren PEACOCK		5 Paul McGRATH ❑	
6 Alan McDONALD		6 Kevin RICHARDSON ❑	
7 Andrew IMPEY		7 Ray HOUGHTON †	
8 Simon BARKER		8 Garry PARKER	
9 Les FERDINAND	67	9 Dean SAUNDERS	
10 Bradley ALLEN	78	10 Dalian ATKINSON	
11 Andy SINTON		11 Tony DALEY	38
Substitutes		*Substitutes*	
Devon WHITE		Martin CARRUTHERS †79	
Rufus BREVETT		Neil COX ‡80	
Gk Jan STEJSKAL		Gk Nigel SPINK	

BEFORE	P	W	D	L	F	A	pts
2 Villa	41	21	11	9	56	38	74
7 QPR	40	15	12	13	58	53	57

AFTER	P	W	D	L	F	A	pts
2 Villa	42	21	11	10	57	40	74
5 QPR	41	16	12	13	60	54	60

FACTFILE

Villa finish with three successive defeats, their worst run of the season... Martin Carruthers makes his only senior appearance of the season... Man United win 2-1 at Wimbledon to finish ten points clear of Villa

Cash incentive drives Rangers

A slightly disturbing element has crept into the scenario with the news that Villa have been charged with irregularities in respect of the signing of Mark Bosnich.

Technicalities regarding the involvement of agents, and how transfer fees are paid, are at the basis of the charge. The worry is that one punishment available to the FA, should a guilty verdict arise, is the deduction of league points.

Notts County are the subject of a similar charge and since they escaped relegation by a whisker there is a modicum of uncertainty at Meadow Lane, too.

However, no such negative waves are in the air as the final match of the season arrives with second place assured along with the accompanying passport to Europe via the UEFA Cup.

Pride alone, linked to the desire to end a fine season on a high, rather than a low, is the motivating force.

A full-strength team is fielded with Tony Daley at No.11, though Martin Carruthers, one of the key figures in the second team's championship success, is on the bench.

While all the media attention is focussed on Villa, this was never going to be a 'typical end of the season' stroll for three easy points.

The prize structure based on finishing position means that while Villa cannot improve their reward QPR distinctly can. An additional £74,000 is at stake for a move up the table by two places, and it shows in the fashion and passion of their play.

For Villa, after successive defeats by Blackburn and Oldham which allowed Manchester United to cruise to their first title win in 26 years, a last-day victory would be more than welcome.

By half-time such a possibility is on the

cards. Although QPR are fizzing their passes around in Villa's own best style, Daley has struck a 36th minute shot under the diving Tony Roberts after taking Garry Parker's pass and rounding David Bardsley.

Villa's goal is frequently under siege in an entertaining game but there is the fleeting chance of a 2-0 lead as Dean Saunders fires from around 20 yards and the ball scrapes the wrong side of the bar.

More frustration on the hour when Dalian Atkinson spurts clear and feeds the ball in to the six-yards line where it hits Deano on the heel and bounces kindly for the defence.

That moment virtually marks the end of Villa's potential goal-scoring for a season which has tailed off disappointingly.

Rangers' striker Les Ferdinand, a recent hit for England in the World Cup qualifier against Holland at Wembley, strikes a left-footed shot past Bosnich in the 67th minute.

A 1-1 draw would be acceptable but even this crumb is snatched away. After 76 minutes Ray Wilkins supplies Bradley Allen with one of his quality passes and Villa's season peters out on the back of three successive defeats.

Villa supporters stage a largely 'friendly' pitch invasion though the misguided elements break one of the crossbars.

Inevitably a vague feeling of anti-climax lingers yet progress in two years under Atkinson has been beyond all expectations.

When he succeeded Jozef Venglos in 1991 relegation had been only narrowly avoided and the club was going nowhere. This was followed by a seventh-place finish in Big Ron's first season and now runners-up and Europe. Gates have gone up by around 20%, the Witton Lane stand is under re-construction and an Holte End all-seater stand will follow 12 months later.

The future for Aston Villa Football Club under chairman Doug Ellis's financial stewardship and Atkinson's footballing expertise and leadership, looks rosy, indeed.

Saturday 25th July 1992 • Dean Court • 3.00pm

AFC BOURNEMOUTH 2 ASTON VILLA 2

Half-time 1-2 • *Attendance 3,722*

Referee John CARTER (Christchurch, Dorset)
Linesmen R. PARSONS and D. ROBERTS

Black and Red Striped Shirts, Black Shorts		Goals	White Shirts, Black Shorts		Goals
1	Vince BARTRAM ·		1	Les SEALEY	
2	Paul MITCHELL		2	Dariusz KUBICKI	
3	Paul MORRELL		3	Steve STAUNTON #	og 29
4	Mark MORRIS		4	Shaun TEALE	
5	Alec WATSON		5	Paul McGRATH †	
6	SCOTT		6	Kevin RICHARDSON ‡	
7	Denny MUNDEE		7	Neil COX	
8	Peter SHEARER		8	Garry PARKER	
9	Steve FLETCHER	45	9	Dwight YORKE	35
10	Shaun BROOKS		10	Dalian ATKINSON §	
11	Keith ROWLAND		11	Stefan BEINLICH	36

Substitutes	*Substitutes*
Sean O'DRISCOLL	Ugo EHIOGU †45
David PUCKETT	Matthias BREITKREUTZ ‡66
Brian McGORRY	Martin CARRUTHERS #68
	Richard CRISP §72

FACTFILE

Ron Atkinson is absent from Dean Court as Villa start their pre-season programme. He's elsewhere persuading Ray Houghton to join Villa in preference to Chelsea. Whilst the match is in progress news comes through that the Liverpool and Republic of Ireland international has said 'yes' to Big Ron. The £900,000 deal is to be completed on Monday... Stefan Beinlich scores his first goal for the Villa first team.

Tuesday 28th July 1992 • Gay Meadow • 7.30pm

SHREWSBURY TOWN 1 ASTON VILLA 2

Half-time 0-0 • Attendance 2,178

Referee Terry HOLBROOK (Wightwick, Staffs)
Linesmen J.H. HOLBROOK and M. IBBOTSON

Amber Shirts with Blue Diamonds, Blue Shorts	Goals	White Shirts, Black Shorts	Goals
1 Paul EDWARDS		1 Nigel SPINK #	
2 Graeme WORSLEY		2 Dariusz KUBICKI	
3 Tommy LYNCH †		3 Bryan SMALL ‡	
4 Steve MacKENZIE		4 Richard CRISP	
5 Mark S. WILLIAMS		5 Ugo EHIOGU	
6 Dean SPINK		6 Earl BARRETT	
7 Mark TAYLOR		7 Neil COX †	
8 Kevin SUMMERFIELD	53	8 Matthias BREITKREUTZ	
9 John BROUGH		9 Dwight YORKE	pen 55, 87
10 Carl GRIFFITHS ‡		10 Dalian ATKINSON	
11 Neil LYNE #		11 Martin CARRUTHERS	
Substitutes		*Substitutes*	
Pat O'TOOLE †		Steve FROGGATT †48	
McDONNELL ‡		Stefan BEINLICH ‡56	
Mark SMITH #		Gk Glen LIVINGSTONE #74	

Ray Houghton, signed the day before from Liverpool, is not considered for this game in which Villa are well below full strength... Dwight Yorke takes his tally to three goals in the two pre-season games. His first is a penalty, awarded for hand-ball, and his late winner comes after he pounces on a mistake by former Villa player Dean Spink.

FACTFILE

Thursday 30th July 1992 • Paul-Zobel-Sportplatz • 7.00pm (local time)

PFV BERGMANN BORSIG 0 ASTON VILLA 5

Half-time 0-3 • Attendance 1,091

No record of the names of the German match officials

Yellow Shirts, Black Shorts	Goals	White Shirts, Blue Shorts	Goals
1 ZÖRN		1 Les SEALEY †	
2 Christian BEECK		2 Dariusz KUBICKI	21
3 Frank WAGNER		3 Bryan SMALL ††	
4 Marcus PETSCH		4 Shaun TEALE	
5 Björn ZAVARKO		5 Ugo EHIOGU	
6 Torsten JOPPIEN		6 Earl BARRETT §	
7 Torsten BAHLO		7 Dwight YORKE ‡	
8 Marek SIWA		8 Garry PARKER #	
9 Mike KOLLOFF		9 Stefan BEINLICH	
10 Eberhard JANOTTA		10 Matthias BREITKREUTZ	35,60
11 Jens ROSALSKI		11 Joe NAGBE	15
Substitutes		*Substitutes*	
SOUPT		Gk Nigel SPINK †45	
SCHÜLD		Dalian ATKINSON ‡45	85
		Richard CRISP #45	
		Tony DALEY §	
		Steve STAUNTON ††	

Stefan Beinlich and Matthias Breitkreutz return to play against their previous club, the latter scoring twice... Liberian international Joe Nagbe scores with a stunning 25 yard drive. He is playing a trial game with a view to a possible move from French club AS Monaco... Villa had hoped to also give a trial to 22-year-old Dynamo Kiev player Oleg Salenko, but he fails to turn up... Cyrille Regis, Neil Cox and Steve Froggatt are left behind in Birmingham to recover from injuries.

Saturday 1st August 1992 • Sachsenstadion

DYNAMO DRESDEN 1 ASTON VILLA 3

Half-time 0-2 • Attendance 4,429

No record of the names of the German match officials

Yellow Shirts, Black Shorts		Goals	Claret and Blue Shirts, White Shorts (91-92 kit)		Goals
1	René MÜLLER		1	Nigel SPINK †	
2	Jens MELZIG		2	Dariusz KUBICKI	
3	Dirk ZANDER		3	Steve STAUNTON	
4	Andreas WAGENHAUS		4	Shaun TEALE	
5	Nils SCHMÄLER		5	Paul McGRATH	20
6	Ralf HAUPTMANN		6	Earl BARRETT	
7	Sven KMETSCH		7	Tony DALEY ‡	44
8	Mici STEVIC		8	Garry PARKER	
9	Uwe JÄHNIG		9	Dwight YORKE #	
10	Hans-Uwe PILZ		10	Dalian ATKINSON	46
11	Thomas RATH	65	11	Ray HOUGHTON	
	Substitutes			*Substitutes*	
			Gk	Les SEALEY †45	
				Joe NAGBE ‡58	
				Stefan BEINLICH #80	

Ray Houghton plays his first game for the club after his £900,000 move from Liverpool and sets up the second goal for Tony Daley with a delightful chip... Dalian Atkinson slots home a long clearance from Paul McGrath for the third goal... Dresden had finished 14th in the previous season's Bundersliga (Germany's premier division), the first to include clubs from the re-united east, of which they were one.

FACTFILE

Tuesday 4th August 1992 • London Road • 7.30pm

PETERBOROUGH UNITED 1 ASTON VILLA 1

Half-time 1-0 • *Attendance* 3,897

Referee Brian HILL (Kettering)
Linesmen M. BULLIVANT and R. NICHOLLS

Blue Shirts, White Shorts	Goals	Yellow Shirts, Blue Shorts	Goals
1 Ian BENNETT		1 Nigel SPINK †	
2 Graham RETALLICK		2 Dariusz KUBICKI ††	
3 Ronnie ROBINSON		3 Steve STAUNTON ‡	
4 Mick HALSALL †		4 Shaun TEALE	
5 Lee HOWARTH		5 Paul McGRATH #	
6 Steve WALSH		6 Kevin RICHARDSON	
7 Worrell STERLING		7 Ray HOUGHTON §	
8 Micky GYNN (Coventry)		8 Earl BARRETT	
9 Tony ADCOCK		9 Dwight YORKE ‡‡	
10 Ken CHARLERY ‡	pen 37	10 Dalian ATKINSON ##	
11 Bobby BARNES		11 Steve FROGGATT	

Substitutes		Substitutes	
Gary COOPER †45		Gk Les SEALEY †45	
Simon WILSON ‡80		Bryan SMALL ‡45	
		Ugo EHIOGU #45	
		Joe NAGBE §45	
		Garry PARKER ††45	
		Frank McAVENNIE ‡‡45	46
		Martin CARRUTHERS ##45	

★ *The game is a benefit for Peterborough manager Chris Turner, who played over 350 games for the Posh between 1968 and 1978. He guided Peterborough to promotion to Division One last season.*

FACTFILE

Villa field virtually a different team after the interval... Former West Ham striker Frank McAvennie, on a month's trial at the club, scores with a six-yard tap-in within a minute of his first appearance for the club... Peterborough's penalty is awarded when Dariusz Kubicki trips Worrell Sterling.

Friday 7th August 1992 • Fratton Park • 7.45pm

PORTSMOUTH 1 ASTON VILLA 0

Half-time 1-0 • Attendance 7,300

Referee Michael PIERCE (Portsmouth)

Linesmen A. FARRAR and D. LAMBWELL

Blue Shirts, White Shorts		Goals	Yellow Shirts, Blue Shorts		Goals
1	Allan KNIGHT		1	Nigel SPINK	
2	Andy AWFORD		2	Earl BARRETT	
3	Ray DANIEL ‡		3	Steve STAUNTON	
4	Alan McLOUGHLIN		4	Shaun TEALE	
5	Kit SYMONS		5	Paul McGRATH †	
6	Lee RUSSELL		6	Kevin RICHARDSON	
7	Warren NEIL		7	Ray HOUGHTON	
8	Mike ROSS †		8	Garry PARKER	
9	Paul WALSH	28	9	Dwight YORKE ‡	
10	Guy WHITTINGHAM #		10	Dalian ATKINSON	
11	Chris BURNS		11	Steve FROGGATT	

Substitutes		Substitutes	
Mark CHAMBERLAIN †45		Ugo EHIOGU †45	
Darryl POWELL ‡		Frank McAVENNIE ‡45	
Colin CLARKE #			

FACTFILE

There's a fright for Villa when Paul McGrath goes down clutching his knee. He is taken off at half-time as a precaution... Frank McAvennie misses a sitter after being set-up by Ray Houghton... Paul Walsh, a summer signing for Pompey from Tottenham, scores from a rebound after Nigel Spink fails to hold his first attempt... Spink later makes two fine stops to deny Mark Chamberlain.

STAN CULLIS TESTIMONIAL MATCH

Sunday 9th August 1992 • Molineux • 12 noon

WOLVERHAMPTON W. 2 ASTON VILLA 2

Half-time 0-2 • *Attendance* 10,000

Referee Terry HOLBROOK (Wightwick, Staffs)

Linesmen P. REJER and B. HARRIS

Old Gold Shirts, Black Shorts	Goals	Claret and Blue Shirts, White Shorts	Goals
1 Mike STOWELL		1 Nigel SPINK	
2 Kevin ASHLEY		2 Earl BARRETT †	
3 Andy THOMPSON		3 Steve STAUNTON ‡	
4 Mark VENUS ‡		4 Shaun TEALE	
5 Shane WESTLEY		5 Ugo EHIOGU	
6 Tim STEELE †		6 Kevin RICHARDSON ‡‡	
7 Paul BIRCH		7 Tony DALEY #	
8 Paul COOK		8 Garry PARKER	
9 Steve BULL	68, 86	9 Matthias BREITKREUTZ	1, 40
10 Andy MUTCH		10 Frank McAVENNIE ††	
11 Robbie DENNISON		11 Steve FROGGATT §	

Substitutes	*Substitutes*
Mark BURKE †11	Dariusz KUBICKI †45
Darren SIMKIN ‡38	Bryan SMALL ‡45
	Cyrille REGIS #45 ##
	Stefan BEINLICH §45
	Martin CARRUTHERS ††54
	Richard CRISP ‡‡66
	Dwight YORKE ##82

★ *The game is a benefit for Wolves' most famous and successful manager Stan Cullis. It also marks the official opening of the new Stan Cullis Stand at the old North Bank end of the ground.*

FACTFILE

Matthias Breitkreutz takes his tally to four goals in four games as he pushes for a place in Villa's starting line-up at Ipswich on Saturday... Ugo Ehiogu and Steve Bull pick up the sponsors' man-of-the-match awards.

Tuesday 8th September 1992 • Villa Park• 7.45pm

ASTON VILLA 2 BIRMINGHAM CITY 0

Half-time 0-0 • *Attendance* 6,998
Referee Michael REED (West Heath, Birmingham)
Linesmen J. BIDDLE and G. HAMBLIN

Claret and Blue Shirts, White Shorts	Goals	Blue Shirts, Blue Shorts	Goals
1 Les SEALEY †		1 Andy GOSNEY †	
2 Dariusz KUBICKI		2 Ian RODGERSON ‡	
3 Bryan SMALL		3 Boban BABUNSKI ‡‡	
4 Shaun TEALE		4 Trevor MATTHEWSON	
5 Earl BARRETT		5 John FRAIN #	
6 Kevin RICHARDSON	51	6 Jason BECKFORD §	
7 Mark BLAKE #		7 Mark COOPER	
8 Garry PARKER		8 Paul TAIT ††	
9 Frank McAVENNIE	68	9 Mark SALE	
10 Dalian ATKINSON ‡		10 Louie DONOWA	
11 Matthias BREITKREUTZ		11 Nigel GLEGHORN	

Substitutes

Gk Mark BOSNICH †45

Alec BUNBURY ‡45

Neil COX #80

Substitutes

Gk Martin THOMAS †45

Ian ATKINS ‡45

Darren ROGERS #45

Dean PEER §45

Darran ROWBOTHAM ††45

Martin HICKS ‡‡75

★ *The match generates receipts of £37,599 for former Villa defender Jimmy Dugdale who has recently had a leg amputated... He played over 250 games for the club between 1955 and '62.*

FACTFILE
Both teams give trials to foreign players - Villa to Canadian international Alec Bunbury, later to join West Ham, and Blues to Yugoslav Boban Babunski... Prior to the main event teams of past Villa and Blues players draw 2-2.

OFFICIAL OPENING OF OAKEY PARK

Thursday 8th October 1992 • Oakey Park • 7.30pm

WITNEY TOWN 1 ASTON VILLA 7

Half-time 1-3 • Attendance 2,156

Referee R. HARRIS (Oxford)

Yellow Shirts, Blue Shorts	Goals	Claret and Blue Shirts, White Shorts	Goals
1 Kevin ALDER †		1 Nigel SPINK †	
2 Mark GEE ††		2 Earl BARRETT	
3 Darren TEGGART ‡ ‡‡68		3 Bryan SMALL	
4 Andy LEACH		4 Shaun TEALE	
5 Gary MURPHY		5 Ugo EHIOGU ‡	
6 Jason MILLAR		6 Dariusz KUBICKI	
7 Terry MERRIMAN	1-2	7 Mark BLAKE #	44
8 Jason CAFFELL		8 Garry PARKER	
9 Kenny CLARKE ††		9 Matthias BREITKREUTZ	1-5
10 Peter HUTTER #		10 Dalian ATKINSON	0-2
11 Shaun BRADBURY §45		11 Dwight YORKE §	13
Substitutes		*Substitutes*	
Gk Robert WILD †45		Gk Mark BOSNICH †45	
Lee HYATT ‡45		Neil COX ‡45	1-6
Darryl KEW #45		Dave FARRELL #45	60
Mickey CARROLL §45		Stefan BEINLICH §45	88
Cliff COUSINS ††56			

Note: Where there is no record of goal times, the order in which they were scored is given (i.e. 0-2)

Just 24 hours after eliminating Oxford United from the Coca-Cola Cup at Villa Park, Villa send a strong team to West Oxfordshire to mark the official opening of Witney Town's new Oakey Park stadium. The Beazer Homes (Southern) League side have named the Downs Road ground after outgoing chairman and new club president Aubrey Oakey.

FACTFILE

Saturday 14th November 1992 • Stadio Comunale, Florence, Italy

FIORENTINA 2 ASTON VILLA 1

Half-time 1-0 • *Attendance* 4,939

Referee Arcangelo PEZZELLA (Frattamaggiore, Italy)

White Shirts with Purple Trim, White Shorts	Goals	Claret and Blue Shirts (91/92), White Shorts (92/93)	Goals
1 Alessandro MANNINI ‡		1 Nigel SPINK	
2 Stefan LACCHI		2 Dariusz KUBICKI	
3 Stefano CAROBBI ††	36	3 Bryan SMALL #	
4 Giuseppe IACHINI ‡‡		4 Shaun TEALE	
5 Mario FACCENDA		5 Earl BARRETT	
6 Lorenzo D'ANNA		6 Kevin RICHARDSON	
7 Antonio DELL'OGLIO	66	7 Dwight YORKE	
8 Diego LATORRE		8 Ugo EHIOGU	
9 Gabriel BATISTUTA #		9 Cyrille REGIS ‡	
10 Massimo ORLANDO §		10 Dalian ATKINSON	
11 Francisco BAIANO †		11 Theo KUMALI †	
Substitutes		*Substitutes*	
Daniele BELTRAMMI †44		Matthias BREITKREUTZ †45	
Gk Gian Matteo MAREGGINI ‡45		Stefan BEINLICH ‡63	74
Mario BARTOLELLI #45		Neil COX #77	
VASCOTTO §45		Mark BLAKE	
Paolo COZZI ††62		Dave FARRELL	
Mario MASINI ‡‡69			

FACTFILE

Ron Atkinson gives South African triallist Theo Kumali half a game against the Italian Serie A side... The game is arranged to fill the blank weekend allowed in the fixtures for the benefit of the forthcoming international games.

Friday 5th March 1993 • Tolka Park, Dublin • 7.30pm

DROGHEDA UNITED 0 ASTON VILLA 0

Half-time 0-0 • Attendance 3,500
Referee M. CAULFIELD (Dublin)
Linesmen L. FITZPATRICK and J. FEIGHERY

Maroon Shirts, Blue Shorts	Goals	Yellow Shirts, Blue Shorts	Goals
1 Jim GRACE		1 Nigel SPINK	
2 Colin TRESSON		2 Earl BARRETT	
3 Joe REYNOLDS		3 Steve STAUNTON	
4 DOOHAN		4 Shaun TEALE	
5 Paul McLAUGHLIN		5 Dariusz KUBICKI	
6 KINSELLA		6 Henrik LARSEN	
7 Trevor CROLLY		7 Ray HOUGHTON	
8 Gavin RYAN		8 Ugo EHIOGU	
9 Noel REID		9 Dean SAUNDERS †	
10 Barry O'CONNOR		10 Dwight YORKE	
11 Denis CUNNINGHAM		11 Stefan BEINLICH	

Substitutes

Alan WELDRICK

Albert MURPHY

Derek CORCORAN

Substitutes

Tony DALEY †67

Neil COX

Matthias BREITKREUTZ

Martin CARRUTHERS

FACTFILE
Villa are without a Premier League fixture this weekend as scheduled opponents Blackburn Rovers have a FA Cup quarter-final tie with Sheffield United, so a trip to Ireland is arranged, mainly to give Tony Daley a run-out... Daley comes through his first 23 minutes of football in just over six months safely and is in line for a shock recall against Spurs on Wednesday... Danish international Henrik Larsen makes his only first team appearance for Villa.

Monday 10th May 1993 • Villa Park • 7.30pm

ASTON VILLA 4 STOKE CITY 1

Half-time 1-1 • Attendance 4,450

Referee Keren BARRETT (Coventry)

Claret and Blue Shirts, White Shorts		Goals	Red and White Striped Shirts, Red Shorts		Goals
1	Nigel SPINK		1	Peter FOX	
2	Dariusz KUBICKI		2	John BUTLER	
3	Bryan SMALL		3	Graham HARBEY	
4	Earl BARRETT		4	David KEVAN	
5	Ugo EHIOGU		5	Mark DEVLIN	
6	Neil COX		6	Nigel GLEGHORN †	
7	David PLATT (Juventus)	58	7	Steve FOLEY	
8	Dwight YORKE	32	8	Paul WARE	
9	Cyrille REGIS ‡		9	Mark STEIN #	30
10	Gordon COWANS (Blackburn)		10	Kevin RUSSELL	
11	Matthias BREITKREUTZ †		11	Dave REGIS ‡	

Substitutes			*Substitutes*		
	Dave FARRELL †	67		Tony KELLY †	
	Martin CARRUTHERS ‡	50		James MULLIGAN ‡	
Gk	Mark BOSNICH			Graham SHAW #	
			Gk	Wayne STARKEY	

Stoke finish the game with 12 players when kit man Neil Baldwin joins in the fun!

FACTFILE

A disappointingly low crowd turn out to honour former Villa favourite Gordon Cowans, although the game does come just a day after Villa's disappointing end to the season at QPR... Cowans made 509 appearances during two spells with the club - only Charlie Aitken (660) and Billy Walker (531) made more - winning League championship, European Cup and League Cup winners medals.

Wednesday 12th May 1993 • Windsor Park, Belfast • 7.30pm

ASTON VILLA 1 MANCHESTER UNITED 1

Half-time 0-1 • *Attendance* 22,000

Referee Frank McDONALD (Newry)

Linesmen N. COWIE and J. DUFFY

White Shirts, Blue Shorts	Goals	Yellow and Green Halved Shirts, Black Shorts	Goals
1 Mark BOSNICH		1 Les SEALEY	
2 Earl BARRETT		2 Paul PARKER	
3 Bryan SMALL		3 Lee SHARPE	
4 Shaun TEALE		4 Brian CAREY	
5 Ugo EHIOGU †		5 Mike PHELAN	32
6 Kevin RICHARDSON		6 Gary PALLISTER	
7 Ray HOUGHTON		7 Bryan ROBSON	
8 Garry PARKER		8 Paul INCE	
9 Dean SAUNDERS		9 Brian McCLAIR †	
10 Dwight YORKE	79	10 Dion DUBLIN	
11 Tony DALEY ‡		11 Ryan GIGGS	
Substitutes		*Substitutes*	
Dariusz KUBICKI †		Colin McKEE †	
Dave FARRELL ‡			

FACTFILE

This game between the Premier League champions and runners-up raises over £100,000 for the trust fund set up in honour of late Irish League secretary Mervyn Brown... Mike Phelan shoots United ahead following a right-wing cross from Paul Ince... Dwight Yorke diverts Kevin Richardson's cross in for Villa's equaliser and forces a stunning save from former Villa 'keeper Les Sealey in the last minute.

Sunday 16th May 1993 • The National Stadium in Mauritius

ASTON VILLA 3 EVERTON 1

Half-time 2-1 • Attendance 21,000
Referee A. LIM KEE CHEONG
Linesmen P. SOHUN and P. RAGHOOPUTH

Yellow Shirts, Blue Shorts	Goals	White Shirts, Blue Shorts	Goals
1 Nigel SPINK †		1 Jason KEARTON	
2 Earl BARRETT	2-1	2 Paul HOLMES †	
3 Bryan SMALL		3 Andy HINCHCLIFFE	1-1
4 Shaun TEALE		4 Barrie HORNE	
5 Ugo EHIOGU		5 Dave WATSON ‡	
6 Kevin RICHARDSON		6 Matthew JACKSON	
7 Ray HOUGHTON		7 Mark WARD	
8 Tony DALEY ‡	1-0	8 Peter BEARDSLEY	
9 Dean SAUNDERS		9 Tony COTTEE	
10 Neil COX		10 Stuart BARLOW	
11 Dave FARRELL	3-1	11 Peter BEAGRIE #	
Substitutes		*Substitutes*	
Gk Mark BOSNICH †45		John DOOLAN †	
Steve STAUNTON ‡82		Neil MOORE ‡	
Cyrille REGIS		Chris PRIEST #	
Martin CARRUTHERS		Gary ABLETT	

FACTFILE

Villa wind up the season with a comprehensive win against Premier League rivals Everton on the sun-kissed Indian Ocean Island of Mauritius... The game is arranged by football mad Mauritius Minister for Tourism Noel Lee Cheong Lem, an avid viewer of the BBC's 'Match of the Day' broadcasts... The game is played in front of a full house at the National Stadium... Other than those listed, three more Villa players made the trip, Paul McGrath, Steve Froggatt and Neil Davis.

THE MANAGEMENT TEAM

Although **Ron Atkinson's** colourful playboy image, which was always largely a media myth, has long-since been modified, very few members of the public actually realise the extent to which he is pure pro behind the scenes.

Big Ron's charismatic presence at Bodymoor Heath owes much more to Stormin' Norman, right down to the appropriate headgear, than it does to Champagne Charlie.

In using his wide experience to steer the team to within sight of the championship with a squad mostly of his own choice, he could never be accused of either over-stating nor under-stating their prospects.

For all his wise-cracks, and there were many, he never lost sight of the basic truths. Only when Norwich City were well in the lead early on did he waver from his conviction that Manchester United were 'red-hot' favourites.

Journalists attempting to prise from him a headline-hitting quote claiming the title was heading for Villa Park, failed totally.

As a manager, his great strength is that he is still a player at heart who seems to know the strengths and weaknesses of every performer worth mentioning throughout the league and with a remarkable memory recall mode.

An atmosphere of pure enjoyment is generated in training because he clearly revels in the five-a-sides.

Self-descriptions of his contribution, reigning from Pele-like through a whole range of past great players, most of whom the youngers ones have never heard of, are always grossly exagerated. A centre is never just a centre. It's a 'Besty' or a 'Finney' or a 'Stan'.

In creating such an environment of hard work mixed in with competitive 'winding up' of each other Atkinson has gathered around him a team of compatible lieutenants.

Jim Barron, a cheerful Geordie ex-goalkeeper who began at Wolves and met up with Atkinson at Oxford, took over Andy Gray's No. 2 role without the merest bleep in the system. He, too, has style and personality, not to mention the physical presence usually associated with the big men who make up the goalkeeping fraternity.

Dave Sexton, as coach, need bend the knee to no-one in the business. You name it, he's been there, done it, emerged as an amiable evergreen who goes about practicising his code with a visible air of contentment. See the football Villa play at all levels, examine the progress kids have made and you know Sexton's hallmark is indelibly there.

The supply of raw material is supervised by another approachable character, **Dave Richardson**, the Director of Youth.

Like Sexton, he is one of the most respected of his breed in football, with a proven record of identifying and capturing some of cream of the nation's schoolboys as YTS trainees. This level of club administration is far more scientific than ever before and Dave Richardson is a brand leader.

Richard Money, the David Essex look-alike, was youth coach at the start of the season and such was his rating that he left to become manager of Scunthorpe United. And, just as Barron had snugly into Gray's former role, when the latter became a full-time BSkyB TV pundit, so Money was succeeded by **Colin Clarke** who now coaches the young players.

The vastly-experienced Clarke is another ex-Oxford United man who played alongside Atkinson in the half-back line before gaining widespread experience at various league clubs.

The fitness factor is supplemented by **Roger Spry** who has muscle-testing schedules of his own unique design and, in the friendliest way, is reckoned to have a sadistic streak...

And the injured brigade are grateful for the re-assuring presence of **Jim Walker**, the expert physiotherapist. It was Jim who supervised the visionary use of the oxygen 'bubble car' in an attempt to speed up the healing process for Dalian Atkinson's abdominal injury, though surgery proved the only answer in the end.

Jim is a courteous, quiet-natured soul whose two main 'stocks in trade' are a deep knowledge of his craft and an ever-present grin.

And when it comes to packing the bags and clearing up the mess, who better than the loyal and trusty **Jim Paul**? A very good team... behind a very good team.

DALIAN ATKINSON

Born Shrewsbury,
21st March 1968
Joined Villa July 1991,
from Real Sociedad,
£1.6m.
Villa debut v Sheff Wed,
Lge (a), 17/8/91. 1 goal.

Had the talented striker finished the
season as he started it Villa would have
remained in the title chase to the last
kick! When he fired two terrific goals at
Hillsborough on December 5th he
completed a haul of 13 goals in 22
games. Then a stomach injury,
eventually requiring surgery, held him
back and, amazingly, he never scored
again for the rest of the season.

His goal at Wimbledon in October was
the BBC's 'Goal of the Season'.

Career Record:

Season	Club	League Apps	Gls	Cups Apps	Gls
85-86	Ipswich T.	- (1)	-	-	-
86-87	Ipswich T.	3 (5)	-	1 (2)	-
87-88	Ipswich T.	13 (4)	8	1	-
88-89	Ipswich T.	33 (1)	10	5	3
89-90	Sheffield W.	38	10	7	5
90-91	Real Sociedad	29	12		
91-92	Aston Villa	11 (3)	1	3	-
92-93	Aston Villa	28	11	4	2
Villa record		39 (3)	12	7	2
TOTAL		155 (14)	52	21 (2)	10

★ *England 'B' international (1 cap).*

( ) indicates appearances as a used substitute.

Cup figures include FA Cup, League Cup, Full
Members' Cup, Associate Members' Cup, Mercantile
Credit Centenary Trophy, Screen Sport Super Cup,
FA Charity Shield, European Champions' Cup,
European Cup Winners' Cup, UEFA Cup, European
Super Cup and World Club Championship.

EARL BARRETT

Born Rochdale,
28th April 1967.
Joined Villa February
1992 from Oldham,
£1.7m.
Villa debut v Man City,
Lge (a), 29/2/92.

Some doubt was expressed at the start of
the season about Barrett's capacity to
switch from his favourite central role to
right back. By the end of the season he
had, however, been named as the
manager's personal choice of the player
of the season. Had spells in midfield and
briefly at centre back performing equally
well and earning himself an England
fringe place. Regarded as the finest
athlete at the club. An ever-present, he
has proved a fine investment at £1.7m.

Career Record:

Season	Club	League Apps	Gls	Cups Apps	Gls
84-85	Man. City	-	-	-	-
85-86	Man. City	1	-	-	-
(loan)	Chester City	12	-	-	-
86-87	Man. City	1 (1)	-	1	-
87-88	Man. City	-	-	-	-
	Oldham Ath.	16 (2)	-	-	-
88-89	Oldham Ath.	44	-	6	-
89-90	Oldham Ath.	46	2	19	2
90-91	Oldham Ath.	46	3	6	-
91-92	Oldham Ath.	29	2	7	-
	Aston Villa	13	-	-	-
92-93	Aston Villa	42	1	9	-
Villa record		55	1	9	-
TOTAL		250 (3)	8	48	2

★ *Full England international (1 cap). Also capped
at 'B' and Under-21 levels.*

STEFAN BEINLICH

Born Berlin, Germany, 13th January 1972. *Joined Villa* October 1991 from Bergmann Borsig, £100,000. *Villa debut* As substitute v Nott'm. Forest, Zenith Cup (h), 19/11/91.

A striker with good control, he took the eye in the reserves where he made a big contribution towards the Central League title, scoring nine goals in 22 games.

He made six Premier League appearances as sub and started a game for the first time against Everton in February.

Scored three goals in seven 'friendly' outings with the first team.

Career Record:

Season	Club	League Apps	Gls	Cups Apps	Gls
91-92	Aston Villa	- (2)	-	- (1)	-
92-93	Aston Villa	1 (6)	-	-	-
TOTAL		1 (8)	-	- (1)	-

★ *Joined Villa from PFV Bergmann Borsig along with Matthias Breitkreutz in a £200,000 deal. When the pair appeared together during the home game with Sheffield United in January, Villa became the first English league club to field two Germans in a game.*

MARK BLAKE

Born Nottingham, 16th December 1970. *Joined Villa* July 1987 as a trainee. July 1989 on professionals forms. *Villa debut* v Luton T., Lge (a), 14/10/89.

The 22 year-old midfielder was sidelined with a hamstring injury at the start of the season, made a first team appearance on September 26 as substitute at Middlesbrough, but by Christmas had undergone an operation for a cyst on the calf. Returned to play a part in helping the reserves win the Central League championship scoring his fourth goal of the campaign in the final game against Bolton.

Career Record:

Season	Club	League Apps	Gls	Cups Apps	Gls
89-90	Aston Villa	6 (3)	-	- (1)	-
90-91	Aston Villa	6 (1)	-	-	-
(loan)	Wolves	2	-	-	-
91-92	Aston Villa	14	2	5	-
92-93	Aston Villa	- (1)	-	-	-
Villa record		26 (5)	2	5 (1)	-
TOTAL		28 (5)	2	5 (1)	-

★ *Capped at under-21, youth and schoolboy levels for England.*

Other players to appear in the Villa first team in 1992-93:

● **Frank McAvennie** - *released by West Ham he started the season on trial with Villa but returned to his native Scotland to rejoin Celtic.*

● **Les Sealey** - *spent the first 11 games on the bench, had a spell on loan at Birmingham City and returned to Manchester United on a free transfer in January.*

● **Michael Oakes** - *the promising young 'keeper made the subs bench on five occasions and earned a call-up for the England under-21 party. Had two spells on loan at Gloucester City and played 11 games for Villa's championship-winning reserve team.*

MARK BOSNICH

MATTHIAS BREITKREUTZ

Born Fairfield, Australia, 13th January 1972. *Joined Villa* February 1992 from Sydney Croatia. *Villa debut* v Luton Town, Lge (a) 25/4/92.

After appearing in the penultimate league game of 1991-92 he was ready to grasp his chance when it came along.

His first appearance of the season was at Hillsborough in December with the big break arriving two months later. He kept his nerve and composure well in the Cup replay at Wimbledon and kept the jersey for the rest of the season.

Before the 0-3 defeat at Ewood Park spoiled his record he had kept nine clean sheets in 15 starts and had never let in more than one in any game.

Career Record:

Season	Club	League		Cups	
		Apps	Gls Ag	Apps	Gls Ag
89-90	Man. United	1	0	-	-
90-91	Man. United	2	1	-	-
91-92	Aston Villa	1	1	-	-
92-93	Aston Villa	17	12	1	0
Villa record		18	13	1	0
TOTAL		21	14	1	0

★ *Full international with Australia. Appeared in the 1992 Barcelona Olympics, where Australia were beaten semi-finalists.*

★ *Won the club's 'Young Player of the Year' award at the end of season gala night at the Holte Suite.*

★ *Villa's home game with Everton in February was the first in this country to feature two Australian goalkeepers when Jason Kearton was Bosnich's counterpart.*

Born Crivitz, Germany, 12th May 1971 *Joined Villa* October 1991 from Bergmann Borsig, £100,000. *Villa debut* As sub v Sheff Wed, Lge (h), 18/1/92.

The German-born midfield player made his first appearance of the season as sub in the Coca Cola Cup defeat at Ipswich having impressed Ron Atkinson with his reserve match form. He later made a couple of senior appearances, showing a nice touch on the ball, but his attention was focussed on helping win the Central League, scoring four goals in 31 games.

Career Record:

Season	Club	League		Cups	
		Apps	Gls	Apps	Gls
91-92	Aston Villa	7 (1)	-	-	-
92-93	Aston Villa	2 (1)	-	- (1)	-
TOTAL		9 (2)	-	- (1)	-

★ *Scored twice when Villa played a pre-season friendly against his previous club PFV Bergmann Borsig in Berlin. Also scored both goals in the 2-2 draw with Wolves at Molineux in the Stan Cullis Testimonial match.*

● *Two young professionals who never made the Villa first team in 1992-93 were* **Lee Williams** *and* **Richard Crisp***. They did taste first team action elsewhere, however. Williams had a spell on loan with Third Division Shrewsbury and scored an FA Cup goal against Mansfield. Crisp was taken on loan by Richard Money at Scunthorpe and made his Football League debut against Chesterfield in March.*

● *NOTE: Career records of goalkeepers Mark Bosnich (left) and Nigel Spink (p133) list number of goals conceded in the goals columns.*

MARTIN CARRUTHERS

Born Nottingham,
7th August 1972
Joined Villa June 1988 as
a trainee. July 1990 on
professionals forms.
Villa debut As sub v
Nott'm Forest, Zenith
Cup (h), 19/11/91.

Although the Nottingham-born striker reached the fringe of the first-team in 1991-92 with a couple of appearances, plus two more as substitute, his chances were limited in 1992-93.

He benefited from a successful loan spell at Hull City. Then, after helping the reserves win their prize in scoring several valuable goals he was given the nod by Ron Atkinson to join the squad for the final Premier League match of the season, at Loftus Road.

Twelve minutes from time he replaced Ray Houghton against QPR so could thus be accurately described as the 'player in possession' when the season closed!

Career Record:

Season	Club	League Apps	League Gls	Cups Apps	Cups Gls
90-91	Aston Villa	-	-	-	-
91-92	Aston Villa	2 (1)	-	- (2)	-
92-93	Aston Villa	- (1)	-	-	-
(loan)	Hull City	13	6	-	-
Villa record		*2 (2)*	*-*	*- (2)*	*-*
TOTAL		15 (2)	6	- (2)	-

★ *Scored his first senior goal, against Mansfield, whilst on loan at Hull.*

★ *Was top scorer for the reserves with 11 goals in 22 appearances including six in the last nine games of the title run in.*

NEIL COX

Born Scunthorpe,
8th October 1971.
Joined Villa February
1991 from Scunthorpe
United, £400,000.
Villa debut v Nott'm F.,
Zenith Cup (h), 19/11/91.

Though it took time for the Jozef Venglos signing to realise his potential he emerged during the season as a valuable squad man.

He proved he could play both in defence and midfield while also scoring a couple of goals. The first of these was as substitute in the 1-1 draw with Bristol Rovers in the FA Cup at Villa Park and the other in the 2-1 home league win over Everton on February 20th.

Made his first appearance of the season as substitute in the Coca-Cola Cup replay at Ipswich in December and made the teamsheet in all but two of the remaining 30 games.

Career Record:

Season	Club	League Apps	League Gls	Cups Apps	Cups Gls
89-90	Scunthorpe	-	-	- (1)	-
90-91	Scunthorpe	17	1	8	-
	Aston Villa	-	-	-	-
91-92	Aston Villa	4 (3)	-	1	-
92-93	Aston Villa	6 (9)	1	3 (2)	1
Villa record		*10 (12)*	*1*	*4 (2)*	*1*
TOTAL		27 (12)	2	12 (3)	1

★ *Won his first England under-21 cap in the goalless draw in Turkey at the end of March and retained his place for the 3-0 defeat of Holland at Portsmouth a few weeks later.*

★ *Qualified for a Central League championship medal after making 21 appearances.*

TONY DALEY

Born Birmingham, 18th October 1967. *Joined Villa* May 1983 as an apprentice. May 1985 on professionals forms. v Southampton, Lge (a), 20/4/85.

After being England's winger in the European Championships in Sweden Daley suffered a season almost of write-off because of cruciate ligament surgery.

Having made little impact before his injury the old breathtaking pace was not quite there when he returned.

Came straight into the team for the visit of Spurs in March after playing just 23 minutes football in a friendly in Ireland.

His one big highlight was when he scored the only goal against Arsenal at Highbury on Easter Monday, a victory which kept Villa in the title race.

Career Record:

Season	Club	League Apps	Gls	Cups Apps	Gls
84-85	Aston Villa	4 (1)	-	-	-
85-86	Aston Villa	16 (7)	2	2 (1)	-
86-87	Aston Villa	25 (8)	3	6 (1)	2
87-88	Aston Villa	10 (4)	3	1	-
88-89	Aston Villa	25 (4)	5	8 (1)	1
89-90	Aston Villa	31 (1)	6	11 (1)	2
90-91	Aston Villa	22 (1)	2	8	2
91-92	Aston Villa	29 (5)	7	7	-
92-93	Aston Villa	8 (4)	2	-	-
TOTAL		170 (35)	30	43 (4)	7

★ *Full England international (7 caps), he appeared in the 1992 European Championship Finals in Sweden. Also capped at 'B' and youth levels.*

UGO EHIOGU

Born Hackney, London, 3rd November 1972. *Joined Villa* July 1991 from West Bromwich Albion, £40,000. *Villa debut* v Arsenal, Lge (h), 24/8/91.

Made captain of the England under-21s late in the season though restricted to a couple of first team appearances and the odd selection on the bench.

A tall, talented player who can play either at right back or in the centre of defence, where he prefers to be.

He was unfortunate to take time to settle when chosen as replacement for Shaun Teale in the home defeat by Norwich. That experience set him back a little but the backroom staff at Bodymoor Heath are convinced that he will become a top player.

Career Record:

Season	Club	League Apps	Gls	Cups Apps	Gls
90-91	W.B.A.	- (2)	-	-	-
91-92	Aston Villa	4 (4)	-	1 (1)	-
92-93	Aston Villa	1 (3)	-	1	-
Villa record		5 (7)	-	2 (1)	-
TOTAL		5 (9)	-	2 (1)	-

★ *Captained the England under-21 side for the first time in the 3-0 win against Holland at Portsmouth in April.*

★ *Captain of Villa's Central League championship winning side, he played 29 games and scored six times, including the goal against Newcastle which clinched the title.*

DAVE FARRELL

Born Birmingham,
11th November 1971
Joined Villa January 1992
from Redditch United,
£45,000.
Villa debut As sub v
Oldham, Lge (a),
24/10/92.

Birmingham-born winger who made one appearance as sub at Oldham and one full appearance, in front of a live TV audience, at home to QPR. The 22-year-old has natural ability but was playing in local club football until fairly recently.

A key member of Villa's title-winning reserve team, finishing the season in dazzling form.

Travelled to Florence and Mauritius with the first team party.

Career Record:

Season	Club	League Apps	Gls	Cups Apps	Gls
91-92	Aston Villa	-	-	-	-
92-93	Aston Villa	1 (1)	-	-	-
(loan)	Scunthorpe	4 (1)	1	1	-
Villa record		*1 (1)*	*-*	*-*	*-*
TOTAL		5 (2)	1	1	-

★ *Scored his first senior goal after coming on as substitute against York City in his final game on loan to Scunthorpe United.*

★ *Scored five goals in 23 league games for the Villa reserve team.*

ANSELLS BIG STEAK PLAYER OF THE MONTH AWARDS IN 1992-93
Earl Barrett (August), Garry Parker (September), Nigel Spink (October), Dalian Atkinson (November & December), Dean Saunders (January), Mark Bosnich (February), Kevin Richardson (March) and Shaun Teale (April).

STEVE FROGGATT

Born Lincoln,
9th March 1973
Joined Villa July 1989 as a
trainee. January 1991 on
professionals forms.
Villa debut As last minute
substitute v West Ham,
Lge (h), 26/12/91.

One of the big hopes for 1992-93 after his bold introduction the previous season. Although spindly and leggy in appearance the teenager's ability to take on and beat strong, mature defenders impressed everyone.

His capacity to measure accurate crosses and cross shots was a valuable asset to the team but unhappily a knee problem, requiring surgery, restricted him to a mere 19 appearances.

Although wanted by Irish Republic boss Jack Charlton on the strength of a family connection, he decided to answer an England Under-21 call before his season was brought to a premature end.

Career Record:

Season	Club	League Apps	Gls	Cups Apps	Gls
90-91	Aston Villa	-	-	-	-
91-92	Aston Villa	6 (3)	-	2 (1)	1
92-93	Aston Villa	16 (1)	1	3 (1)	-
TOTAL		22 (4)	1	5 (2)	1

★ *Made his England under-21 international debut in a September friendly in Spain, setting up the winning goal for Darren Anderton. Also made an appearance as substitute in the 6-0 defeat of San Marino in February.*

★ *Named as the Barclays Young Eagle for the Midlands in August.*

RAY HOUGHTON
DARIUSZ KUBICKI

Born Glasgow,
9th January 1962
Joined Villa July 1992
from Liverpool,
£900,000.
Villa debut v Ipswich,
Lge (a), 15/8/92.

The Irish Republic colleague of Paul
McGrath and Steve Staunton was an
energetic forager on the right of midfield
thoughout the season.

As a member of the midfield which
became something of a TV attraction he
more or less carried on where he left off
at Liverpool. Where he, himself,
expressed disappointment was in his
limited supply of goals.

Career Record:

Season	Club	League Apps	Gls	Cups Apps	Gls
79-80	West Ham	-	-	-	-
80-81	West Ham	-	-	-	-
81-82	West Ham	- (1)	-	-	-
82-83	Fulham	42	5	7	2
83-84	Fulham	40	3	5	-
84-85	Fulham	42	8	4	3
85-86	Fulham	5	-	-	-
	Oxford Utd.	35	4	14	3
86-87	Oxford Utd.	37	5	6	1
87-88	Oxford Utd.	11	1	2	-
	Liverpool	26 (2)	5	7	2
88-89	Liverpool	38	7	14	1
89-90	Liverpool	16 (3)	1	4 (1)	-
90-91	Liverpool	31 (1)	7	7	3
91-92	Liverpool	36	8	15	4
92-93	Aston Villa	39	3	9	1
TOTAL		398 (7)	57	94 (1)	20

★ *Republic of Ireland full international (50 caps,
3 goals - up to 28/4/93)*

Born Warsaw, Poland,
6th June 1963.
Joined Villa August 1991
from Legia Warsaw,
£200,000.
Villa debut
v Southampton, Lge (a),
31/8/91.

The Polish international defender was
an outstanding member of the
championship-winning second team but
enjoyed only limited involvement with
the first team. He was the one most
affected by Earl Barrett's emergence as a
quality right back and also the progress
of Neil Cox.

Barrett's ever-present record in the
No.2 shirt and the use of Cox as cover
when Barrett played in midfield, meant
that the Pole was restricted to one full
senior appearance only, the 2-2 home
draw with Ipswich in the Coca Cola Cup
when Shaun Teale was out injured.

Career Record:

Season	Club	League Apps	Gls	Cups Apps	Gls
91-92	Aston Villa	23	-	7 (1)	-
92-93	Aston Villa	-	-	1	-
TOTAL		23	-	8 (1)	-

★ *Full Poland international (46 caps, 1 goal).*

★ *Made 238 appearances (7 goals) for Stal Mielec
and Legia Warsaw in the Polish First Division
before joining Villa*

★ *Played more games than anyone (32) in Villa's
championship-winning reserve team.*

● *Goalkeeper Glen Livingstone left Villa for York
City during the season, after a spell on loan with
the Bootham Crescent side. He.appeared as a sub
in Villa's pre-season friendly at Shrewsbury.*

PAUL McGRATH

Born Ealing, London, 4th December 1959. *Joined Villa* August 1989 from Man. United, £400,000. *Villa debut* v Nott'm F., Lge (a), 19/8/89.

Widely regarded as one of the best defenders in the World, his magnificent season earned him the accolade of PFA Players' Player of the Year.

Although he trains only lightly because of his troublesome knees he has the remarkable knack of finding clear spaces for himself in various parts of the field. The complete footballer.

Career Record:

Season	Club	League Apps	Gls	Cups Apps	Gls
81-82	Man. United	-	-	-	-
82-83	Man. United	14	3	1 (1)	-
83-84	Man. United	9	1	3	-
84-85	Man. United	23	-	7	2
85-86	Man. United	40	3	8	1
86-87	Man. United	34 (1)	2	4 (1)	-
87-88	Man. United	21 (1)	2	2	1
88-89	Man. United	18 (2)	1	5 (1)	-
89-90	Aston Villa	35	1	12	-
90-91	Aston Villa	35	-	9	-
91-92	Aston Villa	41	1	7	-
92-93	Aston Villa	42	4	8	1
Villa record		*153*	*6*	*36*	*1*
TOTAL		312 (4)	18	66 (3)	5

★ *Republic of Ireland full international (59 caps, 6 goals - up to and including 28/4/93)*
★ *PFA Player of the Year and Midland Soccer Writer's Player of the Year in 1993. Voted Villa Player of the Year for the fourth successive year.*

GARRY PARKER

Born Oxford, 7th September 1965. *Joined Villa* November 1991 from Nottingham Forest, £650,000. *Villa debut* v Oldham, Lge (a), 30/11/91.

The former Nottingham Forest midfield player reached probably a career peak in mid-season and attracted the attention of England boss Graham Taylor.

Unfortunately when included in the England squad he had a troublesome tooth problem and later his club form was affected by his 'carrying' a stomach injury.

Career Record:

Season	Club	League Apps	Gls	Cups Apps	Gls
82-83	Luton Town	1	-	-	-
83-84	Luton Town	13	2	1	-
84-85	Luton Town	13 (7)	1	4 (4)	1
85-86	Luton Town	4 (4)	-	1 (1)	-
	Hull City	12	-	-	-
86-87	Hull City	37 (1)	-	5	1
87-88	Hull City	33 (1)	8	6	-
	Nott'm. For.	1 (1)	-	-	-
88-89	Nott'm. For.	22	7	14 (1)	6
89-90	Nott'm. For.	36 (1)	6	13	1
90-91	Nott'm. For.	35 (1)	3	15	5
91-92	Nott'm. For.	5 (1)	1	4	-
	Aston Villa	25	1	5	1
92-93	Aston Villa	37	9	9	-
Villa record		*62*	*10*	*14*	*1*
TOTAL		274 (17)	38	77 (6)	15

★ *Was in the full England squad for the game with Norway in September. Capped at England under-21, under-19 and youth levels.*

CYRILLE REGIS

Born French Guyana,
9th February 1958.
Joined Villa July 1991 on
a free transfer from
Coventry City.
Villa debut v Sheff Wed,
Lge (a), 17/8/91. 1 goal.

Kicked off the season looking fitter than anyone in the club but at approaching 35 it was almost certain to be his last at Villa Park and so it proved.

He revealed his stylish ability to hold the ball up under pressure but by mid-season needed achilles tendon surgery. Agreed on an amicable parting with the club to seek first-team football elsewhere.

Career Record:

Season	Club	League Apps	Gls	Cups Apps	Gls
77-78	W.B.A.	33 (1)	10	7 (1)	8
78-79	W.B.A.	38 (1)	13	17	4
79-80	W.B.A.	24 (2)	8	4	1
80-81	W.B.A.	38	14	9	3
81-82	W.B.A.	37	17	16	8
82-83	W.B.A.	26	9	3	2
83-84	W.B.A.	30	10	6	3
84-85	W.B.A.	7	1	-	-
	Coventry C.	30 (1)	5	1	-
85-86	Coventry C.	34	5	3	5
86-87	Coventry C.	40	12	11	4
87-88	Coventry C.	30 (1)	10	6	2
88-89	Coventry C.	34	7	4	-
89-90	Coventry C.	32 (2)	4	8 (1)	1
90-91	Coventry C.	31 (3)	4	10	3
91-92	Aston Villa	39	11	7	-
92-93	Aston Villa	7 (6)	1	1 (3)	-
Villa record		*46 (6)*	*12*	*8 (3)*	*-*
TOTAL		510 (17)	141	113 (5)	44

★ *Full England international (5 caps).*

KEVIN RICHARDSON

Born Newcastle-upon-
Tyne, 4th December 1962.
Joined Villa August 1991
from Real Sociedad,
£450,000.
Villa debut v Sheff Wed,
Lge (a), 17/8/91.

The 'quiet man', Geordie skipper who prefers to lead by example, namely simply getting on with the job. Not a spectacular player but one who motors back and forth to fetch and carry.

An ever-present who admitted to getting 'sick and tired' of hearing that he could become the first-ever player to win Championship medals with three different clubs. "This is not a personal ego trip" he said.

Career Record:

Season	Club	League Apps	Gls	Cups Apps	Gls
80-81	Everton	-	-	-	-
81-82	Everton	15 (3)	2	1	-
82-83	Everton	24 (5)	3	3 (2)	-
83-84	Everton	25 (3)	4	11 (1)	3
84-85	Everton	14 (1)	4	3 (1)	-
85-86	Everton	16 (2)	3	7	1
86-87	Everton	1	-	1	-
	Watford	39	2	11	-
87-88	Arsenal	24 (5)	4	10 (1)	2
88-89	Arsenal	32 (2)	1	5 (1)	-
89-90	Arsenal	32 (1)	-	7	-
90-91	Real Sociedad	37	-		
91-92	Aston Villa	42	6	9	-
92-93	Aston Villa	42	2	9	1
Villa record		*84*	*8*	*18*	*1*
TOTAL		343 (21)	31	77 (6)	7

★ *An ever-present since joining the club.*

DEAN SAUNDERS

Born Swansea,
21st June 1964.
Joined Villa September
1992 from Liverpool,
£2.3m.
Villa debut v Leeds, Lge
(a), 13/9/92.

His arrival from Liverpool for £2.3m was a turning point in the season. On his home debut he scored twice in the 4-2 home win over his former club.

Comfortable when in possession and lithe and quick in moving across the line he quickly formed the lethal Deadly Duo partnership with Dalian Atkinson until the latter's injury brought it to an end.

In his best spell he netted 16 goals in 28 games but then went eleven games without scoring.

Career Record:

Season	Club	League Apps	Gls	Cups Apps	Gls
82-83	Swansea C.	-	-	-	-
83-84	Swansea C.	14 (5)	3	- (1)	-
84-85	Swansea C.	28 (2)	9	4 (1)	-
(loan)	Cardiff City	3 (1)	-	-	-
85-86	Brighton	39 (3)	14	9	5
86-87	Brighton	27 (3)	6	5	-
	Oxford Utd.	12	6	-	-
87-88	Oxford Utd.	35 (2)	12	11 (1)	9
88-89	Oxford Utd.	10	4	2	2
	Derby Co.	30	14	6	1
89-90	Derby Co.	38	11	11	10
90-91	Derby Co.	38	17	8	4
91-92	Liverpool	36	10	18	11
92-93	Liverpool	6	1	1	1
	Aston Villa	35	13	9	4
TOTAL		351 (16)	120	84 (3)	47

★ *Full international for Wales (39 caps, 11 goals - up to and including 28/4/93).*

BRYAN SMALL

Born Birmingham,
15th November 1971.
Joined Villa June 1988
from FA School of
Excellence as a trainee.
July 1990 professional.
Villa debut v Everton,
Lge (a), 19/10/91.

Strong, speedy local-born defender who continued the previous season's steady progress to a first-team squad place.

He appeared a couple of times as sub early in the season and went on to reach double figures in appearances. A valuable squad man who could, if required, replace Steve Staunton at left back allowing the Irish cap to move forward.

Progressed to the England under-21 side in the New Year.

Career Record:

Season	Club	League Apps	Gls	Cups Apps	Gls
89-90	Aston Villa	-	-	-	-
90-91	Aston Villa	-	-	-	-
91-92	Aston Villa	8	-	4 (1)	-
92-93	Aston Villa	10 (4)	-	1	-
TOTAL		18 (4)	-	5 (1)	-

★ *Made his England under-21 international debut in the 6-0 defeat of San Marino at Luton in February and retained his place for the games with Turkey and Holland. Also capped at youth level.*

★ *Earned a Central League championship medal for his reserve team appearances.*

● *Dean Saunders was one of the six players shortlisted for the PFA Player of the Year Award, which was won by team-mate Paul McGrath. Villa's Cyrille Regis presented the Young Player of the Year award to Manchester United's Ryan Giggs at the 28th March dinner.*

NIGEL SPINK

Born Chelmsford,
8th August 1958
Joined Villa January 1977
from Chelmsford City
Villa debut v Nott'm
Forest, League (a),
26/12/79.

Having fought his way back into the first team under challenge from Les Sealey in 1991-92 the long-serving goalkeeper set off the season with a new lease of life.

Spink was back to his peak form, missing only one game through injury, until the FA Cup replay at Wimbledon when he was unwell and Mark Bosnich took over. From then on the young Aussie played so well that a disappointed Spink could not get back into the side.

Career Record:

Season	Club	League Apps	Gls Ag	Cups Apps	Gls Ag
79-80	Aston Villa	1	2	-	-
80-81	Aston Villa	-	-	-	-
81-82	Aston Villa	-	-	- (1)	0
82-83	Aston Villa	22	23	8	9
83-84	Aston Villa	28	43	13	16
84-85	Aston Villa	19	22	1	3
85-86	Aston Villa	31	53	11	15
86-87	Aston Villa	32	55	7	9
87-88	Aston Villa	44	41	7	11
88-89	Aston Villa	34	52	8	10
89-90	Aston Villa	38	38	13	14
90-91	Aston Villa	34	54	11	13
91-92	Aston Villa	23	21	3	2
92-93	Aston Villa	25	29	8	7
TOTAL		331	433	90 (1)	109

★ *Full England international (1 cap). Also capped at England 'B' level. Member of Villa's European Cup and European Super Cup winning teams.*

STEVE STAUNTON

Born Drogheda, Ireland,
19th January 1969.
Joined Villa August 1991
from Liverpool, £1.1m.
Villa debut v Sheff. Wed.
League (a), 17/8/91.
Scored the winner.

The Irish Republic cap was constantly outstanding whether in his usual role as an attacking left back, in the centre or grafting and attacking from midfield.

An ever-present who never gave less than 100% in skill and effort. Apart from creating many goals by his forceful play he scored one of the most spectacular and valuable goals of the season, an edge-of-the-area blast for a 1-1 draw at Old Trafford.

Career Record:

Season	Club	League Apps	Gls	Cups Apps	Gls
86-87	Liverpool	-	-	-	-
87-88	Liverpool	-	-	-	-
(loan)	Bradford City	7 (1)	-	3	-
88-89	Liverpool	17 (4)	-	8	1
89-90	Liverpool	18 (2)	-	4 (2)	3
90-91	Liverpool	20 (4)	-	9	2
91-92	Aston Villa	37	4	6	-
92-93	Aston Villa	42	2	9	-
Villa record		79	6	15	-
TOTAL		141 (11)	6	39 (2)	6

★ *Full Republic of Ireland international (38 caps, 3 goals - up to and including 28/4/93). Scored direct from a corner in a World Cup qualifier against Northern Ireland in March. Also capped at under-21 level.*

● *NOTE: Career records of goalkeepers Nigel Spink (left) and Mark Bosnich (p125) list number of goals conceded in the goals columns.*

SHAUN TEALE

Born Southport,
10th March 1964.
Joined Villa July 1991
from Bournemouth,
£300,000.
Villa debut v Sheff Wed,
Lge (a), 17/8/91.

A tigerish defender whose quick tackling and aerial aggression blends superbly with the calm assurance of Paul McGrath in central defence.

Teale has been described as England-class by Ron Atkinson in the way that he defiantly guards his line. The first time he missed a league game, through injury, Villa were beaten at home by Norwich.

He missed four games in all, the last of them through a suspension, the inevitable price paid by all such determined ball-winners.

Career Record:

Season	Club	League Apps	Gls	Cups Apps	Gls
88-89	Bournemouth	19 (1)	-	-	-
89-90	Bournemouth	34	-	6	-
90-91	Bournemouth	46	4	10	1
91-92	Aston Villa	42	-	9	1
92-93	Aston Villa	39	1	8	1
Villa record		*81*	*1*	*17*	*2*
TOTAL		180 (1)	5	33	3

★ *Joined Everton as an apprentice in January 1980 but was released and spent eight months with Huddersfield Town. Then came spells with non-league clubs Burscough, Ellesmere Port, Southport, Northwich Victoria and Weymouth before joining Bournemouth for £50,000 in January 1989.*

DWIGHT YORKE

Born Canaan, Tobago,
3rd November 1971.
Joined Villa December
1989 from Signal Hill in
Tobago, £120,000.
Villa debut v C.Palace,
Lge (a), 24/3/90.

The Trinidad and Tobago international's dramatic impact in 1991-92, was a difficult act to follow.

He missed the opening fixture because of a World Cup qualifier and found it hard to re-establish himself.

Dean Saunders' arrival made it even more difficult for him but he did enjoy a favourable run early in the New Year and the experience of being in a championship-bidding team will have been invaluable for the West Indian youngster.

Career Record:

Season	Club	League Apps	Gls	Cups Apps	Gls
89-90	Aston Villa	- (2)	-	-	-
90-91	Aston Villa	8 (10)	2	3	-
91-92	Aston Villa	27 (5)	11	8	6
92-93	Aston Villa	22 (5)	6	6 (2)	1
TOTAL		57 (22)	19	17 (2)	7

★ *Full international with Trinidad & Tobago.*

★ *Yorke twice won the BBC Goal of the Month award for his efforts against Ipswich and Sheffield Wednesday, the latter finishing third in the Goal of the Season vote.*

● *All international records are up to and including 28th April 1993.*

FIRST TEAM APPEARANCES & GOALSCORERS

	LEAGUE		FA CUP		LGE CUP		TOTAL	
	Apps	Gls	Apps	Gls	Apps	Gls	Apps	Gls
Dalian ATKINSON	28	11	-	-	4	2	32	13
Earl BARRETT	42	1	4	-	5	-	51	1
Stefan BEINLICH	1 (6)	-	-	-	-	-	1 (6)	-
Mark BLAKE	- (1)	-	-	-	-	-	- (1)	-
Mark BOSNICH	17	-	1	-	-	-	18	-
Matthias BREITKREUTZ	2 (1)	-	-	-	- (1)	-	2 (2)	-
Martin CARRUTHERS	- (1)	-	-	-	-	-	- (1)	-
Neil COX	6 (9)	1	2 (1)	1	1 (1)	-	9 (11)	2
Tony DALEY	8 (5)	2	-	-	-	-	8 (5)	2
Ugo EHIOGU	1 (3)	-	-	-	1	-	2 (3)	-
Dave FARRELL	1 (1)	-	-	-	-	-	1 (1)	-
Steve FROGGATT	16 (1)	1	2 (1)	-	1	-	19 (2)	1
Ray HOUGHTON	39	3	4	1	5	-	48	4
Dariusz KUBICKI	-	-	-	-	1	-	1	-
Paul McGRATH	42	4	4	-	4	1	50	5
Garry PARKER	37	9	4	-	5	-	46	9
Cyrille REGIS	7 (6)	1	- (2)	-	1 (1)	-	8 (9)	1
Kevin RICHARDSON	42	2	4	-	5	1	51	3
Dean SAUNDERS	35	13	4	2	5	2	44	17
Bryan SMALL	10 (4)	-	-	-	1	-	11 (4)	-
Nigel SPINK	25	-	3	-	5	-	33	-
Steve STAUNTON	42	2	4	-	5	-	51	2
Shaun TEALE	39	1	4	-	4	1	47	2
Dwight YORKE	22 (5)	6	4	1	2 (2)	-	28 (7)	7

Also Played:
Frank McAvennie (on trial) - (3) Lge Apps.

Unused Substitutes:
Nigel Spink 15, Mark Bosnich 13, Les Sealey 11, Neil Cox 9, Bryan Small 7, Dwight Yorke 7, Ugo Ehiogu 6, Michael Oakes 5, Stefan Beinlich 4, Cyrille Regis 4, Mark Blake 2, Matthias Breitkreutz 2, Dariusz Kubicki 2, Dave Farrell 1 and Frank McAvennie 1.

Goalscorers in friendly games:
Dwight Yorke 6, Matthias Breitkreutz 5, Dalian Atkinson 3, Stefan Beinlich 3, Dave Farrell 3, Tony Daley 2, Frank McAvennie 2, Earl Barrett 1, Mark Blake 1, Martin Carruthers 1, Neil Cox 1, Dariusz Kubicki 1, Paul McGrath 1, Joe Nagbe (triallist) 1, David Platt (guest) 1, Kevin Richardson 1.

FINAL TABLE

		Pl	Home					Away					Total					Pts
			W	D	L	F	A	W	D	L	F	A	W	D	L	F	A	
1	Manchester United	42	14	5	2	39	14	10	7	4	28	17	24	12	6	67	31	84
2	Aston Villa	42	13	5	3	36	16	8	6	7	21	24	21	11	10	57	40	74
3	Norwich City	42	13	6	2	31	19	8	3	10	30	46	21	9	12	61	65	72
4	Blackburn Rovers	42	13	4	4	38	18	7	7	7	30	28	20	11	11	68	46	71
5	Queen's Park Rangers	42	11	5	5	41	32	6	7	8	22	23	17	12	13	63	55	63
6	Liverpool	42	13	4	4	41	18	3	7	11	21	37	16	11	15	62	55	59
7	Sheffield Wed.	42	9	8	4	34	26	6	6	9	21	25	15	14	13	55	51	59
8	Tottenham Hotspur	42	11	5	5	40	25	5	6	10	20	41	16	11	15	60	66	59
9	Manchester City	42	7	8	6	30	25	8	4	9	26	26	15	12	15	56	51	57
10	Arsenal	42	8	6	7	25	20	7	5	9	15	18	15	11	16	40	38	56
11	Chelsea	42	9	7	5	29	22	5	7	9	22	32	14	14	14	51	54	56
12	Wimbledon	42	9	4	8	32	23	5	8	8	24	32	14	12	16	56	55	54
13	Everton	42	7	6	8	26	27	8	2	11	27	28	15	8	19	53	55	53
14	Sheffield United	42	10	6	5	33	19	4	4	13	21	34	14	10	18	54	53	52
15	Coventry City	42	7	4	10	29	28	6	9	6	23	29	13	13	16	52	57	52
16	Ipswich Town	42	8	9	4	29	22	4	7	10	21	33	12	16	14	50	55	52
17	Leeds United	42	12	8	1	40	17	0	7	14	17	45	12	15	15	57	62	51
18	Southampton	42	10	6	5	30	21	3	5	13	24	40	13	11	18	54	61	50
19	Oldham Athletic	42	10	6	5	43	30	3	4	14	20	44	13	10	19	63	74	49
20	Crystal Palace	42	6	9	6	27	25	5	7	9	21	36	11	16	15	48	61	49
21	Middlesbrough	42	8	5	8	33	27	3	6	12	21	48	11	11	20	54	75	44
22	Nottingham Forest	42	6	4	11	17	25	4	6	11	24	37	10	10	22	41	62	40

ROLL OF HONOUR

Champions: Manchester United
Runners-up: Aston Villa
Relegated: Crystal Palace, Middlesbrough and Nottingham Forest
PFA Fair Play Award winners: Norwich City
Runners-up: Aston Villa

FACTS & FIGURES

Of the 462 games played, 214 resulted in home wins, 118 in away wins and 130 in draws. A total of 1,222 goals were scored, that's an average of 2.64 per game, 723 by the home clubs and 499 by the away clubs.

Most goals: 68, Blackburn Rovers
Most home goals: 43, Oldham Athletic
Most away goals: 30, Blackburn & Norwich
Least goals: 40, Arsenal
Least home goals: 17, Nott'm Forest
Least away goals: 15, Arsenal

Least goals conceded: 31, Man United
Least home goals conceded: 14, Man United
Least away goals conceded: 17, Man United
Most goals conceded: 74, Oldham Athletic
Most home goals conceded: 32, QPR
Most away goals conceded: 48, Middlesbrough

Highest goals aggregate: 137, Oldham Athletic
Lowest goals aggregate: 78, Arsenal

Best home record: 47pts, Man United
Best away record: 37pts, Man United
Worst home record: 22pts, Nott'm Forest
Worst away record: 7pts, Leeds United

Highest home score:
Blackburn Rovers 7 Norwich City 1, 3.10.92

Highest away scores:
Blackburn Rovers 2 Coventry City 5, 26.1.93
Manchester City 2 Everton 5, 8.5.93
Everton 3 Queen's Park Rangers 5, 12.4.93

GOALSCORERS & ATTENDANCES

LEADING SCORERS

(Including Cup & European games)

30 Ian Wright (Arsenal)
29 *Teddy Sheringham (Tottenham Hotspur)
24 Les Ferdinand (Queen's Park Rangers)
22 *Mick Quinn (Coventry City)
22 Alan Shearer (Blackburn Rovers)
21 *Mark Bright (Sheffield Wednesday)
21 Mike Newell (Blackburn Rovers)
21 Ian Rush (Liverpool)
20 Brian Deane (Sheffield United)
19 Lee Chapman (Leeds United)
19 *Craig Hignett (Middlesbrough)
19 Dean Holdsworth (Wimbledon)
19 David White (Manchester City)
18 *Dean Saunders (Aston Villa)
18 Matthew Le Tissier (Southampton)
18 Paul Warhurst (Sheffield Wednesday)
17 *Chris Armstrong (Crystal Palace)
17 *Eric Cantona (Manchester United)
17 Chris Kiwomya (Ipswich Town)
16 David Hirst (Sheffield Wednesday)
16 Mark Hughes (Manchester United)
16 Mark Robins (Norwich City)
16 Paul Wilkinson (Middlesbrough)
*Includes goals for other clubs

Most Goals in a Match:
3 Eric Cantona (Leeds) v Spurs, 25.8.92
3 Mark Robins (Norwich) v Oldham, 9.11.92
3 John Hendrie (M'boro) v Blackburn, 5.12.92
3 Andy Sinton (QPR) v Everton, 28.12.92
3 Brian Deane (Sheff. U.) v Ipswich, 16.1.93
3 Teddy Sheringham (Spurs) v Leeds, 20.2.93
3 Les Ferdinand (QPR) v Nottm F., 10.4.93
3 Gordon Strachan (Leeds) v B'burn, 10.4.93
3 Les Ferdinand (QPR) v Everton, 12.4.93
3 Chris Bart-Williams (S.Wed) v Soton, 12.4.93
3 Chris Sutton (Norwich) v Leeds, 14.4.93
3 Mark Walters (L'pool) v Coventry, 17.4.93
3 Matthew Le Tissier (Soton) v Oldham, 8.5.93
3 Rod Wallace (Leeds) v Coventry, 8.5.93

THE GATE LEAGUE

	Best	Average
Liverpool	44,619	37,009
Manchester United	40,447	35,132
Aston Villa	39,063	29,594
Leeds United	34,166	29,228
Tottenham Hotspur	33,707	27,878
Sheffield Wednesday	38,688	27,264
Manchester City	37,136	24,698
Arsenal	29,739	24,403
Nottingham Forest	26,752	21,910
Everton	35,826	20,457
Blackburn Rovers	20,305	16,248
Sheffield United	30,039	18,801
Chelsea	34,464	18,754
Ipswich Town	22,093	18,185
Middlesbrough	24,172	16,724
Norwich City	20,610	16,254
Crystal Palace	30,115	15,726
Southampton	19,654	15,148
Queen's Park Rangers	21,117	15,002
Coventry City	24,429	14,995
Oldham Athletic	17,106	12,864
Wimbledon	30,115	8,391

Highest Attendance:
44,619 Liverpool v Everton, 20.3.93

Lowest Attendance:
3,039 Wimbledon v Everton, 26.1.93

PONTIN'S LEAGUE DIVISION ONE TABLE

	P	W	D	L	F	A	Pts
Aston Villa	34	21	8	5	64	32	71
Nottingham Forest	34	20	8	6	77	46	68
Blackburn Rovers	34	18	10	6	60	37	64
Leeds United	34	15	8	11	59	44	53
Bolton Wanderers	34	15	8	11	48	49	53
Manchester United	34	13	13	8	58	50	52
Liverpool	34	13	10	11	47	43	49
Sheffield Wednesday	34	13	10	11	51	48	49
Leicester City	34	12	12	10	42	38	48
Wolverhampton W.	34	13	6	15	46	55	45
Notts County	34	12	8	14	56	52	44
Newcastle United	34	12	7	15	36	43	43
Sheffield United	34	10	10	14	54	59	40
Sunderland	34	11	6	17	57	57	39
Barnsley	34	9	11	14	48	58	38
Stoke City	34	8	8	18	38	56	32
Manchester City	34	7	9	18	34	68	30
Rotherham United	34	5	6	23	29	69	21

THE F.A. PREMIER LEAGUE

HIGHEST AND LOWEST

Highest home attendance:
39,063 v Manchester United, 7.11.92
Lowest home attendance:
17,120 v Crystal Palace, 5.9.92
Highest away attendance:
40,826 v Liverpool, 9.1.93
Lowest away attendance:
6,849 v Wimbledon, 3.10.92

Biggest victory:
5-1 v Middlesbrough (home), 17.1.93
Heaviest defeat:
0-3 v Coventry (away), 26.12.92
0-3 v Blackburn Rovers (away), 21.4.93

Most goals in a match:
2 Garry Parker v Sheff. Utd. (a) 29.8.92
2 Dean Saunders v Liverpool (h), 19.9.92
2 Dean Saunders v M'brough (a), 26.9.92
2 Dean Saunders v Wimbledon (a), 3.10.92
2 Dalian Atkinson v Sheffield W. (a), 5.12.92
2 Dean Saunders v Bristol R. FAC (a), 20.1.93
2 Dwight Yorke v Sheffield W. (h), 20.3.93

Most goals against:
2, Chris Kiwomya (Ipswich, CCC), 2.12.92
2, Mick Quinn (Coventry), 26.12.92
2, Mike Newell (Blackburn), 21.4.93

Clean sheets: 18
Failed to score: 13

Villa scored first: 31
Scored first and won: 21
Scored first and drew: 8
Scored first and lost: 2

Opponents scored first: 16
Lost after opponents scored first: 10
Drew after opponents scored first: 2
Won after opponents scored first: 4

Highest League position: 1st
Lowest League position: 16th

SEQUENCE RECORDS

Most matches undefeated:
13, Sep 5 - Nov 21
Most home matches undefeated:
14, Dec 2 - Apr 18
Most away matches undefeated:
8, Aug 29 - Dec 15
Most wins in succession:
5, Sep 19 - Oct 7
Most home wins in succession:
4, Jan 27 - Feb 27
Most away wins in succession:
3, Sep 23 - Oct 3
Longest run without a win:
4, Aug 15 - Aug 25
Longest run without a home win:
3, Aug 19 - Sep 2
Longest run without an away win:
3, Dec 15 -26 and Jan 30 - Feb 10
Most defeats in succession: 3
Goals for in successive matches:
9, Aug 29 - Oct 7
Goals against in successive matches:
7, Nov 28 - Dec 26
Longest run without scoring:
242 minutes, Jan 27 - Feb 6
Longest run without conceding a goal:
449 minutes, Oct 24 - Nov 28
Most consecutive appearances:
102, Kevin Richardson, 2 full seasons. Other
ever-presents (51 games) in 1992/93 were
Earl Barrett and Steve Staunton.

DEBUTANTS

Four players made their Villa first team
debuts (Ray Houghton, Frank McAvennie,
Dean Saunders and Dave Farrell) compared
to 19 last term.

EARLY BATH!

The only player sent off in a Villa match was
Bristol Rovers' Billy Clark, in the FA Cup
replay at Twerton Park.

SUSPENSIONS

Two Villa players served suspensions during the season. Shaun Teale missed the home game with Manchester City after passing the disciplinary points limit with a booking at Nottingham Forest. Mark Bosnich was sent off playing for the reserves at Forest and was unfortunate that his ban started after returning to the first team at Sheffield Wednesday.

QUICK OFF THE MARK

Dwight Yorke scored Villa's fastest goals of the season after 3 minutes of the home games with Wimbledon and Sheffield Wednesday. The earliest goal conceded was from Crystal Palace's Bobby Bowry after 8 minutes.

HOLTE v WITTON

Of the 64 goals scored at Villa Park 34 were netted at the Holte End (26 for Villa, 8 against) and 30 at the Witton End (17 for, 13 against).

Villa kicked towards the Witton End in the first half on 20 occasions, winning 12, drawing 6 and losing 2.

On the 6 occasions Villa attacked the Holte End first, 3 games were won, 2 drawn and 1 lost.

PENALTIES

There were just 5 penalties, 3 scored and 2 saved:

Game	Mins	Taker v Goalkeeper	Outcome
v Arsenal (h)	41	**Dean Saunders** v David Seaman	Goal
v Bristol Rovers (h)	51	**Dean Saunders** v Gavin Kelly	Saved
v Bristol Rovers (a)	28	**Ray Houghton** v Gavin Kelly	Saved
v Everton (h)	24	Peter Beardsley v **Mark Bosnich**	Goal
v Man City (h)	67	**Garry Parker** v Tony Coton	Goal

There was also, of course, the FA Cup penalty shoot-out at Wimbledon (see page 74) which Villa lost 6-5.

0-15 mins   16-30 mins   31-45 mins   46-60 mins   61-75 mins   76-90 mins

GOAL TIMES

The last half hour proved Villa's most productive in terms of goals scored, with the last 15 minutes the period when most were conceded, as our goal chart (above) shows.

Nottingham Forest's Roy Keane was the only visiting player to score in the first 15 minutes at Villa Park.

● *This statistical review of 1992-93 covers all of the 51 League, FA Cup and League Cup games played.*

SCORELINES

1-0 wins - 7
2-0 wins - 4
3-0 wins - 2
2-1 wins - 6
3-1 wins - 2
5-1 wins - 1
3-2 wins - 2
4-2 wins - 1
0-0 draws - 5
1-1 draws - 9
2-2 draws - 1
0-1 defeats - 5
0-2 defeats - 1
0-3 defeats - 2
1-2 defeats - 1
1-3 defeats - 1
2-3 defeats - 1

PONTIN'S CENTRAL LEAGUE *All home games played at Walsall's Bescot Stadium*

Aug	17	H	Wolverhampton W.	3-0	Gillhaus 2, McAvennie
	26	A	Manchester United	0-0	-
	29	A	Liverpool	2-5	Carruthers, Crisp
Sept	3	H	Stoke City	2-1	Blake, McAvennie
	16	A	Notts County	1-1	Ehiogu
	30	H	Barnsley	1-0	Fenton
Oct	10	A	Sheffield United	1-0	Ehiogu
	14	A	Bolton Wanderers	0-1	-
	21	H	Manchester City	4-2	Farrell 2, Blake, Yorke
	28	A	Sunderland	0-0	-
Nov	2	H	Leeds United	2-0	Fenton, Williams
	9	A	Leicester City	1-1	Beinlich
	18	H	Rotherham United	3-0	Breitkreutz, Beinlich, Davis
	25	A	Nottingham Forest	3-3	Ehiogu, Cox, Yorke
Dec	16	H	Sheffield Wednesday	2-1	Breitkreutz 2
Jan	6	H	Notts County	3-1	Beinlich 2, Davis
	11	A	Leeds United	2-0	Berry, Farrell
	21	A	Stoke City	3-0	Beinlich 2, Davis
	30	H	Manchester United	1-2	Fenton
Feb	5	A	Blackburn Rovers	1-0	Davis
	9	A	Wolverhampton W.	1-0	Carruthers
	24	A	Barnsley	2-0	Blake, Carruthers
Mar	3	H	Sheffield United	3-1	Larsen, Carruthers, Berry
	11	H	Leicester City	3-3	Regis, Carruthers, Own Goal
	17	A	Newcastle United	0-0	-
	31	H	Nottingham Forest	1-3	Carruthers
Apr	7	A	Rotherham United	1-0	Carruthers
	13	A	Sheffield Wednesday	2-2	Parker, Breitkreutz
	20	H	Blackburn Rovers	4-1	Cox 2, Beinlich, Farrell
	24	H	Liverpool	2-1	Carruthers, Farrell
	28	H	Sunderland	3-1	Beinlich 2, Carruthers
May	4	A	Manchester City	5-0	Ehiogu 2, Carruthers 2, Cox
	6	H	Newcastle United	1-0	Ehiogu
	12	H	Bolton Wanderers	1-2	Blake

BIRMINGHAM SENIOR CUP

Nov	11	A	Boldmere S.M. (Rnd 2)	7-0	Davis 2, Crisp, Berry, Fenton, Regis, Cox
Dec	7	A	Wolves (Rnd 3)	3-2	Davis 2, Farrell
Jan	19	A	Nuneaton Bor. (Rnd 4)	2-3	Fenton 2

Reserves win championship

Skipper Ugo Uhiogu was the goalscoring hero as the Reserves went one better than the first team and claimed the Central League title for the first time in 29 years with a 1-0 home win over Newcastle on May 6.

Their exciting and successful exploits for home fixtures were staged at Walsall's Bescot Stadium in order to protect the Villa Park playing surface.

"It must augur very well for the future that our first and second teams can be in the top two of their respective leagues," said chairman Doug Ellis.

"Apart from two or three members of the squad all of the Reserve team are under-21 years of age, a very healthy sign."

The young team, featuring a host of players who are knocking on the first team door, won the title in style leaving such clubs as Nottingham Forest, Blackburn Rovers, Leeds and Manchester United trailing behind.

Like the first team the Reserves had a cosmopolitan look with such players as the Pole Dariusz Kubicki, the two Germans Matthias Breitkreutz and Stefan Beinlich, West Indian Dwight Yorke and the Dane Henrik Larsen enhancing the squad at various times.

Kubicki, Larsen and Yorke are full internationals while, early in the season, the side also featured internationals Frank McAvennie (Scotland) and Hans Gilhaus (Holland) who were on trial with Villa.

Four of the Reserves won England Under-21 honours - Ehiogu, Bryan Small, Neil Cox and Mark Blake while goalkeeper Michael Oakes was a squad member awaiting his first cap.

The Youth team also made fine progress with some outstanding displays in the Midland Purity Youth League.

During the season Colin Clarke took over as coach in succession to Richard Money who became manager of Scunthorpe.

The youth scheme has continued to flourish under the supervision of the club's Director of Youth, Dave Richardson.

A record number of twelve YTS apprentices have been engaged from July 1993 and Richardson, looking ahead to building on the first team's solid foundation for future years, pointed out: "This is probably as well-balanced a group as we have had for a while.

"They have got a fair bit to learn but the potential is there. This intake has not arrived by magic, it is a reflection of the work done by the scouts and coaches during the last three years."

Aston Villa's future is clearly in very good hands.

Reserve team skipper Ugo Ehiogu with the Central League trophy

MIDLAND PURITY YOUTH LEAGUE

Aug	15	H	**Birmingham City**	5-1	King (pen), Harrison 2, Cowe, D.Pearce
	22	A	Coventry City	2-3	D.Pearce 2
	29	H	**Derby County**	3-4	D.Pearce, C.Pearce, Harrison
Sept	5	A	Grimsby Town	3-0	Harrison 2, Own Goal
	12	H	**Leicester City**	1-0	P.Browne
	19	A	Lincoln City	4-0	King, C.Pearce, Finney, Wiltshire
Oct	3	A	Northampton Town	3-4	Cowe, C.Pearce, D.Pearce
	10	H	**Notts County**	2-0	Cowe 2
	17	A	Nottingham Forest	1-4	Berry
	30	A	Port Vale	0-1	-
Nov	7	A	Leicester City	2-1	Cowe, D.Pearce
	14	H	**Shrewsbury Town**	1-2	Aston
	21	A	Stoke City	4-1	Harrison 2, Evans, Cowe
Dec	11	H	**Peterborough Utd.**	2-0	Harrison, C.Pearce
	19	H	**Wolverhampton W.**	2-1	Cowe, C.Pearce
Jan	9	A	Birmingham City	0-1	-
	23	A	Shrewsbury Town	2-0	Scimeca, Harrison
	30	A	Derby County	0-4	-
Feb	6	H	**Grimsby Town**	1-0	C.Pearce
	13	H	**Lincoln City**	1-1	Cowe
	20	A	Mansfield Town	2-2	Scimeca, P.Browne
	27	H	**Northampton Town**	6-0	Aston 3, Scimeca, P.Browne, Farrelly
Mar	6	A	Notts County	1-2	Cowe
	13	H	**Walsall**	1-2	P.Browne
	20	H	**Nottingham Forest**	0-1	-
	23	H	**Coventry City**	1-2	Cowe
	27	A	Peterborough United	3-0	Berry 2, King
Apr	2	H	**Port Vale**	1-1	Cowe
	16	H	**Stoke City**	2-0	Scimeca 2
	24	A	Walsall	7-0	Cowe 2, D.Pearce, Henderson, Aston, Scimeca, Byfield
	30	A	Wolverhampton W.	2-0	Aston, Scimeca
May	1	A	West Bromwich Albion	3-0	P.Browne, Aston, Scimeca
	8	H	**Mansfield Town**	0-0	-
	12	H	**West Bromwich A.**	0-3	

FA YOUTH CUP

Nov	3	A	Nottingham F. (Rnd 1)	2-4	Berry, Harrison

SOUTHERN JUNIOR FLOODLIT CUP

Oct	13	A	Southend Utd. (Rnd 1)	2-1	P.Browne 2
Nov	23	A	Leyton Orient (Rnd 2)	2-3	C.Pearce, Wiltshire

MIDLAND YOUTH CUP

Sept	21	A	Stoke City (Prelim Rnd)	2-4	Cowe 2

MIDLAND PURITY YOUTH LEAGUE CUP

Oct	24	H	B'ham City (Rnd 2)	1-3	P.Browne

RESERVE & YOUTH TEAM APPEARANCES

	CENTRAL LGE		SENIOR CUP		YOUTH LGE		YOUTH CUPS	
	Apps	Gls	Apps	Gls	Apps	Gls	Apps	Gls
Lee ASTON	-	-	-	-	11 (10)	7	- (1)	-
Stefan BEINLICH	22	9	1	-	-	-	-	-
Trevor BERRY	17 (1)	2	3	1	9	3	4	1
Mark BLAKE	23	4	-	-	-	-	-	-
Paul BLENKINSHIP	-	-	-	-	18	-	2	-
Chris BODEN	18 (4)	-	3	-	-	-	-	-
Mark BOSNICH	16	-	-	-	-	-	-	-
Matthias BREITKREUTZ	31	4	-	-	-	-	-	-
Ian BROWN	-	-	-	-	18 (2)	-	1	-
Paul BROWNE	4 (1)	-	2	-	30	5	5	3
Martin CARRUTHERS	20 (2)	11	-	-	-	-	-	-
Steven COWE	- (1)	-	- (2)	-	29	13	5	2
Neil COX	21 (1)	4	1	1	-	-	-	-
Richard CRISP	10 (6)	1	2	1	-	-	-	-
Tony DALEY	1	-	-	-	-	-	-	-
Neil DAVIS	11 (9)	4	3	4	-	-	-	-
Ugo EHIOGU	29	6	1	-	-	-	-	-
Darren EVANS	1	-	3	-	31	1	5	-
Dave FARRELL	15 (8)	5	3	1	-	-	-	-
Gareth FARRELLY	-	-	-	-	10 (1)	1	3	-
Graham FENTON	11 (5)	3	3	3	-	-	-	-
Nicki FINNEY	-	-	-	-	12 (6)	1	2 (1)	-
Stephen FROGGATT	2	-	-	-	-	-	-	-
Garry HARRISON	-	-	-	-	26	9	5	1
Ian KING	-	-	-	-	12	3	1	-
Dariusz KUBICKI	32	-	-	-	-	-	-	-
Henrik LARSEN	13	1	-	-	-	-	-	-
Glen LIVINGSTONE	-	-	1	-	-	-	-	-
John MURPHY	-	-	-	-	21 (5)	-	3	-
Michael OAKES	11	-	2	-	-	-	-	-
Garry PARKER	1	1	-	-	-	-	-	-
Chris PEARCE	-	-	-	-	29	6	5	1
Dennis PEARCE	-	-	1 (1)	-	32	7	5	-
Mark PUGH	-	-	-	-	11	-	2 (1)	-
Adam RACHEL	-	-	-	-	12	-	3	-
Cyrille REGIS	8	1	1	1	-	-	-	-
Riccardo SCIMECA	-	-	- (1)	-	18	8	-	-
Les SEALEY	1	-	-	-	-	-	-	-
Bryan SMALL	23	-	-	-	-	-	-	-
Nigel SPINK	5	-	-	-	-	-	-	-
Lee WILLIAMS	11 (9)	1	1	-	-	-	-	-
John WILTSHIRE	-	-	-	-	11 (5)	1	2 (1)	1
Dwight YORKE	8	2	-	-	-	-	-	-
Own Goals	-	1	-	-	-	1	-	-

Also played for the reserves (All triallists except Thomas, who was on loan from Birmingham City):
Christian Beeck 1 app (Lge); Steve Donnelly 1 app (Cup); Hans Gillhaus 1 app, 2 goals (Lge); Frank McAvennie 3 apps, 2 goals (Lge); Joe McGuinness 1 app (Lge), 1 app (Cup); Tommy Staunton 1 app (Lge); Martin Thomas 1 app (Lge).

Also played for the youth team (triallists/schoolboys):
Brock 4 apps (Lge); Burchell 2 (1) (Lge); Buxall -(1) (Lge); Byfield 1(4), 1 gl (Lge); M.Davis 2 (Lge); B.Henderson 8(3), 1 gl (Lge); I.Henderson 1 (Lge); Hendry 4(1) (Lge); Hynes -(1) (Lge); McLaughlin -(1) (Lge); Mitchell 1 (1) (Lge); Moore 2(4) (Lge); Petty 1 (Lge); Ryan 1 (Lge); Scally 1 (Lge); Senior 1(1) (Lge); Williams 5 (Lge), 2 (Cup).

VILLA'S ALL-TIME LEAGUE RECORD

Season	Div	Teams	Pos	P	W	D	L	F	A	W	D	L	F	A	Pts	Cup Honours
1888-89	1	12	2nd	22	10	0	1	44	16	2	5	4	17	27	29	*(FAC Winners in 1886-87)*
1889-90	1	12	8th	22	6	2	3	30	15	1	3	7	13	36	19	
1890-91	1	12	9th	22	5	4	2	29	18	2	0	9	16	40	18	
1891-92	1	14	4th	26	10	0	3	63	23	5	0	8	26	33	30	*FAC Runners-up*
1892-93	1	16	4th	30	12	1	2	50	24	4	2	9	23	38	35	
1893-94	**1**	**16**	**1st**	**30**	**12**	**2**	**1**	**49**	**13**	**7**	**4**	**4**	**35**	**29**	**44**	
1894-95	1	16	3rd	30	12	2	1	51	12	5	3	7	31	31	39	*FAC Winners*
1895-96	**1**	**16**	**1st**	**30**	**14**	**1**	**0**	**47**	**17**	**6**	**4**	**5**	**31**	**28**	**45**	
1896-97	**1**	**16**	**1st**	**30**	**10**	**3**	**2**	**36**	**16**	**11**	**2**	**2**	**37**	**22**	**47**	*FAC Winners*
1897-98	1	16	6th	30	12	1	2	47	21	2	4	9	14	30	33	
1898-99	**1**	**18**	**1st**	**34**	**15**	**2**	**0**	**58**	**13**	**4**	**5**	**8**	**18**	**27**	**45**	
1899-00	**1**	**18**	**1st**	**34**	**12**	**4**	**1**	**45**	**18**	**10**	**2**	**5**	**32**	**17**	**50**	
1900-01	1	18	15th	34	8	5	4	32	18	2	5	10	13	33	30	*FAC Semi-finalists*
1901-02	1	18	8th	34	9	5	3	27	13	4	3	10	15	27	34	
1902-03	1	18	2nd	34	11	3	3	43	18	8	0	9	18	22	41	*FAC Semi-finalists*
1903-04	1	18	5th	34	13	1	3	41	16	4	6	7	29	32	41	
1904-05	1	18	4th	34	11	2	4	32	15	8	2	7	31	28	42	*FAC Winners*
1905-06	1	20	8th	38	13	2	4	51	19	4	4	11	21	37	40	
1906-07	1	20	5th	38	13	4	2	51	19	6	2	11	27	33	44	
1907-08	1	20	2nd	38	9	6	4	47	24	8	3	8	30	35	43	
1908-09	1	20	7th	38	8	7	4	31	22	6	3	10	27	34	38	
1909-10	**1**	**20**	**1st**	**38**	**17**	**2**	**0**	**62**	**19**	**6**	**5**	**8**	**22**	**23**	**53**	
1910-11	1	20	2nd	38	15	3	1	50	18	7	4	8	19	23	51	
1911-12	1	20	6th	38	12	2	5	48	22	5	5	9	28	41	41	
1912-13	1	20	2nd	38	13	4	2	57	21	6	8	5	29	31	50	*FAC Winners*
1913-14	1	20	2nd	38	11	3	5	36	21	8	3	8	29	29	44	*FAC Semi-finalists*
1914-15	1	20	13th	38	10	5	4	39	32	3	6	10	23	40	37	
First World War																
1919-20	1	22	9th	42	11	3	7	49	36	7	3	11	26	37	42	*FAC Winners*
1920-21	1	22	10th	42	11	4	6	39	21	7	3	11	24	49	43	
1921-22	1	22	5th	42	16	3	2	50	19	6	0	15	24	36	47	
1922-23	1	22	6th	42	15	3	3	42	11	3	7	11	22	40	46	
1923-24	1	22	6th	42	10	10	1	33	11	8	3	10	19	26	49	*FAC Runners-up*
1924-25	1	22	15th	42	10	7	4	34	25	3	6	12	24	46	39	
1925-26	1	22	6th	42	12	7	2	56	25	4	5	12	30	51	44	
1926-27	1	22	10th	42	11	4	6	51	34	7	3	11	30	49	43	
1927-28	1	22	8th	42	13	3	5	52	30	4	6	11	26	43	43	
1928-29	1	22	3rd	42	16	2	3	62	30	7	2	12	36	51	50	*FAC Semi-finalists*
1929-30	1	22	4th	42	13	1	7	54	33	8	4	9	38	50	47	
1930-31	1	22	2nd	42	17	3	1	86	34	8	6	7	42	44	59	
1931-32	1	22	5th	42	15	1	5	64	28	4	7	10	40	44	46	
1932-33	1	22	2nd	42	16	2	3	60	29	7	6	8	32	38	54	
1933-34	1	22	13th	42	10	5	6	45	34	4	7	10	33	41	40	*FAC Semi-finalists*
1934-35	1	22	13th	42	11	6	4	50	36	3	7	11	24	52	41	
1935-36	*1*	*22*	*21st*	*42*	*7*	*6*	*8*	*47*	*56*	*6*	*3*	*12*	*34*	*54*	*35*	
1936-37	2	22	9th	42	10	6	5	47	30	6	6	9	35	40	44	
1937-38	**2**	**22**	**1st**	**42**	**17**	**2**	**2**	**50**	**12**	**8**	**5**	**8**	**23**	**23**	**57**	*FAC Semi-finalists*
1938-39	1	22	12th	42	11	3	7	44	25	5	6	10	27	35	41	
Second World War																
1946-47	1	22	8th	42	9	6	6	39	24	9	3	9	28	29	45	
1947-48	1	22	6th	42	13	5	3	42	22	6	4	11	23	35	47	
1948-49	1	22	10th	42	10	6	5	40	36	6	4	11	20	40	42	
1949-50	1	22	12th	42	10	7	4	31	19	5	5	11	30	42	42	

SEASON-BY-SEASON

Season	Div	Teams	Pos	P	W	D	L	F	A	W	D	L	F	A	Pts	Cup Honours
1950-51	1	22	15th	42	9	6	6	39	29	3	7	11	27	39	37	
1951-52	1	22	6th	42	13	3	5	49	28	6	6	9	30	42	47	
1952-53	1	22	11th	42	9	7	5	36	23	5	6	10	27	38	41	
1953-54	1	22	13th	42	12	5	4	50	28	4	4	13	20	40	41	
1954-55	1	22	6th	42	11	3	7	38	31	9	4	8	34	42	47	
1955-56	1	22	20th	42	9	6	6	32	29	2	7	12	20	40	35	
1956-57	1	22	10th	42	10	8	3	45	25	4	7	10	20	30	43	*FAC Winners*
1957-58	1	22	14th	42	12	4	5	46	26	4	3	14	27	60	39	
1958-59	*1*	*22*	*21st*	*42*	*8*	*5*	*8*	*31*	*33*	*3*	*3*	*15*	*27*	*54*	*30*	*FAC Semi-finalists*
1959-60	2	22	1st	42	17	3	1	62	19	8	6	7	27	24	59	*FAC Semi-finalists*
1960-61	1	22	9th	42	13	3	5	48	28	4	6	11	30	49	43	*LC Winners*
1961-62	1	22	7th	42	13	5	3	45	20	5	3	13	20	36	44	
1962-63	1	22	15th	42	12	2	7	38	23	3	6	12	24	45	38	*LC Runners-up*
1963-64	1	22	19th	42	8	6	7	35	29	3	6	12	27	42	34	
1964-65	1	22	16th	42	14	1	6	36	24	2	4	15	21	58	37	*LC Semi-finalists*
1965-66	1	22	16th	42	10	3	8	39	34	5	3	13	30	46	36	
1966-67	1	22	21st	42	7	5	9	30	33	4	2	15	24	52	29	
1967-68	2	22	16th	42	10	3	8	35	30	5	4	12	19	34	37	
1968-69	2	22	18th	42	10	8	3	22	11	2	6	13	15	37	38	
1969-70	*2*	*22*	*21st*	*42*	*7*	*8*	*6*	*23*	*21*	*1*	*5*	*15*	*13*	*41*	*29*	
1970-71	3	24	4th	46	13	7	3	27	13	6	8	9	27	33	53	*LC Runners-up*
1971-72	**3**	**24**	**1st**	**46**	**20**	**1**	**2**	**45**	**10**	**12**	**5**	**6**	**40**	**22**	**70**	
1972-73	2	22	3rd	42	12	5	4	27	17	6	9	6	24	30	50	
1973-74	2	22	14th	42	8	9	4	33	21	5	6	10	15	24	41	
1974-75	2	22	2nd	42	16	4	1	47	6	9	4	8	32	26	58	*LC Winners*
1975-76	1	22	16th	42	11	8	2	32	17	0	9	12	19	42	39	
1976-77	1	22	4th	42	17	3	1	55	17	5	4	12	21	33	51	*LC Winners*
1977-78	1	22	8th	42	11	4	6	33	18	7	6	8	24	24	46	
1978-79	1	22	8th	42	8	9	4	37	26	7	7	7	22	23	46	
1979-80	1	22	7th	42	11	5	5	29	22	5	9	7	22	28	46	
1980-81	**1**	**22**	**1st**	**42**	**16**	**3**	**2**	**40**	**13**	**10**	**5**	**6**	**32**	**27**	**60**	
1981-82	1	22	11th	42	9	6	6	28	24	6	6	9	27	29	57	*EC Winners*
1982-83	1	22	6th	42	17	2	2	47	15	4	3	14	15	35	68	*ESC Winners*
1983-84	1	22	10th	42	14	3	4	34	22	3	6	12	25	39	60	*LC Semi-finalists*
1984-85	1	22	10th	42	10	7	4	34	20	5	4	12	26	40	56	
1985-86	1	22	16th	42	7	6	8	27	28	3	8	10	24	39	44	*LC Semi-finalists*
1986-87	*1*	*22*	*22nd*	*42*	*7*	*7*	*7*	*25*	*25*	*1*	*5*	*15*	*20*	*54*	*36*	
1987-88	2	23	2nd	44	9	7	6	31	21	13	5	4	37	20	78	
1988-89	1	20	17th	38	7	6	6	25	22	2	7	10	20	34	40	
1989-90	1	20	2nd	38	13	3	3	36	20	8	4	7	21	18	70	*FMC Area Finalists*
1990-91	1	20	17th	38	7	9	3	29	25	2	5	12	17	33	41	
1991-92	1	22	7th	42	13	3	5	31	16	4	6	11	17	28	60	
1992-93	P	22	2nd	42	13	5	3	36	16	8	6	7	21	24	74	

	P	W	D	L	F	A	Pts
Home	1851	1080	397	374	3930	2121	2683
Away	1851	498	439	914	2374	3375	1494
Total	3702	1578	836	1288	6304	5496	4177

FAC = FA Cup
LC = League Cup
FMC = Full Members' Cup
EC = European Champions' Cup
ESC = European Super Cup
Championship seasons highlighted in **bold** type, relegation seasons in *italics*.

2pts for a win up to season 1980-81
3pts for a win from season 1981-82

Other honours: World Club Championship runners-up 1982-83
FA Charity Shield joint winners 1981-82
FA Charity Shield runners-up 1910-11, 1957-58, 1972-73

VILLA'S ALL-TIME LEAGUE RECORD...

		Home					Away			
	P	W	D	L	F	A	W	D	L	F	A
Accrington Stanley	10	4	0	1	26	12	1	2	2	9	10
Arsenal	128	36	13	15	132	87	19	12	33	76	108
Barnsley	10	3	2	0	9	2	4	1	0	13	2
Birmingham City	96	23	13	12	82	60	16	12	20	68	74
Blackburn Rovers	122	33	17	11	135	81	17	11	33	85	132
Blackpool	62	16	9	6	65	39	10	7	14	44	51
Bolton Wanderers	126	34	15	14	137	81	15	13	35	64	126
Bournemouth	4	1	1	0	3	2	1	0	1	2	4
Bradford Park Avenue	10	4	0	1	12	4	1	2	2	8	16
Bradford City	28	9	2	3	32	12	4	4	6	17	23
Brentford	6	2	1	0	12	4	3	0	0	8	3
Brighton & Hove Albion	16	6	2	0	16	4	3	2	3	8	7
Bristol City	32	10	3	3	27	19	5	6	5	18	14
Bristol Rovers	8	3	1	0	8	3	2	1	1	4	4
Burnley	94	28	12	7	109	47	11	8	28	71	113
Bury	52	17	6	3	59	31	10	6	10	39	39
Cardiff City	44	14	3	5	39	20	8	2	12	23	30
Carlisle United	10	4	1	0	5	1	2	2	1	6	6
Charlton Athletic	38	10	6	3	41	18	5	6	8	22	33
Chelsea	92	25	12	9	100	67	15	8	23	58	71
Chesterfield	8	2	1	1	7	4	3	0	1	8	3
Coventry City	38	11	8	0	30	10	7	6	6	26	26
Crystal Palace	20	7	1	2	18	7	2	4	4	5	9
Darwen	4	2	0	0	16	0	1	1	0	6	2
Derby County	104	33	10	9	130	58	17	11	24	71	90
Doncaster Rovers	4	1	1	0	4	3	0	0	2	1	3
Everton	156	37	17	24	149	112	19	19	40	95	147
Fulham	34	8	5	4	30	22	2	5	10	20	34
Gillingham	2	1	0	0	2	1	0	1	0	0	0
Glossop	2	1	0	0	9	0	0	0	1	0	1
Grimsby Town	20	5	3	2	29	19	5	1	4	16	20
Halifax Town	4	1	1	0	2	1	1	0	1	2	2
Huddersfield Town	64	20	9	3	74	31	7	10	15	32	51
Hull City	16	4	3	1	21	8	2	2	4	7	12
Ipswich Town	36	10	6	2	38	16	3	4	11	17	29
Leeds United	58	13	9	7	51	40	6	10	13	31	51
Leicester City	66	17	5	11	69	48	6	8	19	47	86
Leyton Orient	10	4	1	0	8	3	1	2	2	3	6
Lincoln City	2	0	1	0	1	1	0	1	0	0	0
Liverpool	136	33	16	19	143	89	12	14	42	75	155
Luton Town	32	10	1	5	29	15	1	3	12	8	24

...CLUB BY CLUB

	P	Home W	D	L	F	A	Away W	D	L	F	A
Manchester City	118	32	17	10	113	65	14	14	31	77	112
Manchester United	120	31	15	14	129	88	10	13	37	60	128
Mansfield Town	4	0	0	2	0	2	0	1	1	1	3
Middlesbrough	102	29	9	13	120	59	17	14	20	66	78
Millwall	18	4	4	1	14	8	3	2	4	9	12
Newcastle United	110	31	12	12	114	58	12	9	34	73	120
Northampton Town	2	0	0	1	1	2	0	0	1	1	2
Norwich City	42	14	4	3	41	24	3	6	12	25	39
Nottingham Forest	100	32	9	9	105	50	15	14	21	71	95
Notts County	66	23	7	3	83	29	12	8	13	49	52
Oldham Athletic	28	9	3	2	33	6	7	5	2	28	16
Oxford United	14	4	2	1	9	3	1	3	3	8	11
Plymouth Argyle	14	5	1	1	19	9	2	2	3	12	12
Portsmouth	60	19	7	4	73	39	8	7	15	42	65
Port Vale	4	2	0	0	3	0	0	1	1	4	6
Preston North End	98	37	3	9	108	44	13	11	25	64	90
Queen's Park Rangers	32	5	4	7	22	22	3	2	11	12	24
Reading	4	2	0	0	4	2	2	0	0	7	3
Rochdale	4	2	0	0	3	0	0	1	1	1	2
Rotherham United	8	3	0	1	8	3	2	1	1	6	3
Scunthorpe United	2	1	0	0	5	0	1	0	0	2	1
Sheffield United	118	39	12	8	144	55	16	16	27	83	110
Sheffield Wednesday	114	42	6	9	147	57	14	7	36	81	126
Shrewsbury Town	6	3	0	0	6	0	1	1	1	4	4
Southampton	36	10	6	2	32	13	2	7	9	15	32
Stockport County	2	1	0	0	7	1	1	0	0	3	1
Stoke City	88	31	7	6	108	36	13	13	18	54	66
Sunderland	138	45	11	13	143	88	14	21	34	88	134
Swansea City	14	7	0	0	19	0	4	0	3	12	10
Swindon Town	8	2	1	1	5	5	1	2	1	4	3
Torquay United	4	1	0	1	5	2	0	1	1	2	3
Tottenham Hotspur	100	20	13	17	78	73	16	8	26	80	103
Tranmere Rovers	4	2	0	0	3	0	1	1	0	2	1
Walsall	4	0	2	0	0	0	0	1	1	1	4
Watford	12	3	2	1	11	6	0	2	4	9	16
West Bromwich Albion	124	39	8	15	118	74	19	15	28	86	99
West Ham United	60	17	4	9	65	41	4	9	17	38	75
Wimbledon	12	2	1	3	4	7	2	1	3	7	8
Wolverhampton Wan.	96	26	10	12	109	64	15	12	21	67	86
Wrexham	4	1	0	1	5	4	2	0	0	5	2
York City	4	2	0	0	5	0	1	1	0	2	1

SUBSCRIBERS ROLL CALL

1 Neil Gallagher
2 Jim 'CCTC' Flint
3 Pamela Harris
4 Suzanne Michelle French
5 Paul Simon Waterfield
6 Mick Brown
7 Karen Jeffery
8 Mr J. R. Onyon
9 David Hodges
10 David Bridgewater
11 Pamela Bridgewater
12 Philip Gray
13 Steven Coates
14 Robert Edward Garratt
15 Mr Andrew Harris
16 Richard Cushenan
17 Gregory Upton
18 Tony Broadhurst
19 Michael Louis Wilde
20 Robert Hughes
21 Peter Harold
22 Nigel Follos
23 Harry Follos
24 Adrian Dawson
25 J. T. O'Brien
26 Colin J. Lydon
27 Frank McNally
28 Nicholas Goff
29 Dean Strange
30 David Aston
31 John Walsh
32 Brett Rotheroe
33 Mike Ruston
34 Anthony J. Beaman
35 Kim Sykes
36 Richard Allen
37 Carol Maguire
38 Tim Farazmand
39 David Nicholson
40 Lesley J. Meacham
41 Andrew Clark
42 Philip R. Haynes
43 Kevin Lowbridge
44 Gary Blyth
45 Terry, Richard, Alex
   & Katie Penny
46 Joanne Dacosta
47 Rob Bedington
48 Gregory Hayes
49 Anthony Lee Harper
50 Graham J. Sutton

51 Brian Flanagan
52 Tim Bradley
53 Mr Nigel Iwanski
54 P. J. Connaughton
55 Leslie James Odley
56 Darren Woodfield
57 Ivan McDouall
58 The Kimberley Family
59 Rob Rodway
60 John Michael Derry
61 Calum Dewar
62 Eustace Smith
63 Robert F. Rea
64 Edward McNeill
65 Brian William Hughes
66 Kevin Buttery
67 Mr Philip John Shakespeare
68 Brenda Perkins
69 D. S. Mitchell
70 Stephen Dickens
71 Adam France
72 Aston Villa Colclough
73 B.R. Fitter
74 T. A. Fitter
75 P. T. Reeves
76 Martyn C. Thomas
77 David Barrett
78 Louise Bowdler
79 Andrew Boynton
80 Guy Eden
81 Stephen Adrian Mann
82 Stuart Bailey
83 Peter Perrins
84 Phillip Bagnall
85 John A. Gould (1934)
86 Gary Walden
87 Robin D. Wilkes
88 Ian R. Shave
89 Brian C. Seadon
90 T. Woollatt
91 Jackson Hunt
92 Stephen Holbeche
93 Jan Ibrahim
94 Simon Blake
95 Robert H. Perry
96 Christopher John Reed
97 Mr C. P. Dickens
98 Carl Thornton
99 Paul Tierney
100 Stephen Knott
101 Ian Harris

102 Alan Bennett
103 Sophie Edwards
104 Louise Morrell
105 Dayle Biddulph
106 Adaya Monique Henry
107 Joseff Aeron Fletcher
108 Georgie Boothroyd
109 John K. Knowles
110 Jonathan Betts
111 Junior Upton
112 G. M. Howard
113 R. M. Howard
114 Paul Joiner
115 Tim Allcott
116 Russell Simpson
117 Kim New
118 Paul Jones
119 Andrew Gibbons
120 Richard Bolger
121 Nicholas & Michael Heaven
122 Rob Smith
123 F. E. Oldham
124 Jule
125 Adrian Thorne
126 Mark Simkin
127 Richard R. Carter
128 Bobby Mendonca
129 Campbell Wiseman
130 Andrew James Harper
131 Ian Tetsill
132 Mark H. Whitehouse
133 Alan Robert Wilkinson
134 Lee Adams
135 Paul Desmond Brittain
136 Andrew Oakes
137 Michele & Clive Platman
138 Warren H. McDivitt
139 Richard Winter
140 Stuart T. Swann
141 Steven Duff
142 Mark Glyn Jones
143 Martin Andrew Bird
144 Esther & Ray Rawlings
145 Siân Nolan
146 Mark Pearce
147 R. Pearson
148 Mr Philip R. Jones
149 Bernard R. Bemand
150 John Crouch
151 Chad Weaver
152 Mr A. Seal

SUBSCRIBERS ROLL CALL

153 Neil Harrison	204 Daniel Stefan O'Gorman	255 Kathleen Wendy Brookin
154 Mrs S. M. Scott	205 David Colin Bird	256 Leni D. Ward
155 Rod Snelson	206 Martin Jones	257 Ronald W. Perkins
156 Simon K. Green	207 Mick & Darren Wilkins	258 Norman Stinchcombe
157 John Ward	208 John Lynch	259 Matthew Dale
158 Mark Hughes	209 Malcolm Taylor	260 Mrs Jane Hancox
159 Mark J. O'Neill	210 Benito De Rosa	261 Ralph Schulz
160 Greg Trappett	211 Andy Wale	262 Mr Charles Stephens
161 Mr I. Day	212 Brian Moloney	263 Scott Edward Wayne
162 Gordon Reynolds	213 Gary S. Winterton	264 Mr W. T. Chamberlain
163 Nicholas Casseldine	214 Adrian J. Mullis	265 Paul Harris
164 Jeff Corfield	215 Stefan Rance	266 Mr John Haynes
165 John Donohoe	216 Dougie Jones A.V.	267 David Peachey
166 Ian Humphreys	217 Richard Linley	268 Michael Butler
167 Christopher James Price	218 Andrew Webb	269 Daniel Perry
168 Mr M. K. Whorton	219 Vincent Cade	270 Andrew Burley
169 Neil Barrett	220 Alfred Hoe	271 Paul William Taylor
170 Andrew Archer	221 David Alan Ostojitsch	272 David John Edward Clayton
171 John Emerson	222 Craig Millard	273 Paul Roy Mosley
172 Derek Day	223 David Woodley	274 Caroline Burrill
173 Jonathan Muir	224 Wayne Lee Spencer	275 Kris Michael Hinde
174 Neil Humphreys	225 Mark Lewis	276 John Patrick Walsh
175 Colin Hough	226 Darran Boulter	277 Peter Brett
176 Wayne Beddoes	227 Beckie Drakeley	278 David Smith
177 Sidney Ronald Stokes	228 Peter Vale	279 Steve Loats
178 Peter Bishop	229 B. M. Dain	280 B. R. Veal
179 Elizabeth Medcraft	230 Robert M. Hyland	281 Andy Perry
180 Darren M. G. Wilkes	231 Elizabeth Britton	282 Darren Harness
181 William J. Mottram	232 Michele Willis	283 Dr L. I. Liebling
182 Marc Varnish	233 Dean Lewis Aston	284 James Leghorn
183 Clive W. Cross	234 Mr Paul Palmer	285 Wayne Titmus
184 Cormac Sheedy	235 Oliver Eagle	286 Graham Leslie Garvey
185 Darren Paul Hunt	236 Alan Bowdler	287 Jackie Mills
186 Nicholas Peter Taylor	237 Mark Thomas Randle	288 Simon Lawrie Turner
187 Simon Smith	238 John Frederick Walford	289 Paul Lyes
188 J. W. Smith	239 Kevin Murphy	290 A. L. Brusch
189 David Seabourne Snr.	240 W. Finney	291 P. W. Shakespeare
190 Anthony Hynes	241 Norman Hughes	292 John Hobbs
191 Steven John Smith	242 Susan Pudge	293 Mr Steve Buet
192 Ian Robert Culbert	243 K. A. Trethowan	294 Sidney Vale
193 Stephen Cullen	244 Philip Jennings	295 Mark Kenny
194 William Marron	245 Tony Spraggon	296 Thomas Jeffrey Green
195 Robert Gough	246 Keith & Graham Rickett	297 Simon Mark Wheeler
196 Martyn Bacchus	247 Gerard J. McGovern	298 Gilbert & Elaine McWhirter
197 K. W. Powell	248 Ken Noon	299 Dr Robert Tighe
198 Lee Yale	249 Paul Noon	300 Paul Edwards
199 Peter Aldridge	250 Peter Noon	301 Matthew Seymour
200 Ian Winter	251 Becky Willis	302 Craig Reading
201 Mr V. & Mrs A. Clements	252 Michael Ireland	303 Neil Byrne
202 David Bytheway	253 John Alan Dunn	304 Steve Hayward
203 Scott Miles	254 Neal Sawyer	305 Paul Cummins

306	Julian Smith	357	Leslie Woodhall	408	Alan Robinson
307	Mark Probin	358	Elaine Wardle	409	Tony A. Bill
308	Peter & Martin Hartshorne	359	Mike Jeffries	410	James Merrick
309	Steve Yeomans	360	Ron Jeffries	411	Robin Peck
310	David White	361	Philip Emonson	412	Sam Gamble
311	P. L. Day (Tenby)	362	Mark Goodwin	413	Robert Wilson
312	Jason Davis	363	Phil Wells	414	Luke Farrington
313	Pamela Wood	364	Geir-Morten Hansen	415	Mr C. J. England
314	Nicholas Leach	365	Miss Lisa Collins	416	Mr Paul Newbold
315	Ian Andrew Devey	366	Paul Jarvis	417	Paul Vultaggio
316	Kevin Portley	367	Scott Campbell	418	Keith Jones
317	Stephanie Thorpe	368	P. J. R. Griffiths	419	Sean Escritt
318	Matthew Lycett	369	Gavin Harris	420	Robert Taylor
319	Ian Levell	370	Robert Young	421	Andrew Taylor
320	Stephen Lloyd	371	Anthony Mullen	422	Steve Fletcher
321	Johnathon M. Barber	372	L. N. E. Barlow	423	Colin M. Spencer
322	Mario Menton	373	G. L. Burrows	424	S. R. Haywood
323	Nikki Long	374	Keith Puttick	425	Mark Ingram
324	Paul Perry	375	Paul Kenna	426	Julie Harrison
325	Paul Fitzpatrick	376	Chris Jameson	427	James Close
326	Mr Stephen Tovey	377	Mark Keylock	428	Tony C. Dacey
327	Simon Rawlins	378	C. R. Aldous	429	Russell Adam Higgins
328	Matt J. P. Dolton	379	Gareth Stokes	430	James Marcantonio
329	Edward Mills	380	Dave Skinner	431	Andrew Cole
330	Andrew Simms	381	Gido Kirfel	432	Brian Thomas Berry
331	Anne Edwards	382	Mr M. J. Parker	433	Debbie Hinks
332	Keith Andrew Birch	383	Charles John Williams	434	Roger Wooldridge
333	Nigel Thompson	384	R. H. Rose	435	Graham Wooldridge
334	Matthew Jones	385	James Michael Deeley	436	Alan Bobbett
335	Russell Poulton	386	Steven McCabe	437	Rikki Martin Ravenhill
336	Adrian J. Hill	387	R. A. J. Butler	438	Baily Martin Ravenhill
337	Robert & Liza Giles	388	David Smart	439	Scott Anthony Whitehouse
338	Christine & Ian Rossiter	389	Joanne Gaitskell	440	Mr H. G. Harrison
339	Robert D. Peach	390	Alexander David Smith	441	Nigel Leaver
340	Andy Downes	391	Mr B. Baxter	442	Mark J. Downes
341	J. Thornley	392	Mr D. Baxter	443	David Ball
342	David William Scriven	393	Sue & Mick Tilt	444	A. J. Breckles
343	Joanne & Mark Weetman	394	Paul Jones	445	Alan Norton
344	Jason Cooke	395	Richard Chester	446	Alice McPake
345	Stephen Sturman	396	Louise J. Mullany	447	W. H. J. Ward
346	David & Peter Hitchman	397	Kate Williams	448	Barrie Bailey
347	James Edkins	398	Robert Taylor	449	Anthony Woolley
348	Simon Smith	399	Mary Knowles	450	Damian Barrow
349	Mark Smith	400	J. A. Reynolds	451	T. G. Ashington
350	Kieran Robert Hand	401	Paul Rostance	452	Steve Pritchard
351	Shaun Patrick Hand	402	Anita Glaudot	453	M. A. Foley
352	Bob Nicholls	403	Mick Hinton	454	Clive Goodman
353	Clive Nicholls	404	Gary Beale	455	Martin Lockley
354	Chris Paling	405	Jim McDonald	456	Martell Beckford (10)
355	Andy Sinclair	406	James C. Layne	457	Mathew Kendrick
356	Kevin A. Williams	407	Ralph Willis	458	John Slim

SUBSCRIBERS ROLL CALL

459 Michael Price	509 Gareth Marsh	560 John Leader
460 Sam Jones	510 Simon Daykin	561 David Brueton
461 David Partridge	511 David Allan Jones	562 Guy Spreadbury
462 Keith Johnstone	512 Tony Shanley	563 Martin Greenslade
463 Michael Knight	513 Oliver Richardson	564 Jonathan Clucas
464 Marcus Somerfield	514 Craig Winstone	565 Martin Jenkins
465 Mr S. James-Dyke	515 Clive Foster	566 W. Baylis
466 Graeme B. Reid	516 Gary Foster	567 Miss Kayleigh Rogers
467 Tom Holland (The Guard)	517 Paul, Jenny & Lucy Bailey	568 Paul Hatch
468 Ian McGivern	518 John Ball	569 Alexander Kasperczyk
469 Glyn Barlow	519 Derek Michael Ford	570 Mr Kevin Williams
470 Richard Lee Goodwin	520 Alex D. Rowley	571 C. J. Whitaker
471 C. J. Riordan	521 Joanne Barber	572 Jordan Trouth
472 Richard Jones	522 Theresa Donner	573 Steve Todd
473 Michelle A. McDonough	523 Jon Owen	574 Anthony Ellis
474 David Tiller	524 L. & S. Carter	575 Sue Smith
475 John & Craig Harris	525 Martin Weaver	576 David I. Phillips
476 Malcolm Bache	526 Craig Harrison	577 Kevin Whittick
477 Roy Brandreth	527 Martin Primmer	578 Darren Gidman Hassall
478 Maurice Mackie	528 Trevor John Baker	579 Miss Julie McGregor
479 Shaun Plant	529 Adrian Spray	580 Scott Wheeldon
480 John Peter Reidy	530 David Clarkson	581 Christopher Hartshorne
481 R. M. Noott	531 Jim Stelfox	582 Ted Baxter
482 Terry Wright	532 Mr Roy M. Peters	583 Brendan Shields
483 Stephen R. Palmer	533 John Cartlidge	584 Gary Potter
484 Aston Villa,	534 Mark Griffiths	585 David Bray
Police Liaison Officer	535 Mark & Jason Varley	586 John Millward
485 Master James Cookson	536 Oliver Tate	587 Maria Ganner
486 Charles R. J. Clarke	537 Raymond Warr	588 Sheila A Collins
487 Dave Buet	538 Keith G. Wilkinson	589 Daniel Ray
488 Frank Francies	539 D. P. Shipley	590 Derek Anthony Price
489 Raymond Craig	540 Roger Levicki	591 M. E. C. Wilson
490 Rebecca Craig	541 Tim Levicki	592 Samuel Wetson
491 Roy A. Foster	542 Andrew Levicki	593 Matthew Evans
492 David L. Astley	543 David Higgins	594 Rachel Farrell
493 Michael Newill	544 Talia Homer	595 Paul John Hinckley
494 Mr S. R. Hill	545 Ciaran F. Nixon	596 Carl Morton
495 David Spencer	546 Michael A. Birch	597 Harry W. McDivitt
496 Robert Bell	547 Peter Rodgers	598 Stephen Delaney
497 Jason Marshall	548 Peter John Tennant	599 James W. Johnstone
498 Peter J. Davies	549 Tom Kirk	600 David Pinner
499 Phillip Hunt	550 Mr R. M. Daniels	601 George Johnson
500 Jamie Cash	551 Gary Adams	602 Geoffrey Wright
501 Brian J. Maybury	552 Thomas Johansson	603 Mrs Jane Dainty
502 Christopher Calder	553 Reine Bladh	604 H. John De Saulles
503 Tracy Haines	554 Martin Lockley	605 Richard Ian Stait
504 Kevin Gledhill	555 Stephanie Clay	606 Sheena Meredith
505 Peter Gledhill	556 Tina Clay	607 Wendy Blizard
506 Edmund Gajny	557 Mrs B. R. Warman	608 Richard Hudson
507 Michael Alfred Milne	558 Mr D. P. Warman	609 Ben Lingard
508 Darren P. Rowley	559 Stuart Jones	610 Adrian Paul Rogers

611 John Moore	662 D. J. Lycett	713 Graham D. Cockayne
612 Rob Emery	663 Robert Patterson	714 Martin & Carol Jones
613 Jason Myers	664 Robert York	715 Colin Roy Pheasant
614 John A. Darby	665 Matthew John Collinge	716 Stephen Murphy
615 Jodie Gibson	666 Joseph H. Tildesley	717 Carl Priest
616 Antony Clark	667 John Foster	718 Thomas Forbes
617 Jon Jackson	668 John J. Neeson	719 Tanya M. Firkin
618 Gerald Roberts	669 Steven Behan	720 Christian Garland
619 Barry Curtis	670 Jamie Blundell	721 Thomas W. H. Rudge
620 Mr A. W. Clayton	671 James Flynn	722 Martha Osborne
621 Thomas Blomberg	672 Katie Flynn	723 Adrian Chamberlain
622 S. J. Lavery	673 M. T. Thornley	724 Sid Conway
623 D. S. Tansey	674 Mr & Mrs Iain Rawlings	725 Thomas Fraser
624 John Clayton	675 Toby Seth	726 Tracey Louise Blizard
625 Ian Clayton	676 Adam Robson	727 James C. Flood
626 Christopher Dicken	677 Mr J. Richmond	728 Chris J. Flood
627 Graham Byworth	678 Amanda Tormey	729 Frank Worsey
628 John A. Williams	679 Byron Preece	730 Martin John Watson
629 Neil Ian Walker	680 Ian Thrupp	731 Gavin W. Handley
630 Barbara Acock	681 Kieran James Gennoy	732 R. S. Kesterton
631 Christopher Swann	682 Cheryl Pountney	733 Mr A. P. Kane
632 Kelly Neal	683 Sam & Kate Rylance	734 Colin Renshaw
633 Caroline Crutchley	684 Stuart Grant	735 Matthew Pond
634 Philip Michael Wood	685 Ian Stringer	736 Paul Easter
635 Dejan Tomic	686 Nicholas Cox	737 Julia Strevens
636 Nick Marple	687 George Edgar Myatt	738 M. A. Loxley
637 Jonathan Rich	688 Michael V. Jones	739 Paul Loxley
638 Victoria Jones	689 Colin Holmes	740 Howard Loxley
639 C. R. Walster	690 Mark Davies	741 Andrew Leedham
640 Asten & Graham Perry	691 Louise Eagles	742 Gavin Thelwell
641 Stephen Donnelly	692 Philippa Downing	743 Julia Greenfield
642 Robert D. Brown	693 Harry White	744 John Treadwell
643 Peter David Perry	694 Thomas Algernon Taylor Snr.	745 Michael Torrington
644 Geoff Underhill	695 Thomas Algernon Taylor	746 Stewart J. Draper
645 R. A. Clarkson	696 Thomas Algernon Taylor Jnr.	747 Sean Christopher Edkins
646 Robert James Upton	697 Michelle Diggins	748 Matthew John Curley
647 Allen Souch	698 Paul Sweetman	749 Bruce Woodcock
648 Mr Andrew Mycock	699 Carl Morris	750 Paul Hayward
649 Andrew Hart	700 David O. Cox	751 Simon Bartholomew
650 Andrew Stacey	701 John Madeley	752 Gareth C. Jones
651 Vincent R. Green	702 Mr Philip Holder	753 Adrian Goddard
652 Lynette Barr	703 Adrian Mark Curran	754 Marek Kukula
653 Christopher Tamburro	704 Lou Daniel Brandrett	755 Tudor Botan
654 David Oliver	705 Mark A. J. Ward	756 The Dirty Dingo
655 Ian Steane	706 Dean Beresford	757 Neil A. Pearson
656 Mark Lench	707 Geoff Baker	758 Christopher Lewis
657 Karl Raymond Fisher	708 Kenneth Graham Davies	759 Gavin & Craig Roberts
658 Andrea Warren	709 Roger L. Elwell	760 Desmond Brennan
659 Kenneth Spizz Spiers	710 Mrs Edith Jones	761 Tom, love Ally
660 Andrew Webster	711 Richard Moss	762 Louise Haydon
661 Carl Danson	712 Stephen Crossley	763 Esmé Jayne

SUBSCRIBERS ROLL CALL

764 Marie Pagett	815 The Martyn Family	866 Ian Stuart Gauld
765 Kieran Collins	816 Edward J. Higgs	867 Robert Beagrie
766 Richard & Andrew Candlin	817 W. V. Trott	868 Kieran Sheridan
767 Darren P. Archer	818 Ian Checkley	869 David John Stevens
768 John Stephens	819 Martin S. Buck	870 Barry J. Davies
769 Christopher Abbotts	820 Dave M. Smith	871 Keith Burrows
770 N. J. Yates	821 Gordon Cull	872 Margaret O'Grady
771 Paul Crease	822 Francis Arthur Wright	873 Miss Sarah Conroy
772 Gavin John Rickett	823 Andrew Bemand	874 Tomas Jalowiecki
773 Mr V. A. P. Kiely	824 Jane M. Wooley	875 Michelle Ellis
774 Jeff C. Brown (Los Angeles)	825 Paddy Fenlon	876 W. A. Southam
775 Bob Curry	826 M. D. Pitcher	877 Andy O' Neill
776 Edward Michael Newton	827 Stephen J. Ellis	878 Debbie O'Neill
777 Ian Habbits	828 Frank MacDonald	879 John Hague
778 Mark Barington Stewart	829 Tony & Liam Hall	880 Dave Crathorne
779 Robin Dean	830 Arron Dosanjh	881 Mr Ted Dudley (Canada)
780 Miss Elizabeth May Alsop	831 Kenton J. Ballard	882 Alan West
781 Nicholas & John Timothy	832 Mr M. Slater	883 Matthew Paul Smith
782 John Reading	833 Michael John O'Callaghan	884 Christopher Woodhams
783 Mr R. J. Butler	834 Mst Philip Wright	885 Thomas Woodhams
784 Kieran O'Connor	835 Jane Dormer	886 Audrey Evans
785 David Sims	836 Antony Butler	887 David Allen
786 Carl Jeffrey Brown	837 Jim Ardron	888 John Figures
787 Iain Fenwick	838 Neil Alcock	889 Craig Holman
788 Stephen Baxter-Smith	839 Robert John Kench	890 H. E. Holman
789 Stuart Allan Nelmes	840 Jason Ashley	891 Claire Round
790 Paul Dunn	841 Denise Allibone	892 Jeremy N. Smith
791 Wayne Batsford	842 Jakob Leslie John Witcomb	893 Kabir Ganguly
792 Sue Hall	843 Terry Wright	894 Mr John W. Fairfield
793 Jamie Howe	844 Nigel Tustain	895 Mr Gary Miles
794 Debbie Johnstone	845 Adam Hotton	896 Mick Clarke
795 William Robert Byrne	846 Mandy Shaw	897 Joshua Vincent Ricketts
796 Andrew Collins	847 Saul C. Gray	898 Jackson T. Brown
797 Ross Carcary	848 Keir Hardy	899 Danny Flanagan
798 Brendan Matthews	849 Paul Robert Eccles	900 Mr Ian Crackle
799 Wall Matthews	850 Andrew Phillips	901 Michael J. Gihon
800 Tony Matthews	851 Simon John Lane	902 Gary Fletcher
801 Stephen Rooke	852 Donna-Marie Dowdall	903 Carrie Fisher
802 Simon Booker	853 Ian Galloway	904 Miss Ruth Underhill
803 Lee Russell Jordan	854 Andrew Galloway	905 A. M. P.
804 James A. Powell	855 Michael Parker	906 Pam (Deano) Pedley
805 Bryan Harte	856 Mathew John Chapman	907 Cliff Paget
806 Matthew Lay	857 Ian Smith	908 Mark Green
807 Lucy Foster	858 Steven Anthony Butler	909 C. Duncan T. Brown
808 Pete J. Harris	859 Nicholas Blewer	910 Tony D. Wilkes
809 Gareth Wilmshurst	860 Gary Corbett	911 R. Sheehan
810 Steven Brown	861 Patrick Twigg	912 S. J. Tovey
811 Martin Lawlor	862 Vincent O'Connor	913 Eamonn Christopher Smith
812 Nadine Lawlor	863 Paul Mabbett	914 Steve Wright
813 Trevor Plant	864 Peter Charles Bell	915 Robert Strafford
814 Graham Salisbury	865 Philip Cotterell	916 Oliver A. Morgan-Walsh

SUBSCRIBERS ROLL CALL

917	Stewart J. Oseman	968	Matthew Myers	1019	Alex Ashford
918	Karl M. Mills	969	Carl Gough	1020	Andrew Shergold
919	Lorna Summers	970	Timothy Field	1021	Mark Dodd
920	Paul 'Parv' Harvey	971	Gareth Robert Powell	1022	Peter, Margaret &
921	Keith Gleadall	972	Stephen Hood		Gary James
922	Robert Taylor	973	Philip Leighton	1023	Antony Lawrence McAllister
923	Gary Keeling	974	Bill Willcox	1024	Damian Mark Evans
924	Neil Keeling	975	Stephen Cash	1025	Gareth Humpage
925	Steve 'Aussie' Rake	976	Peter L. Styler	1026	Vicky Lee
926	Stephen Shannon	977	Peter Lee Maddocks	1027	Dave Parsons
927	Jennifer Sanders	978	Cyril Doughty	1028	James Evans
928	Mark Sanders	979	Mr Ronald E. Nicholls	1029	Richard James Godfrey
929	Warren Paul Rees	980	Andrew Howard Mole	1030	Mark Freer
930	Ben Atkins	981	Robert P. Copus	1031	Richard Marshall
931	Matthew Kings	982	Peter J. Nally	1032	Miss Julie Fox
932	Malcolm Hughes	983	Keith Wallace	1033	Ian Stokes
933	Shaun Walsh	984	Jamie McWilliams	1034	Mr A. Nicholls
934	Lawson Baker	985	Paul John Ford	1035	Mr P. Nicholls
935	Andrew Regan	986	Peter Gibbs	1036	C. Morey
936	Phillip Foxall	987	Stuart Pullen	1037	Michael Pagettt
937	Damien Brennan	988	Mr Brent Aston	1038	Martin Ward
938	Patrick James Fenelon	989	Gordon Parton	1039	Corrina Ansbro
939	Danielle Tonks	990	Allan Rhodes	1040	Paul Michael Virgo
940	Rebecca Tonks	991	G. S. Clarke	1041	Michael Peter Redmond
941	Mr T. D. Measey	992	Nicholas Becerra	1042	Nick Harper
942	Matthew Orme	993	Bob Keene	1043	Fred Gray
943	Brian F. Nevett	994	Paul Emes	1044	David Goodyear
944	Reece Jones	995	Simon Foxall	1045	Simon Goodyear
945	Richard Rex	996	Angela Webber	1046	Robert Brooke
946	Ryan Logan Pemberton	997	Philip Bayliss	1047	C. R. Brown
947	Mark Farrington	998	Gavin Richard Savage	1048	Steve Ewer
948	Daniel Coomber	999	Mark Lees	1049	Michelle Rennison
949	Andrew J. Poole	1000	Marc Thomas	1050	Paul Hawkins
950	Gary Sinnott	1001	Bob Read	1051	Bryan Reid
951	Peter Hosier	1002	David Cooley	1052	Kevin Green
952	Keith Nigel Lloyd Griffith	1003	Balbinder Auluk	1053	Colin & James Daly
953	Lewis Graham	1004	Allun Edwards	1054	Christopher Willis
954	Sophie Parkes	1005	Darren Wall	1055	Kieran Mooney
955	David Davies	1006	Keith Thomas Smith	1056	Kevin John Williams
956	Luke John Clarke	1007	Gail Dean	1057	Spencer Gregg
957	Carl Richard Tallis	1008	Rachel C. Wyers	1058	Martin & David George
958	Ian Wilkinson	1009	Edgar C. Lunn	1059	Sue Glenton
959	Ian Hughes	1010	Richard A. Hales	1060	P. J. Stocker
960	Adam Pipe	1011	Chris Rigby	1061	Philip Cookes
961	James P. McCusker	1012	Robert Connelly	1062	Dennis Cookes
962	Chris Yates	1013	Steve Southall	1063	Nick M. Salter
963	Thomas Chapman	1014	Andrew Philip Lewis	1064	David Phillips
964	Martin Morris	1015	Kevin McGovern	1065	Andrew Friel
965	Adrian Stewart	1016	Paul Richard Daly	1066	Benjamin Bradburn
966	Nigel Groves	1017	Joan Taylor	1067	Philip John White
967	Paul Richard Webb	1018	Simon Grose	1068	Stein Carlsson

SUBSCRIBERS ROLL CALL

1069 Patrick Joseph Butler
1070 Lucie Michelle Winspur
1071 Brian Hession
1072 Robert Cleminson
1073 Stuart H. Blackmore
1074 Joseph John Fallows
1075 Adam Fallows
1076 Sean Troth
1077 Paul Ford
1078 Mark Waldren
1079 Andrew Alford
1080 Steven Righton
1081 Gary & Neil Cooksey
1082 Gerald Henry Lodwick
1083 Shane Nicholls
1084 Sam Flynn
1085 Norman Haigh
1086 Garry Faulkner
1087 Kevin Joynes
1088 Mr Neville T. W. Jones
1089 Gary Simcox
1090 Kathleen Stewart
1091 Tim Langridge
1092 David Ward
1093 Darren Murray
1094 Jon G. Jones
1095 William Gwillym
1096 James Stuart Cooper
1097 Andy Smith
1098 Thomas Evans
1099 Neil P. Gaskell
1100 R. Abbotts
1101 Mr Colin Askey
1102 Mr C. J. Lally
1103 Antony Rogers
1104 Russell Mark Field
1105 Chris Johnson
1106 Miss Alison Royles
1107 Miss Nicola Royles
1108 Philip Kimberley
1109 Joseph F. Boden
1110 Andrew M. Boden
1111 Richard John Mortimer
1112 Barbara Talbot
1113 Alex Weir
1114 James Isham
1115 Paul Darlington
1116 David J. Williams
1117 Robert Tonks
1118 John F. Hudson
1119 Ted Harper

1120 Kenneth J. Marriott
1121 Christopher Bloodworth
1122 Steven David Coles
1123 Russell Daxter
1124 Craig Talbott
1125 Neil Cowley
1126 Mark Lakin
1127 James Kinneir
1128 Thomas Ryan
1129 Barbara Acock
1130 Ryan Toner
1131 James Morgan
1132 Nicholas Morgan
1133 S. J. Humpherson
1134 George E. Lenton
1135 John Lane
1136 Andrew Lane
1137 Ian, Andrew & Paul
      Thompson
1138 Emily Alexandrina McLeod
1139 Mark Rowland
1140 Tim Young
1141 John Brealey
1142 Ben Ashford
1143 Jason M. Smith
1144 Helen Veale
1145 Wayne Philip Perry
1146 Greg Dollery
1147 Michael C. Wedge
1148 Julia Wilson
1149 Philip Clover
1150 Hannah Richards
1151 Jessica Richards
1152 Paul Simon Williamson
1153 Vassos Georgiadis
1154 James Bonner
1155 Erica Jessop
1156 Kevin J. Powell
1157 Robert Mark Feasey
1158 Ian R. Wilson
1159 James McNaught
1160 C. J. Turner
1161 Michael J. F. Doyle
1162 David Foster
1163 Adrian Batsford
1164 David F. Harrison
1165 Geoff Thornton
1166 Tracy Motorny
1167 Mark T. Lowndes
1168 David W. Lowndes
1169 Robert Aston

1170 Pete Abrahams
1171 Robbie Marsden
1172 Darren Bedford
1173 Paul James Davies
1174 Terence Anthony Barker
1175 Russell Simon Adams
1176 Mr E. C. Ashenford
1177 Keith Newbury
1178 Adam Philip Joyce
1179 Vass Georgiadis
1180 Philip & Nicola Wright
1181 Russ Jeynes
1182 Colin J. Ball
1183 Sharon Clarke
1184 Gordon Wilfred Price
1185 Nicholas Pinfold
1186 Adam Mobley
1187 Roy Joyner
1188 Philip Brown
1189 Brian Martin Wood
1190 Michael Perkins
1191 Shaun Clarke
1192 Darren Forth
1193 Peter Alec Roberts
1194 Gary Arthurs
1195 David Poole
1196 Sharon Ann Smith
1197 John Bannister
1198 Andrew Clarke
1199 Kristian Long
1200 Russell Faulkner
1201 Eric George Williams
1202 Cheryl Monckton
1203 Neil F. Ingram
1204 Anthony Ayre
1205 Graham N. Willetts
1206 Jamie Madders
1207 Joshua Madders
1208 Peter Wildrianne
1209 Ali Green
1210 Danny Green
1211 Felice Riccobono
1213 Dominic James Moore
1214 Vera Ellen Ragsdale
1215 Sylvia Neal
1216 Scott Marsden
1217 Neil Thorne
1218 Rebecca Lowe
1219 Jennifer Beale
1220 James Matthew Willis
1221 Derek T. Hough

1222	Rebecca Lee Williams	1273	Michael Burgin	1324	Ian Goodfellow
1223	Fredrick Jelphs	1274	Miss Lisa Farmiloe	1325	Paul George Willetts
1224	Philip Chandler	1275	John S. Griffiths	1326	Mr Leonard Stanton
1225	John Doyle	1276	Tony Lennon	1327	Ian Dance
1226	Graham & Neil Jinks	1277	Kevin Lennon	1328	Daniel Wale
1227	Ian K. J. Wilkinson	1278	Chris Ashmore	1329	Robert Bartlett
1228	Adam Richard Harrison	1279	Roy Attenborough	1330	Stanley T. T. Jones
1229	Richard Shutt	1280	Sam Newsome	1331	Andrew Morgan
1230	J. M. Pearce	1281	Joanne Ruth Miller	1332	Master Darryn Picknell
1231	Joe Hankinson	1282	Richard John Clark	1333	Lee Pendrey
1232	Reg Shelley	1283	Stuart Wyse	1334	Peter Reid
1233	Lee Mason	1284	Gary Davis	1335	Aaron Mathew Clinton
1234	Helen Garfield	1285	Matthew Edgington	1336	Mr Cyril M. Plant
1235	William John Horne	1286	John Mee (Saudia Arabia)	1337	F. J. Cox
1236	Mr Andrew Twigger	1287	I. R. Hoskison	1338	D. J. Cox
1237	Liam Kiernan	1288	David Cox	1339	Peter Raffety
1238	Michael Blakeway	1289	Charlie Wesley	1340	Kevin Melaney
1239	Steve Taylor	1290	Anthony Hayes	1341	Michael Shrimplin
1240	Natalie Langford	1291	Janet Farren	1342	James M. Grove
1241	Georg Baden Allen	1292	Nicola Stonehouse	1343	Harold Green
1242	Kelly Louise Barnes	1293	Michelle Wesley	1344	Beth Lury
1243	Mr Thomas Latham	1294	Andrew John Francis	1345	Esther Lury
1244	Craig Bradley	1295	Bill Allen	1346	Tony Starbuck
1245	Mr J. A. Powell	1296	Matthew James Jenkins	1347	Dee Everitt
1246	Martin Attwood	1297	Martyn Whitby	1348	David Barron
1247	Stephen Williams	1298	Ashley Ward	1349	David Taylor
1248	Daren Reynolds	1299	Jason 'Nobby' Crowley	1350	John Turner
1249	Andy Dale	1300	Matthew Bond	1351	Spencer Alan Malpass
1250	Gregory Waddington	1301	Patrick O'Reilly	1352	Gordon Taylor
1251	Jason Hunt	1302	Ian & Shanice Willetts	1353	Mark Preston
1252	Carl John Roberts	1303	Peter Bullock	1354	Lisa & Bully
1253	Julie Edkins	1304	Jonathan Paul Burton	1355	Philip Whelan
1254	Mr Dennis Thomas	1305	Bernard Hall	1356	Thomas Irvine
1255	Mark H. Homer	1306	Sarah Hall	1357	KF, ER, CKF Davis
1256	Thomas Shakespeare	1307	John Hall	1358	Gerald Keith Richards
1257	Mr R. J. Bunn	1308	Nigel Kelly	1359	Julie Bellfield
1258	Steve Godwin	1309	Mr Dennis Rebbeck	1360	Michael Morgan
1259	Jonathan Giffin	1310	George Lawrence	1361	Ian R. Lane
1260	Mrs Susan J. Gentry	1311	Craig Ramsey	1362	Martin Lane
1261	Mark Santy	1312	Russell Turvey	1363	Claire Cooper
1262	Alexander Berwick	1313	Safter Karim	1364	Paul Abraham
1263	Brian Hartley	1314	Stanley Harold Harvey	1365	Mark Wood
1264	Paul Mannion	1315	Maurice Gavin	1366	George Martin
1265	Mr Peter Caunt	1316	Gary Christian Smith	1367	Colin Crowe
1266	Paul Reaves	1317	Keith Richardson	1368	Julie Hughes
1267	James H. W. T. Soden	1318	D. Bellis	1369	Anne Hughes
1268	Ian Denis Hopkins	1319	Richard & Steven Baker	1370	Nicola Ferriday
1269	Mr Gordon A. Dawson	1320	Justine Taylor	1371	Carly Nichols
1270	Paul Anderton	1321	R. F. Harris	1372	Craig Nichols
1271	Vaughn Parker	1322	S. M. Goodall	1373	Howard Nichols
1272	Michael Kerlin	1323	Andrew Mateer	1374	Timothy Jackson

SUBSCRIBERS ROLL CALL

1375 Andy Congrave	1426 Stephen K. Adams	1477 Andrew Baldwin
1376 Andrew Russell Miller	1427 John A. Tooth	1478 Owen McHugh
1377 Mark Hamblett	1428 Phillip D. Allen	1479 Christopher Bloore
1378 Kevin Stratford	1429 Hilary Cole	1480 Miss Megan Deakin
1379 David Seal	1430 H. C. Gee	1481 Christopher James Trumper
1380 Mark Napier	1431 Steven John Ash	1482 Mr Malcolm Wattrus
1381 Terence Stone	1432 Paul Wright	1483 Tracey Page
1382 Steve Bowden	1433 David Whittaker	1484 Sid Jeewa
1383 Teena Harcombe	1434 Steven James Hunt	1485 Michael T. Booth
1384 Stephen J. Lammas	1435 Daniel Everett	1486 Jane Thomas
1385 Mr Neal Harvey	1436 C. C. Smith	1487 Susan Myatt
1386 Lawrence Rigby	1437 Garry Foden	1488 David Byrne
1387 Nigel Carr	1438 James Harper	1489 Ian Nicholls
1388 Chris Russell	1439 Terry Hall (South Africa)	1490 Norman Nicholls
1389 John Simmonds	1440 Carole Jones	1491 Martin K. James
1390 Neil Powell	1441 M. J. Hone	1492 Steve Sands
1391 Gary Wood	1442 T. McHale	1493 Robert Bruce Veitch
1392 Patricia Ibbotson	1443 Andrew John Pitt	1494 M. Murphy
1393 Neil A. Harvey	1444 Geoff Blick	1495 Keith Potter
1394 Darren J. Delaney	1445 Michelle Marie Allen	1496 Simon Padmore
1395 Maxim Metalnikov	1446 Helen Louise Coles	1497 Susan Glaves
1396 Nicholas J. Morton	1447 W. A. Harvey	1498 Darren Seaton
1397 Michael Goode	1448 Nigel Dudley	1499 Martyn Jones
1398 Linda Davies	1449 Andrew Dudley	1500 Kevin Joseph Murphy
1399 Ben Kirby	1450 Andrew Perry	1501 Ian Walker
1400 Mark Byrne	1451 Michael Coombes	1502 T. Evans
1401 Emma Jane Lockey	1452 Shuhei Mori	1503 Andrew Dawes
1402 Birmingham Central Library	1453 Fiona Richards	1504 Ben Caulkett
1403 Matthew Campbell	1454 Jon Sapey	1505 Dieter Backmann
1404 Stephen Drew	1455 Mark Osborne (Oz)	1506 Mark Simon Slater
1405 Benjamin Bennett	1456 Trevor Hartley	1507 Phillip Buglass
1406 Robert Mark Evans	1457 Paul Gilks	1508 Ted Geary
1407 Andrew James Dennis	1458 D. H. Perry	1509 Peter M. J. Fox
1408 Clive Barnwell	1459 Nicola Hobbis	1510 Paul Anthony Halling
1409 James Wood	1460 Joe Ward	1511 Matthew Plant
1410 Martin Darren Hughes	1461 Nick Watts	1512 Robert James Jones
1411 Robert Thomas Mallaber	1462 Carl Ian Horton	1513 Robbie Deakin
1412 Des Suckling	1463 Harry Gatward	1514 Alan Stevens
1413 Courtney Lewis	1464 Alan S. Johnson	1515 Tim Boswell
1414 Michael P. Field	1465 Philip McDonald	1516 G. A. Millard
1415 Phillip J. Bryant	1466 Mike Washington	1517 Andrew Summers
1416 David Moon	1467 P. Lawrence	1518 Ian M. Jones
1417 Eric Cartwright	1468 R. J. Haywood	1519 Stephen Marshman
1418 Alan Perkins	1469 Christian Wilson	1520 W. J. Kitley
1419 Stuart L. Deller	1470 Michael John Cooper	1521 Gordon T. V. Shepherd
1420 Thomas J. Maguire	1471 Craig, Angela & Tony Webb	1522 Kevin Sanders
1421 Harry Brentnall	1472 Maurice Carter	1523 Jonathan Tebbutt
1422 Daniel Steven Beasley	1473 Jack Robert Welch	1524 Alan Jones
1423 Keith Aston	1474 Andy Parkes	1525 Mr D. Cowan
1424 Paul Gray-Davis	1475 Phil Gautrey	1526 Carl Davies
1425 Robert Meadows	1476 Derek Hollis	1527 Oliver Moore

1528	Jason Wardle	1579	John French	1630	Brian Taylor
1529	Neil Harris	1580	Nicholas Forde	1631	Philip Piper
1530	Kevin Meyer	1581	Allan John Baldwin	1632	Kevin Philip Piper
1531	Paul Harris	1582	Colleen Evelyn Bates	1633	Miss Tracy Diane Piper
1532	Simon Burchell	1583	Steven Elvis	1634	Martin Conway
1533	Alice Pursglove	1584	Simon Kerr- Edwards	1635	Angelina Day
1534	Antony Richard Joyner	1585	James Sabey	1636	Darren Yapp
1535	Jonnie Barker	1586	Paul R. Vos	1637	Glynn C. Miller
1536	Bradley Elson	1587	Liam Davis	1638	Martin Colin Roberts
1537	Neil L. Styring	1588	Tim Cotter	1639	Peter Moore
1538	Paul Parker	1589	Phillip Cotter	1640	Barry Moore
1539	D. K. S. Laws	1590	Kelly Beynon	1641	Julie Ann Stratford
1540	Mark Wheeler	1591	Paul Michael O'Connor	1642	Christopher Hageney
1541	Stuart Sturmey	1592	Joel Nathan Copson	1643	Mark Pugh
1542	Gerald Leek	1593	WP, SA & FA Duff	1644	Philip Corbett
1543	Andrew & Stephen Martin	1594	R. G. K. Griffith	1645	James Hart
1544	Dean Sutton	1595	Jane Howdle	1646	Mr John De Sousa
1545	Claire Matthias	1596	Alan F. Jasper	1647	Sarah Kinsman
1546	John Lacey	1597	Peter Jennings	1648	Jason Russell Perry
1547	Gary Lacey	1598	Russell Brown	1649	Peter Beardshaw
1548	Philip J. Horgan	1599	Simon Bull	1650	John Cunnington
1549	Michael A. Horgan	1600	S. Razaque	1651	Michael Holton
1550	Neil John Binks	1601	George Guest	1652	Jack Pinnock
1551	Carl Dickens	1602	Alec Beach	1653	Neil F. Jones
1552	Pauline A. Holloway	1603	Alan Watton	1654	George E. R. H. Auster
1553	David Halford	1604	David Knight	1655	Martin Dean
1554	Marie Weedall	1605	Roy Stringer	1656	Iain Hill
1555	R. Hemus	1606	Dr Julian Stringer	1657	Raymond John Paul Feely
1556	Stephen Daly	1607	Harvey Stringer	1658	John R. Feely
1557	J. R. Meek	1608	Simon Protheroe	1659	M. D. McDonald
1558	Suzanne Moloney	1609	Owen Suter	1660	Jean Gledhill
1559	Charles D. Dewsbery	1610	Michael Field	1661	Graham Padmore
1560	Neil Mason	1611	Tony Preece	1662	Sean Christopher Starrs
1561	David Fortnam	1612	Simon Preece	1663	Nick Bevan
1562	Raj Vaswani	1613	Philip Williamson	1664	Michael J. Dando
1563	Morgan Courtney	1614	Mike Turner	1665	Rebecca Smith
1564	James Richard Bray	1615	Mark Howes	1666	Adele Ross
1565	Kevin Morton	1616	Simon Smith	1667	Lee Marshall
1566	Scott Hemmens	1617	Geoff Elkington	1668	Paula Thirtle-Watts
1567	Richard Jensen	1618	Donald Grisdale	1669	Peter Stoner
1568	Michelle Louise Jeffcoate	1619	Steven Bampton	1670	Kevin George Walker
1569	Michael Bishop	1620	David Wallis	1671	Miss Lisa Whitmore
1570	Richard Lowe	1621	David J. Pike	1672	Matthew Woodhouse
1571	Jeff Winters	1622	Roger Linney	1673	Albert Lumley Humphreys
1572	P. Rogers	1623	T. M. Newcombe	1674	Paul Mervyn Arscott
1573	Nigel Sadler	1624	M. J. Smith	1675	Neil Loveridge
1574	David Alyn Harris	1625	Peter Keyte	1676	Michael P. McTiernan
1575	Neil Brailsford	1626	Mr George Holloway	1677	Mark H. Cooper
1576	Lisa Robinson	1627	Lee Overthrow	1678	Michael Taylor
1577	David Charles Baldock	1628	Richard Atkins	1679	Ray Brennan
1578	Anthony J. C. Hughes	1629	John C. Atkins	1680	Sam Smith

SUBSCRIBERS ROLL CALL

1681 Richard Evans	1732 Michael F. Weller	1783 Wayne Tandy
1682 Neil Edwards	1733 Lee Harrison	1784 Michael Hewlett
1683 Laith K. Mustafa	1734 Julie A. Bowcott	1785 John W. Daw
1684 Vicki Bennett	1735 David A. Phillips	1786 Catherine Thompson
1685 Gwyn Brewer	1736 Michael D. Mitic	1787 Paul Thompson
1686 Charles Southby	1737 Karen Downes	1788 David French
1687 Mr Paul Randle	1738 Paul Michael Trilloe	1789 Mrs Eileen Ellaway
1688 Peter William James	1739 Ben Davey	1790 Mr Peter Hemmings
1689 Peter Curry	1740 Stephen Smith	1791 Neil Houghton
1690 Leonard Rawlings Layton	1741 Keith Smith Jnr	1792 Sioned Enlli & Sion Ynyr
1691 Paul Sadler	1742 Mr M.O'Brien	1793 Robin Raymond Sully
1692 Brian Broome	1743 Martin Binks	1794 David Alexander Galbraith
1693 Craig Sargeant	1744 David J. Bate	1795 Keith Stubbs
1694 Frank Smith	1745 Mark Robinson	1796 Hugh Swindell
1695 Lee Derek Robinson	1746 Tracey Stockley	1797 West Heath Library
1696 Matthew Fitch	1747 Karen Hasson	1798 Warren Hodson
1697 Luke Thomas	1748 Terence Butler	1799 Lynn-Marie May
1698 Brian Tomlinson	1749 Paul Lawrence	1800 Kirk Wheeler
1699 Gregg Easteal	1750 Fiona and Alex Skeoch	1801 Hugh Thomas
1700 Mervyn Aston Arscott	1751 Adam Robins	1802 Katherine Palmer
1701 Mr C. I. Deakin	1752 John Joe Madigan	1803 Stuart Palmer
1702 Scott Ellison	1753 Paul Madigan	1804 David Palmer
1703 Steven Pricehunt	1754 S. Clayton	1805 Mick Bannister
1704 Phil Lees	1755 Gary Morton	1806 Miss Susan Wheeldon
1705 Elaine Virginia Howells	1756 Matthew Holt	1807 John and Andrew Gillingham
1706 Miss Sarah Peagram	1757 Rebecca Holt	1808 Ian Baker
1707 Miss Tracie Peagram	1758 Margaret Downey	1809 Justine Rose
1708 Mr Jon Lambert	1759 Anish Desai	1810 Denis Jones
1709 Dr Glenn Lambert	1760 Karen Green	1811 Michael Breen
1710 James Pratt	1761 Vickie Gold	1812 Joseph Michael Hopkins
1711 Craig Marriott	1762 Michael Harnett	1813 Simon Giles
1712 Sarah Head	1763 Keith Andrew Busst	1814 Mrs Rosemary Bidey
1713 Steven Davis	1764 Adam Clarke	1815 Mike DJ Leeming
1714 Alan Hipkiss	1765 James Booth	1816 Paul 'Sportsco' Bayliss
1715 Philip J. Etheridge	1766 Nathan Atterbury	1817 Michael Coleman
1716 Steven Thomas Attewell	1767 Adam Peter O'Connor	1818 Natalie Hardware
1717 D. S. Willetts	1768 Naomi Stowell-Smith	1819 Mark McCormack
1718 Antony Morris	1769 Mark Sumner	1820 Karl Court
1719 Cathryn Evans	1770 Sharron Philpot	1821 Karl Court Jnr
1720 Ian David Parkes	1771 The Wildigs	1822 Chris Ballantine
1721 David Lock	1772 Tony Kiely	1823 Ron Parry
1722 Mark Clews	1773 Daniel Elliott Griffin	1824 Craig Vigurs
1723 Richard D. Bradley	1774 Ian D. Strong	1825 Graham Carlin
1724 Peter James Cashin	1775 Keith John Carton	1826 Joanne Hunt
1725 Greg Rose	1776 Robert Adam Lerner	1827 Christopher Biggs
1726 John Adkins	1777 Tony Warren	1828 Miss R. L. Davies
1727 Brian Cowling	1778 Gordon W. Price	1829 Melvin James Thickett
1728 Nigel Rose	1779 Malcolm P. Price	1830 Anthony J. Thickett
1729 Peter W. Parrock	1780 David England	1831 Sharon Thickett
1730 Clive Parrock	1781 Ian O'Brien	1832 Amanda Ann Evans
1731 Christopher C. Fleming	1782 Mr Sydney Pride	1833 Darren Bray

1834 Steve Matthews	1889 David Edwards	1944 Caroline James
1835 Nigel Snowden	1890 Mr N. C. Geldard-Williams	1945 Matthew Owens
1836 Stefan Wally	1891 David Gilbert	1946 Greg Spawton
1837 Mark A. Barton	1892 Steven David Giles	1947 Christopher Pritchard
1838 Caroline Bush	1893 Sean Colin Verhoest	1948 Mr R. E. Utting
1839 Dave Alan Turner	1894 Andrew R. Blythe	1949 Michael Atkinson
1840 Chris Bradbury	1895 Mick Richards	1950 Ian Drew
1841 Angela Weir	1896 Jason Davies	1951 Paul Johnson
1842 Doris Moylan	1897 David Victor Michael Heeley	1952 Mr S. W. Walton
1843 Paul Taylor	1898 Andrew Parsons	1953 Arthur A. Bent
1844 David Corfield	1899 Chris Messer	1954 Desmond O'Donoghue
1845 Robert Cooley	1900 Dean Philip Allen	1955 T. J. Noden
1846 K. N. Ashman	1901 Mark H. Russell	1956 Robert E. Barrett
1847 John Arthur Westwood	1902 Steve Farr	1957 Trevor Bragg
1848 Nig Hardy	1903 Gary Daniel Costello	1958 Matthew Shrimpton
1849 Ian Vickers	1904 Charlotte Ball	1959 Philip Shrimpton
1850 Dave Harrison	1905 Andrew Paul Beard	1960 Karl Sephton
1851 Chris Newton	1906 Tony 'Fant' Green	1961 Gareth Wayne Perry
1852 David Michael Buttery	1907 Lee Chapman	1962 Malcolm Morley
1853 Martin James Bond	1908 Mark S. Waldron	1963 Stuart J. L. Dingley
1854 Alan & Sarah	1909 Peter J. Ross	1964 David Daniel
1855 Martin Montgomery	1910 Adam Conniff	1965 Tony Wright
1856 Anthony Middleton	1911 Stephen Lynch	1966 Lee Coton
1857 Reg Evans	1912 Mr Barry Bindhoff	1967 Jeff Coton
1858 Michael Parker	1913 Mr Nigel Bindhoff	1968 Nicholas Godward
1859 Kevin Brown	1914 Master Gary Bindhoff	1969 Frank Croft
1860 Steven James Taylor	1915 Stephen Bayliss	1970 Andrew J. Harding
1861 Andrew Mark Neale	1916 Christopher Hinsley	1971 Nicholas Townson
1862 R. R. Vincent	1917 Steven John Green	1972 Andrew Owen
1863 Robert Cooper	1918 Daniel 'Tonga' Taylor	1973 Mr Denis S. Cooper
1864 Ben Moseley- Deakin	1919 David Hockenhull	1974 Ben Gurney
1865 Mark Mumford	1920 Dr Mark Wilson	1975 Daniel Cuthell
1866 Lesedi Chilume	1921 Marc Troth	1976 Michael A. Smith
1867 Rob Hale	1922 Philip Goldie	1977 Mark Bowyer
1868 Mike Bull	1923 Michael J. Medforth	1978 Warren Enon
1869 Roger Nicklin (Tamworth)	1924 Nicola Dowell	1979 Adrian Rushton
1870 Dean John Aldington	1925 Richard Pike	1980 Gary Shaw
1871 Gavyn Dean Eade	1926 Amanda & Gordon Grove	1981 Mark Shaw
1872 Lee Rose	1927 John Michael Anthony Burns	1982 Dean Williams
1873 Benjamin John Turvill	1928 Ian Edward Beesley	1983 Jeanette James
1874 Mr Derek Thornton	1929 Mark Antony Lewis	1984 Gail Taylor
1875 Steven Baker	1930 Stephen Underhill	1985 Graham Jauncey
1876 Neil Cox	1931 Richard Hill	1986 Ian Murphy
1877 Richard Weston	1932 Stephen Bloomer	1987 Robert & Karen Wardle
1878 M. Waite	1933 Edward Knott	1988 David Jones
1879 Derek Taylor	1934 Leighton Bullivant	1989 Peter Gokes
1880 Richard Wilson	1935 Nicholas Hogan	1990 Jamie Bell
1881 Brian Wilson	1936 R. O. Evans	1991 Paul Biddlestone
1882 Wayne Cole	1937 Philip John Badhams	1992 Jim Foat
1883 Steve Louden	1938 Andrew J. Cox	1993 Frank Beach
1884 Andrew Wibberley	1939 Dawn Rabone	
1885 Steve Gough	1940 Michael McMaster	
1886 Samantha Abberley	1941 Keith Thomas	
1887 Nicholas Jennison	1942 Helen Hollywell	
1888 David Tysall	1943 Neil Jarvis	